See the **Wider** picture

Unbelievable umbrella street art

A colourful umbrella art installation floats above this promenade in Águeda, Portugal. It casts a shadow of geometric shapes on the ground below and fills the streets with a fairy tale-like atmosphere. As well as providing shade in the heat of summer it also brings uplifting energy and colour into a quiet street.

Is there anything similar in your country or town?

CONTENTS

0

A new start at Belmont Academy

VOCABULARY
Relationships | School | Everyday technology | Holidays and travel | Means of transport | Opinion adjectives

GRAMMAR
Present Simple | *Wh-* questions | Adverbs of frequency | Comparatives and superlatives | Present Continuous | Past Simple | Present Perfect Simple with *for* and *since*

0.1 HI, I'M SKYE!

Relationships; School; Present Simple; *Wh-* questions; Adverbs of frequency; Comparatives and superlatives

1 1.02 **Read the text. What changes does Skye mention?**

her daily routine her friends her hobbies her home her school

My name is Skye Winter-Fox and I'm sixteen. After a year in Woodley Bridge with my gran, I now live in the city again with my parents. My parents usually travel abroad a lot for their jobs, but now they work in London. I'm really happy to be home with my mum and dad again. I sometimes stay with my gran at weekends. Her home is really nice but quite small. At my parents' house, I have a big bedroom and so there's more space to hang out with my friends. I love taking photos of my classmates. When I'm on my own, I also like writing songs. I start my new school, Belmont Academy, on Monday. My neighbour, Jay, goes to the same school. We get on really well. My friend Dan also starts there on Monday. Dan's going to Belmont Academy because his mum wants him to go to an international school. Dan's not worried at all, but I am. I hope my first day goes OK!

2 Read the text again. Mark the sentences T (true) or F (false).

1 ☐ Skye's grandmother lives in a large city.
2 ☐ Skye's parents no longer work abroad.
3 ☐ Skye's grandmother always comes to visit at weekends.
4 ☐ Skye likes writing songs with her friends.
5 ☐ Jay lives near Skye.

3 Study the Vocabulary A box. Which of these people does Skye mention?

Vocabulary A | **Relationships**

best friend classmate gran (grandmother) great-grandfather half-brother neighbour parents relative stepfather uncle

4 **I KNOW!** **Work in pairs. How many relationship words can you add to the Vocabulary A box in three minutes? Compare your answers with another pair.**

aunt, …

5 Study the Grammar A box. Find more examples of the Present Simple in the text.

Grammar A | **Present Simple and *wh-* questions**

Present Simple

I live in the countryside.	She works abroad.
I don't like doing sports.	She doesn't take photos.
Do you live in London?	Yes, I do./No, I don't.
Does she go to your school?	Yes, she does./No, she doesn't.

Adverbs of frequency

always, never, often, rarely, sometimes

***Wh-* questions**

Where do you live?	Why do you like your house?
When do you have breakfast?	What sports do you play?
Who do you hang out with?	How often do you visit your gran?
Which school do you go to?	

6 Complete the questions with the Present Simple form of the verbs in brackets. Write answers that are true for you.

1 Where *do you relax* (you/relax) in the evenings?
2 What ______ (you/usually/eat) for breakfast?
3 Who ______ (you/often/see) at the weekend?
4 ______ (you/have) many cousins?
5 ______ (you/often/visit) your neighbours?
6 ______ (you/live) in a city or a small town?

7 1.03 Read and listen. What are the differences between Belmont Academy and Skye's old school?

Jay: Skye, you don't need a prospectus for Belmont Academy. Just ask me!
Skye: OK. Do you like it there, Jay?
Jay: It's great. I'm sure you'll love it too.
Skye: But I don't know what it's like at an international school. And it's bigger than my old school in Woodley Bridge.
Jay: Well, you hear lots of different languages every day because there are students from about forty countries. I think it's the friendliest school round here.
Skye: That's cool. And they don't have a uniform!
Jay: No, you can wear what you like. It's more relaxed than other schools.
Skye: That will be a nice change. The curriculum looks good too. I might try some different after-school classes.
Jay: You should come to the Astronomy class with me. It's more interesting than chess or football.
Skye: I might try that. And maybe Mandarin Chinese!

8 Look at the highlighted words. Check your understanding. Use a dictionary if necessary.

9 I KNOW! Study the Vocabulary B box. How many words can you add in three minutes? Compare your answers with another pair.

Vocabulary B | **School**

School subjects
Citizenship, Philosophy, Physics
Places at school
canteen, computer lab
Types of assessment
practical exam, project
Verbs
learn, revise, take exams

10 Study the Grammar B box. Find examples of comparative and superlative forms in the dialogue.

Grammar B | **Comparatives and superlatives**

The classrooms are bigger.
It's more exciting than a normal school.
Sports lessons are better/worse than in my old school.
The classrooms have the latest technology.
The first day is the most difficult.
It's the best/worst school in the area.

11 Complete the sentences with the comparative or superlative form of the adjectives in brackets.

1 Jay thinks Belmont Academy is *the friendliest* (friendly) school in the area.
2 Skye is ______ (nervous) than Jay.
3 Belmont is ______ (big) school in the area.
4 The curriculum is ______ (interesting) than at Skye's old school.
5 Languages are ______ (important) subjects at Belmont.
6 Skye is ______ (happy) than she was before.
7 Jay thinks Astronomy is ______ (good) than chess or football.

0.2 HI, I'M JAY!

Present Continuous; Everyday technology

1 1.04 **Read Jay's blog entry and complete the personal profile below.**

Hi! My name's Jay and I'm from London. My family are originally from Jamaica. I live with my parents and my brother and sister. My brother's still at school, but my sister's training to be a web designer. I go to Belmont Academy and my favourite subjects are Physics, Chemistry and ICT. My neighbour, Skye, is joining the school this term. I'm really looking forward to hanging out with her more. When I'm not at school, I love spending time on my computer. Right now I'm writing my weekly blog. It's about science and I write about things I hear in the news and upload interesting pictures. I also love anything about Physics. At the moment I'm reading an e-book about Helen Sharman, the first British person in space. I'd love to go to another planet one day!

Name: *Jay*
Lives with: ______
Name of school: ______
Favourite subjects: ______
Interests: ______
Dream: ______

2 In pairs, cover the text and see how many other facts you can remember about Jay.

3 Study the Grammar box. Find more examples of the Present Continuous in Jay's blog.

Grammar | **Present Continuous**

She's studying Art this year.
I'm not looking forward to my exams.
Are you reading a good book at the moment?
Yes, I am./No, I'm not.

Time words and phrases
at the moment, now, right now, this month, this year, today

4 Complete the short dialogues with the Present Continuous form of the verbs in brackets.

1 A: What *are* you *doing* (do) on the laptop?
B: I ______ (look for) information about the Amazon for my Geography homework.
2 A: Is that a German book you ______ (read)?
B: Yes, I ______ (study) German literature at school this year.
3 A: ______ you ______ (enjoy) the party?
B: Yes, it's great! Everyone ______ (dance)! Come on, let's dance!

5 WORD FRIENDS **Find phrases from the Word Friends box in Jay's blog.**

Word Friends

chat with friends	**watch** music videos
upload pictures	**make** a film/video
download songs	**write** a blog
text friends/parents	**read** an e-book
go online	

6 1.05 **Complete the text with verbs from the Word Friends box. Listen and check.**

My favourite subject is French. During the school year I use a course book to learn French and I do lots of grammar exercises. When I'm on holiday, I often [1]*go* online to watch short films in French. I also [2] ______ with friends in French. I have two French friends and we often Skype. I sometimes [3] ______ a film to send them – usually it's a film of me playing my guitar. I love music and my French friends always send me French songs to [4] ______ or they recommend good music videos to [5] ______ .

7 In pairs, talk about your favourite subject at school. Say what you are learning about at the moment and why you like the subject. And YOU

My favourite subject is Chemistry. At the moment we're learning about chemical reactions. I like Chemistry because …

0.3 HI, I'M DAN!

Holidays and travel; Past Simple (regular and irregular verbs); Means of transport

1 1.06 **Study the Vocabulary box. Write the words in the correct categories. Listen and check.**

B&B campsite city break coach cruise ferry hiking sightseeing

Vocabulary | **Holidays and travel**

Means of transport
canoe, plane, train
Types of holiday
activity camp, beach holiday
Accommodation
hostel, hotel
Activities
horse-riding, sunbathing

2 I KNOW! **How many more words related to holidays and travel can you think of in one minute?**

3 1.07 **Read the text about Dan. Who are the people in the picture with him? Name three facts about them.**

My name's Dan Garcia and I'm half American and half Mexican. I came to England over a year ago with my mum. My brother stayed at home in the USA to study at university there. This is a picture of me, Alisha and Tommo. Alisha moved to Scotland because of her dad's job. I sometimes see Tommo, but we don't go to the same school anymore. My mum wanted me to speak more Spanish and there are lots of Spanish-speaking students at my new school, Belmont Academy. I didn't want to leave my old school at first, but now I'm quite excited. I'm not ready for school yet though! I only flew back from the USA yesterday. I spent the summer with my brother, Ed. We took the train down to Florida and we had a great time. Although he's annoying, I really miss him!

4 **Study the Grammar box. Find more examples of the Past Simple in the text. Which verbs are regular and which are irregular?**

Grammar | **Past Simple**

Regular verbs

She started a new school.	They didn't play any sports.
Did you enjoy your trip?	Yes, I did./No, I didn't.

Irregular verbs

I met my friend.	He didn't go on holiday.
Did we forget anything?	Yes, we did./No, we didn't.

Time expressions
earlier this morning, in 2001, last week, over a year ago, the day before yesterday, yesterday

5 **Complete the sentences about Dan and his family with the Past Simple form of the verbs in brackets.**

1 Dan's brother *didn't come* (not come) to England because he's at an American university.
2 Dan ______ (leave) his old school because his mum wants him to speak more Spanish.
3 Dan ______ (not want) to change schools at first.
4 Dan ______ (not spend) the summer in England.
5 Dan and his brother ______ (go) to Florida.
6 They ______ (travel) by train.
7 They ______ (enjoy) their holiday together.

6 1.08 WORD FRIENDS **Study the Word Friends box. Choose the correct option in the questions below. Listen and check.**

Word Friends

catch a train/a ferry/a bus **drive** a car **fly** a helicopter
ride a horse/a bicycle **sail** a yacht/a boat
take a bus/a train **travel** by bus/abroad

1 When was the last time you *took* / *rode* a train?
2 Do you know anyone who can *fly* / *drive* a helicopter?
3 When did you learn to *ride* / *drive* a bike?
4 Do you have to *travel* / *catch* a bus to get to school?
5 Would you like to learn to *drive* / *sail* a boat?

7 **In pairs, ask and answer the questions in Exercise 6.**

8 **In pairs, talk about an enjoyable trip or holiday you went on. Talk about where you went, how you travelled and what you did.**

And YOU

0.4 HI, I'M NINA!

Opinion adjectives; Present Perfect Simple; *for* and *since*

1 1.09 **Read the text and find:**

1 two countries *Colombia, …*
2 two cities
3 two languages
4 eight adjectives

Hi! I'm Nina and I'm from Colombia. We moved to the UK this summer and I've been here for about a month. London is all right, but it still feels strange. It's very different from Medellin, where I grew up. For a start, there are no mountains or cable cars. In Medellin we have some awesome views. They're both big, noisy cities, though.

I'll start a new school on Monday. I visited it last week, but there weren't any pupils there as it's the summer holidays now. I speak Spanish at home, but I learned English at school in Medellin. I'm worried about the language in the UK as American English is a bit different to British English. I've had an English tutor for two weeks and I've also tried to watch loads of English TV since I arrived. It's quite funny and it has helped a lot. My accent isn't perfect yet, but I think I'll be able to make friends easily.

2 I KNOW! **Work in pairs. How many more adjectives can you add to the Vocabulary box in one minute?**

Vocabulary **Opinion adjectives**

all right amazing awesome awful exciting funny lovely noisy perfect strange terrible unusual useful

3 Find the opposites of these words in the Vocabulary box.

1 amazing a*wful*
2 terrible a______
3 serious f______
4 quiet n______
5 common u______
6 horrible l______
7 boring e______
8 normal s______

4 Study the Grammar box. Find more examples of the Present Perfect Simple in the text.

Grammar **Present Perfect Simple**

Affirmative
I have lived abroad.
I have never lived abroad.
My parents have just/already arrived.

Negative
I haven't lived in Europe. They haven't arrived yet.

Questions
Have you ever lived abroad? Yes, I have./No, I haven't.
Has she arrived yet? Yes, she has./No, she hasn't.

for* and *since
She's been in London for a month. (a period of time)
They've lived here since August. (a point in time)

5 Complete the sentences with the Present Perfect Simple form of the verbs in brackets.

1 We *haven't lived* (not live) here very long.
2 The film ______ (not start/yet).
3 Mum and Dad ______ (never/meet) my school friends.
4 ______ you ever ______ (have) a pet dog?
5 Oscar ______ (not eat) lunch today.
6 Ella ______ (always/like) foreign languages.
7 I ______ (not see) my grandparents since September.
8 Amanda ______ (be) my best friend for years.

6 Write questions about Nina using the Present Perfect.

1 how long / Nina / live / in London / ?
How long has Nina lived in London?
2 why / Nina's parents / move / to the UK / ?
3 Nina / see / her new school / yet / ?
4 Nina / ever / be / to Spain / ?
5 what lessons / she / have / with a tutor / ?
6 TV programmes / help / Nina's English / ?

7 In pairs, ask and answer the questions in Exercise 6.

8 Complete the sentences so they are true for you. And YOU

1 My family has lived here since …
2 I've been at this school for …
3 My best friend has never …
4 Our English teacher has just …
5 I've liked [band/singer] for …

9 In pairs, ask and answer questions about your sentences in Exercise 8.

0.5 CHARACTER QUIZ

1 1.10 Look at the photo. Describe what is happening. Match the speech bubbles with the people in the photo. Listen and check.

> Have you learned how to juggle yet?

> Yeah, I've just got the hang of it.

2 1.10 Listen again. Answer the questions.

1. Has Jay met Tommo and Dan before?
2. Who has the longest journey to school?
3. When do the friends plan to meet up with Tommo?
4. Who has learned to juggle?
5. Has Jay tried juggling before?
6. Is Skye good at juggling?

3 Look at the quiz. Choose the correct option.

The big character quiz

1. Has the school term started *just* / *yet*?
2. Has Skye *ever* / *never* lived in London before?
3. Are Skye's parents *travel* / *travelling* abroad at the moment?
4. What kind of things does Jay *post* / *posts* on his blog?
5. Where *has* / *have* their friend Alisha moved to?
6. Where did Dan and his brother *go* / *gone* this summer?
7. Have Nina and her family moved to the UK *yet* / *just*?
8. Why is Nina *watch* / *watching* lots of TV programmes?
9. Whose sister has *never* / *already* left school?
10. Who has *never* / *ever* met the other characters?
11. Who has *just* / *ever* decided to try some new after-school classes?
12. Who *was* / *were* at Belmont Academy last year?

4 In groups, do the quiz in Exercise 3. Use the texts in Lessons 1–4 to help you. How much can you remember?

And YOU

5 In pairs, write two similar questions about your partner. Hand the questions to your teacher and have a class quiz with two teams.

When did Eduardo move to Madrid?
What instrument does Leila play?

1 Out of your comfort zone

VOCABULARY
Adjectives of emotion | Phrases with *yourself* | New experiences | Personality adjectives

GRAMMAR
Present tenses | Past tenses

Grammar: New beginnings

Speaking: First day nerves

BBC Culture: The adventure begins

Workbook p. 17

BBC VOX POPS

A week of challenges

Love the Cinnamon Challenge? What about a week of challenge? Try it, take photos and win a prize.

1.1 VOCABULARY New experiences

I can talk about challenging new experiences and emotions.

1 CLASS VOTE **Read about the Ice Bucket Challenge. Would you do it? Why? / Why not?**

The Ice Bucket Challenge is an activity involving dumping a bucket of ice water on someone's head. It's done to encourage people to donate money for research on a serious disease called ALS.

2 Your friend has invited you to do the Ice Bucket Challenge. How do you feel?

I feel excited because I love all challenges.
I'm scared. I'd never do anything like this; it might be dangerous.
I'm worried I might look silly, but it's worth trying – it's for charity.

3 1.11 **Study the Vocabulary A box. Write the adjectives in the correct group in the table. Listen and check.**

Vocabulary A Adjectives of emotion

afraid annoyed anxious confused determined disappointed joyful miserable relaxed satisfied stressed surprised uneasy

Positive	______	______	______	______
	______			
Negative	*afraid*	______	______	______
	______	______	______	______

4 Which adjectives could go in both columns?

'Surprised' could be positive or negative, depending on the situation.

5 Look at Claudia's notes and pictures on page 11. Choose the correct option.

1 Claudia was *determined* / *miserable* to try all the challenges.
2 Claudia was *disappointed* / *relaxed* with the Yoga Challenge because it didn't go well.
3 She felt really *confused* / *anxious* about the Ice Bucket Challenge.
4 She was *satisfied* / *miserable* with the Chubby Bunny Challenge.
5 When Claudia was doing the Behaviour Challenge, she tried not to get *annoyed* / *uneasy* with her little brother.

A week of challenges

Monday	Do the One Leg Yoga Challenge. Stand on one leg for as long as you can!
Tuesday	Try the Be Really Nice Challenge on your brother or sister. Be extra nice until they ask you why you're being so nice!
Wednesday	Take the Chubby Bunny Challenge: say 'chubby bunny' with marshmallows in your mouth!
Thursday	This is the big one – video your Ice Bucket Challenge!

6 I KNOW! How many other adjectives of emotion can you think of in one minute?

7 Work in pairs. Choose an adjective from the Vocabulary A box. Your partner says when he or she last felt like that.

A: Satisfied.

B: I felt satisfied when I won the Maths competition.

8 1.12 Study the Vocabulary B box. Listen to five people and tick the phrases you hear.

Vocabulary B Phrases with *yourself*

- ☐ express yourself
- ☐ surprise yourself
- ☐ tell yourself
- ☐ know yourself
- ☐ challenge yourself
- ☐ congratulate yourself
- ☐ make yourself (do sth)
- ☐ be yourself

9 1.12 Listen again and complete the sentences.

1 It's important to ________ yourself when you meet new people.
2 You should ________ yourself for the challenges you try, even if you aren't successful.
3 It's a good thing to ________ yourself and give your opinion.
4 You should ________ yourself do certain things, even if they aren't easy.
5 You need to ________ yourself that you aren't the only person with problems.

10 Do you agree with the sentences in Exercise 9? Why? / Why not?

11 1.13 WORD FRIENDS Complete the verbs in the phrases. Listen and check.

Word Friends

g*ive* an opinion	b________ your confidence
g________ sth a go	h________ an adventure
ch________ your routine	g________ a buzz (out of sth)
m________ plans	t________ sth on board

12 1.14 Read the blog post. Choose the correct option. Listen and check.

How to ... get out of your comfort zone!

It's the start of a new school year. Everyone's getting back into their 'normal' routine, so it seems like a good time to challenge yourself.

Here's a simple idea. Why not surprise yourself and [1]*change* / *make* your daily routine? You could travel a different way to school. You never know – you might [2]*have* / *make* an adventure! Why not eat your meals in a different place or get up early and do some yoga? Our brains [3]*have* / *get* a buzz out of change, so it helps you to enjoy your day and focus on what you're doing.

I love making videos, but I was always too shy to share them. Then last month I made myself post my work online. Now people like to comment, [4]*give* / *get* their opinions and criticise, but I don't mind. Good comments [5]*make* / *boost* my confidence, but I try to [6]*take* / *get* on board negative comments too. **Marco**

I tried this idea on my birthday: allow a friend to [7]*boost* / *make* plans for you! Your friend chooses a place to go. You have to see a film you wouldn't normally choose or try a new activity. I was really excited about my day – and a bit anxious too. But I decided to [8]*have* / *give* it a go and now I have a new hobby: juggling! **Carly**

GRAMMAR Present tenses

I can use different tenses to talk about the present.

VIDEO NEW BEGINNINGS

Nina: Excuse me. I'm waiting for the number 7 bus. What time does it arrive?

Woman: Sorry. The number 7 doesn't stop here. It goes from the other bus stop, around the corner.

Nina: Thank you! Oh no, the bus is leaving. I don't believe it! Wait!

Skye: Hi. Are you going to Belmont Academy? A lot of students get this bus. I'm Skye. This is Jay.

Nina: I'm Nina.

Jay: Oh, here comes another bus.

Nina: Thank goodness for that!

Skye: Hey, Dan. This is Nina. She's starting at Belmont too.

Dan: It's nice to meet you, Nina. Where are you from?

Nina: I'm from Colombia, but I'm living in London now. Is it always this cold here?

Dan: Erm, yes, quite often. What's it like in Colombia? I'd really like to go there. I love travelling. Oh, by the way …

Thank goodness for that!
… by the way.

OUT of class

1 CLASS VOTE **How do you normally travel to school? Tell the class.**

I usually go by car. My dad takes me.

2 1.1 1.15 **Watch or listen. What problems has Nina got?**

3 Study the Grammar box. Find more examples of these tenses in the dialogue.

Grammar Revision of present tenses

Present Simple
Buses usually come past every ten minutes. (routine)
She lives in London. (permanent situation)

Present Continuous
I'm looking for the bus stop. (present action)
She's living in Brighton now. (temporary situation)

State verbs
state verbs: *belong*, *know*, *prefer*, etc.
state or dynamic verbs:
I think she's shy. (state verb: opinion)
What are you thinking about? (dynamic verb: mental process)

GRAMMAR TIME > PAGE 118

4 Complete the sentences with the Present Simple or Present Continuous form of the verbs in brackets.

1 I live near the school, so I *don't usually get* (usually/not get) the bus.
2 Mum ______ (not pick) us up today, so we ______ (walk) home from school.
3 ______ you ______ (usually/give) new after-school clubs a go?
4 Why ______ you ______ (do) your homework now?
5 My brother ______ (not go) to this school.

5 1.16 **Choose the correct option. Listen and check.**

Hi Gran,

How are you? I [1]*have / am having* lunch in the school canteen, so this is just a quick message. First of all, the school and the teachers are great – I [2]*prefer / am preferring* them to the old ones. We usually [3]*discuss / are discussing* things in groups. Everybody can say what they [4]*think / are thinking* about something and teachers often [5]*encourage / are encouraging* students to share their experiences.

This is an international school, so I [6]*hear / am hearing* lots of different languages every day. I [7]*know / am knowing* my Spanish will improve quickly! I've got to go! We can talk on Skype soon.

Besos (that's 'kisses' in Spanish),

Skye

1.3 READING and VOCABULARY Moving to the USA

I can identify specific detail in an article about immigrants and talk about the problems they face.

1 CLASS VOTE Could you cope with moving to another country? Vote *yes* or *no*. What problems do you think you might face? Think about the things below.

friends family home language school

2 1.17 Read the text and complete the table.

	Name	Country of origin	Languages spoken	How long in the USA
Student 1				
Student 2				
Student 3				

3 Read the text again. Mark the sentences T (true) or F (false).

1 ☐ Mateo says some Americans think of Mexicans in a fixed way.
2 ☐ Mateo feels people should have some knowledge of the countries around them.
3 ☐ Ji-Min agrees with Obama's views on immigration.
4 ☐ Americans are usually familiar with Ji-Min's home country.
5 ☐ Vanessa guessed correctly about the problems she would have in the USA.
6 ☐ Adele helps immigrants with more than just learning the language.

4 Look at the highlighted words in the text. Check your understanding. Use a dictionary if necessary.

5 In pairs, discuss the questions.

1 Which migrant do you think has the most problems at the moment?
2 What did you learn about the USA?
3 What did you learn about immigrants?
4 What would you find difficult if you moved to the USA?

Fitting in

Have you ever felt that it's hard to fit in with the people around you? Wanting to belong is part of growing up, but it's definitely more difficult when you move to a new country. This group of young migrants talk about the challenges they face in the USA.

Mateo Martinez is fifteen but his family moved to the USA from Mexico when he was a few years old. Although he loves his life in the USA, Mateo still faces stereotypes. 'Some Americans expect me to be lazy,' he explains. 'That's what they think of Mexicans. I don't take it personally, but I don't like that kind of label.' Another thing which annoys Mateo is when other students ask if he speaks Mexican at home. 'Some people don't know that we speak Spanish,' he says. 'Our countries are neighbours, so people should be aware of our language and culture.'

Ji-Min Choy arrived a few months ago. When I meet her, she's searching for a video on YouTube. In the video, Barack Obama is speaking about immigrants as a big part of American history: 'We don't simply welcome new arrivals – we are born of immigrants.' 'I love this speech,' says Ji-Min. 'It makes me feel welcome. Do you know that almost one quarter of the US population are first or second generation migrants?' That definitely makes life in this big country easier, but there are still awkward moments for Ji-Min. 'Many Americans don't really know where South Korea is!' she says.

Vanessa Defay, from Haiti, was anxious before she arrived last year. She thought that finding new friends would be her biggest problem, but she was wrong. 'Making friends is simple because some other students speak Creole, which is my language, and Spanish, which I learned at school. But I often don't understand the teachers when they speak fast.' Adele Parker, an English teacher, is helping Vanessa. Adele knows that many children move here due to various problems in their home countries. 'Learning a new language is a huge challenge for immigrants. I teach students about the culture too, and help them integrate through extra social activities.'

6 [VOX POPS ▶ 1.2] What problems do immigrants face in your country? How can we make a difference in these areas?

And YOU

culture jobs language
stereotypes tolerance

1.4 GRAMMAR Past tenses

I can use different tenses to talk about past events and experiences.

1 CLASS VOTE **Have you or has anybody in your school done something exciting? What was it?**

2 **Read the article quickly. What was Malavath's challenge?**

3 **Read the text again. In pairs, ask and answer the questions.**

1 What did Malavath do in 2014?
2 Why did Malavath want to do the challenge?
3 How did she get to the training centre?
4 Why did they have to walk slowly?
5 Why has Malavath gone back to school?
6 What famous person did Malavath meet after the climb?
7 How has this experience changed Malavath?

4 **Study the Grammar box. Find more examples of past tenses in the article.**

Grammar | **Past tenses**

Past Simple
She became a good climber. (finished action)
They trained in the countryside. (repeated action)

Past Continuous
At nine o'clock she was studying for her exam. (action in progress)
It was raining. (background description)

Past Simple and Past Continuous
They were sleeping when we arrived.

Present Perfect
She has gone home. (result in the present)
I have never been to Paris. (experience)

She's gone home. She went home an hour ago. (recent event + completed action)
I've been to Paris. I went there three years ago. (experience + completed action)

GRAMMAR TIME > PAGE 118

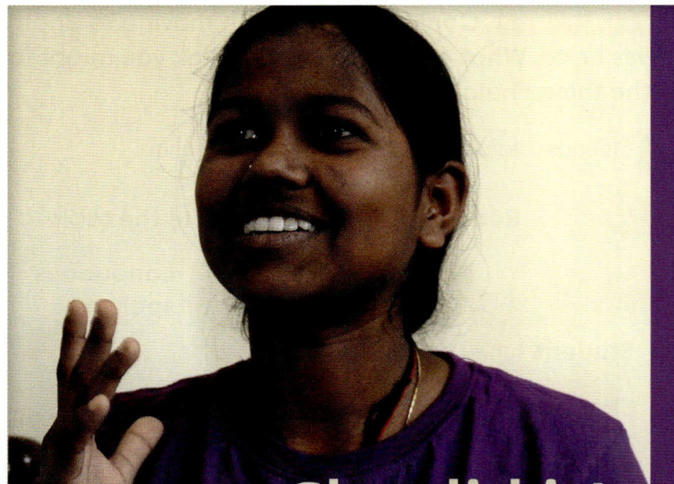

She did it!

In 2014 thirteen-year-old Malavath Poorna became the youngest girl to climb Mount Everest. She was living in a village in the countryside with her parents when a government organisation chose her and a friend for the mountain challenge. At the time, Malavath was looking for a chance to do something different and she was happy to go. She flew for the first time in her life to a special mountain centre where she trained for eight months. The training was hard and sometimes the temperature dropped as low as -35°C. Malavath also hated the packaged food that she had to eat. It didn't smell nice and she missed her mum's cooking! The climb lasted fifty-two days. At times it was dangerous and they had to walk very slowly, but Malavath didn't give up. When she finally raised India's flag on the highest peak in the world, she said she felt great and very proud of herself. Since the climb, Malavath has gone back to school because she couldn't study while she was training. She's also met the Prime Minister, who encouraged her to complete her studies. Has the climb changed her? Definitely! Now she wants to climb more mountains around the world.

5 **Write questions using the correct past tense. Write answers that are true for you.**

1 you / climb / a mountain / recently / ?
Have you climbed a mountain recently?
No, I haven't.
2 what / you / do / at 5 p.m. / yesterday / ?
3 you / ever / eat / packaged food / ?
4 you / start / English classes / five years ago / ?
5 it / rain / when / you / get up / this morning / ?
6 you / ever / be / abroad / ?

And YOU

6 [VOX POPS ▶ 1.3] **Describe a past experience when you were away from home. Did you enjoy it? Was it difficult?**

- Where did you go and why?
- Who were you staying with?
- What did you like/not like about it?

I've been away from home a few times. Once I stayed with a family in France. They were very friendly, but I didn't like the food much.

1.5 LISTENING and VOCABULARY Projection mapping

I can identify specific detail in a conversation and talk about personality.

1 CLASS VOTE **Do you like trying new things? Why? / Why not?**

2 1.18 **Complete the sentences with words from the Vocabulary box. Listen and check.**

Vocabulary Personality adjectives

calm confident creative curious fussy generous gentle organised punctual reliable sensible

1 Someone who always has new ideas is ________ .
2 Someone you can trust is ________ .
3 Someone who worries about things that aren't important is ________ .
4 Someone who is sure about him- or herself is ________ .
5 Someone who wants to learn new things is ________ .
6 Someone who always arrives on time is ________ .

3 **Write definitions for the other five words in the Vocabulary box.**

4 I KNOW! **In pairs, add more adjectives to the list in Exercise 2. Use two words to describe a person you know.**

My best friend is always kind and calm.

5 **This photo is an example of 'projection mapping'. Have you ever seen this on TV or where you live? How do you think it works?**

6 1.19 **Listen to Ivan telling Marisa about a workshop. Tick the correct option.**

1 ☐ Marisa has seen the information and has decided she isn't interested.
2 ☐ Marisa has bought tickets for her and Ivan to go to the workshop.

7 1.19 **Listen again. Complete the information with a word or phrase.**

Projection mapping workshop
new, easy and great fun!

Location: [1]*Science Museum*
Address: [2]________ Road
Title: 'Bringing the [3]________ '
For: fourteen- to [4]________-year-olds
Time: [5]________ to 4 p.m.
Please bring: [6]________ and a drink.
Cost per person for this special event:
[7]£________

8 1.19 **Listen again. In pairs, answer the questions.**

1 What did Marisa think the workshop was about?
2 Where do you create the videos in a projection mapping workshop?
3 Where did Marisa see an example of projection mapping?
4 Is Ivan creative or curious?
5 Why can't Marisa go on her own to the workshop?
6 Why does Marisa have to go to Ivan's house on Saturday?

9 **In pairs, talk about these classes and workshops. What type of person are they right for? Are they right for you? Why? / Why not?** And YOU

chess cooking creative writing
gardening photography
sewing singing

You have to be organised if you do the cooking class because you plan recipes and shopping lists.

I joined a singing class after school. I'm not very confident but the teacher was very gentle and kind.

1.6 SPEAKING Asking for and offering help

I can ask for and offer help, and respond to offers of help.

VIDEO FIRST DAY NERVES

Dan: OK, here we are. Do you need anything else?
Nina: No, I'm fine. Thanks for your help!
Skye: Good luck with the Head. I hope you're in our class.
Dan: Catch you later.
Student: Do you need any help?
Nina: Oh hi. You made me jump! I'm meeting the Head at 8.30 but she isn't here.
Student: No surprise there! Just take a seat. She won't be long.
Nina: Excuse me. Can you help me?
Woman: Of course. I'll be with you in a minute. Now, what can I do for you?
Nina: I'm looking for the Head.
Woman: Oh, Nina! I'm so sorry. I'm Ms Holiday, the Head. Wecome to Belmont Academy. It's always crazy on the first day. Let's find your class. Can I give you a hand with that?
Nina: No, I'm fine, but thanks anyway.
Woman: Don't worry. I've asked Dan to look after you.
Nina: Dan? I've just met him by the bus!

Catch you later!
You made me jump!
OUT of class

1 CLASS VOTE Can you remember the first day at your school? What was it like?

Everything seemed so big. I didn't know where to go.

2 Look at the photo. How do you think Nina is feeling?

3 1.4 1.20 Watch or listen and answer the questions.

1 Who is Nina waiting for?
2 What's the surprise for Nina at the end?

4 Study the Speaking box. Find more examples in the dialogue.

Speaking Asking for and offering help

Asking for help
Can/Could you help me?
Excuse me. Would you mind helping me?
Can/Could you give me a hand (with sth)?

Replying
Of course./Sure!
I'll be with you in a minute.

Offering help
Do you need any help?
Do you need anything else?
Can I give you a hand with ...?
Can I get you anything?
May I help you?
What can I do for you?

Replying
That would be great, thanks.
Thanks for helping/your help.
That's really nice of you, thanks.
No, I'm fine, but thanks anyway.

Be careful!
Would you mind helping me? No, of course not.

5 1.21 Complete the dialogue with phrases from the Speaking box. Listen and check. Then practise the dialogue.

A: Excuse me. Would [1]*you mind helping me*? I don't know where the school office is.
B: No, of [2]_________. It's over there. I'll show you.
A: Thanks for your [3]_________.
B: Do you [4]_________ else?
A: No, [5]_________, but thanks anyway.

6 In pairs, read the situations and take it in turns to ask for and/or offer help.

Student A
- Ask your teacher to help you with you homework.
- Offer to help your friend to carry a big bag and a guitar.

Student B
- Ask your friend to help you buy food and drink for your party.
- A classmate isn't feeling well. Offer to help.

WRITING A description of a personal challenge

I can write a description of a personal challenge.

1 CLASS VOTE
Are you afraid of heights? Where are the worst places to be if you are?

2 **Look at the photo. Where is the girl and how do you think she's feeling?**

3 **Study the Vocabulary box. In pairs, take it in turns to use the words in a sentence.**

I gasped at the end of the film because it was a surprise.

Vocabulary	Verbs that express emotion
gasp scream shake shiver sweat yawn	

4 **Read Jo's description of a personal challenge. Which paragraph describes:**

a ☐ a challenge that helped Jo?
b ☐ how the experience changed Jo?
c [1] a bad experience in the past?

My personal challenge by Jo

I've always loved trying new things, so when Dan invited me to go climbing, I was confused. The problem is I'm scared of heights. I first realised this when I was crossing Tower Bridge in London on a school trip. Suddenly, somebody screamed and I saw that part of the floor was glass. I started shaking and my hands were sweating. I was disappointed with myself and sad.

Soon after that, I heard about the climbing class and I decided to give it a go. When I arrived and saw the climbing wall, I gasped. It was quite high, but the instructor helped me and showed me how to climb slowly and safely. At the beginning it was quite difficult, but gradually I felt less anxious although I had to concentrate very hard.

The experience has made me more confident. That day, I got a buzz out of climbing and I couldn't stop smiling. Now I climb regularly and I'm never scared.

5 **Find more examples of the verbs in the Vocabulary box in Jo's description. In pairs, discuss how Jo felt before, during and after the challenge.**

6 **Study the Writing box. Find examples of these phrases in Jo's description.**

Writing A description of a personal challenge

Reason for the challenge
I've always loved/wanted/dreamed about ...
The problem is/was, I ...
I first realised this when ...

Description of the challenge
Soon after that, I heard about/saw ...
... I decided to give it a go.
When I arrived at/started/saw ... , I gasped/screamed.
At the beginning it was difficult/impossible to do, but gradually I felt ...
In the end, I ...

After the challenge
The experience has made me ...
That day, I ...
Now I'm not afraid of ...
Now I ... regularly.
I'm thinking of becoming a ...

7 **In pairs, choose one of these challenges and answer the questions below.**

- joining a new sports team
- performing in front of your school mates
- staying with a family in another country
- taking an important exam

1 Why is the challenge difficult?
2 How would you feel before, during and after the challenge?

Writing Time

8 **Write a description of a personal challenge. In your description, you should write about:**

- why you wanted to do the challenge.
- what the challenge was like.
- how you felt after the experience.

TIP
Use the verbs in the Vocabulary box to make your writing more interesting.

WORDLIST Adjectives of emotion | Phrases with *yourself* | Personality adjectives

afraid /əˈfreɪd/
annoyed /əˈnɔɪd/
anxious /ˈæŋkʃəs/
arrival /əˈraɪvl/
be aware /bi əˈweə(r)/
be yourself /bi jə(r)ˈself/
belong /bɪˈlɒŋ/
calm /kɑːm/
challenge /ˈtʃæləndʒ/
challenge yourself / tʃæləndʒ jə(r)ˈself/
chubby /ˈtʃʌbi/
concentrate /ˈkɒns(ə)nˌtreɪt/
confident /ˈkɒnfɪd(ə)nt/
confused /kənˈfjuːzd/
congratulate yourself /kənˈgrætʃʊleɪt jə(r)ˈself/
creative /kriˈeɪtɪv/
criticise /ˈkrɪtɪsaɪz/
curious /ˈkjʊəriəs/
determined /dɪˈtɜː(r)mɪnd/
disappointed /ˌdɪsəˈpɔɪntɪd/
due to /dju tə/
dump /dʌmp/
encourage /ɪnˈkʌrɪdʒ/
express yourself /ɪkˈspres jə(r)ˈself/
face /feɪs/
fit in /fɪt ɪn/
fixed /fɪkst/
focus /ˈfəʊkəs/
fussy /ˈfʌsi/
gasp /gɑːsp/
generous /ˈdʒenərəs/
gentle /ˈdʒent(ə)l/
government organisation /gʌvə(r)nmənt ˌɔː(r)gənaɪˈzeɪʃ(ə)n/
gradually /ˈgrædʒuəli/
grow up /grəʊ ʌp/
immigrant /ˈɪmɪgrənt/
integrate /ˈɪntɪˌgreɪt/
international /ˌɪntəˈnæʃnəl/
joyful /ˈdʒɔɪf(ə)l/
know yourself /nəʊ jə(r)ˈself/
label /ˈleɪb(ə)l/
make yourself (do sth) /meɪk jə(r)ˈself/
marshmallow /ˌmɑːʃˈmæləʊ/
migrant /ˈmaɪgrənt/
miserable /ˈmɪz(ə)rəb(ə)l/
organised /ˈɔː(r)gənaɪzd/
peak /piːk/
population /ˌpɒpjʊˈleɪʃ(ə)n/
Prime Minister /praɪm ˈmɪnɪstə(r)/
projection mapping /prəˈdʒekʃən mæpɪŋ/
punctual /ˈpʌŋktʃuəl/
raise (a flag) /reɪz ə flæg/
relaxed /rɪˈlækst/
reliable /rɪˈlaɪəb(ə)l/
satisfied /ˈsætɪsfaɪd/
scream /skriːm/
search /sɜː(r)tʃ/
sensible /ˈsensəb(ə)l/
shake /ʃeɪk/
shiver /ˈʃɪvə(r)/
social /ˈsəʊʃ(ə)l/
speech /spiːtʃ/
stereotype /ˈsteriəˌtaɪp/
stressed /strest/
surprise yourself /sə(r)ˈpraɪz jə(r)ˈself/
surprised /sə(r)ˈpraɪzd/
sweat /swet/
take it personally /teɪk ɪt pɜː(r)s(ə)nəli/
talk to yourself /tɔːk tə jə(r)ˈself/
tell yourself /tel jə(r)ˈself/
tolerance /tɒlərəns/
uneasy /ʌnˈiːzi/
workshop /ˈwɜː(r)kˌʃɒp/
yawn /jɔːn/

WORD FRIENDS

boost your confidence
change your routine
get a buzz (out of sth)
give an opinion
give sth a go
have an adventure
make plans
take something on board

VOCABULARY IN ACTION

1 Use the wordlist to find:

1 three people *migrant, ...*
2 four adjectives to describe positive emotions *satisfied, ...*
3 three actions people do when they're nervous or frightened *shake, ...*
4 one expression that means 'try new things'

2 Use the wordlist to find an adjective which describes:

1 your best friend's personality
2 a good student
3 how you feel when you have a test at school
4 how you feel if you get bad marks in an essay
5 how you feel if a friend argues with you

3 Complete the sentences with the correct form of verbs from Word Friends.

1 My friends and I are always ready to ________ an adventure.
2 I find ________ negative comments on board difficult.
3 I've already ________ plans for the next school holiday.
4 A nice comment from my teacher can ________ my confidence.
5 I don't like ________ my opinion in class.

4 In pairs, discuss if the sentences in Exercise 3 are true for you.

5 1.22 PRONUNCIATION **Listen to the words below and decide how the underlined vowels are pronounced.**

disappointed integrate migrant miserable organised
reliable satisfied surprised

6 1.23 **Write the words from Exercise 5 in the correct category. Listen and repeat.**

/ɪ/ *disappointed*, ________, ________
/aɪ/ *migrant*, ________, ________, ________, ________

Revision

VOCABULARY

1 **Write the correct word for each definition.**

1. If you can make yourself climb to the top of a mountain, you are d*etermined*.
2. People who worry about unimportant things are f__________.
3. The total number of people in a country is the p__________.
4. You work with others to learn something new at a w__________.
5. When you have a fixed opinion about something or somebody, this is a s__________.

2 **Complete the personality quiz with the verbs below.**

be challenge ~~speak~~ surprised

1. **Name one situation when you might *speak* to yourself.**
2. **Name one situation when you could __________ yourself to try something difficult.**
3. **Name one time when you __________ yourself by doing something unexpected.**
4. **Name one situation when you can just __________ yourself and relax.**

3 **In pairs, discuss the situations in Exercise 2. Then tell the class about your partner.**

GRAMMAR

4 **Complete the letter with the Present Simple or Present Continuous form of the verbs in brackets.**

Dear Student,

[1]*Are* you *starting* (start) a new term at Belmont Academy this year? Then this advice might help.

On the first day, all students [2]__________ (go) to their classrooms at 8.30 for registration, so everyone [3]__________ (meet) their new tutor before lessons. Your tutor has your timetable. Like most secondary schools, Belmont [4]__________ (have) six fifty-minute periods a day.

We hope you [5]__________ (not feel) anxious! But if you are worried, please contact me. At Belmont Academy, we [6]__________ (believe) that it's good to ask questions!

Best wishes,

Ms Holiday, Head Teacher

5 **Complete the sentences with the Past Simple, Past Continuous or Present Perfect form of the verbs in brackets.**

1. A: *Have* you *ever taken* (ever/take) part in a dance workshop?
   B: Yes, I __________. I __________ (take) part in a salsa workshop in May.
2. I've got so much homework to do! I can't believe that a week ago we __________ (sit) on a beach and I __________ (not think) about school at all!
3. The Prime Minister __________ (give) a speech when, suddenly, the microphone __________ (break).
4. Maria is really generous. She __________ (already/give) a lot of money to an organisation which helps immigrants.
5. A: So, what __________ you __________ (do) on Bornholm?
   B: Lots of things. We __________ (ride) bicycles and we __________ (take) lots of photos!

SPEAKING

6 **Choose the best response for each question.**

1. Excuse me, would you mind helping me? I can't open this door.
   a That would be great, thanks.
   b Could you give me a hand?
   c Of course not!
2. Those bags look heavy. Do you need any help?
   a I'll be with you in a minute.
   b No, I'm fine, thanks.
   c Sure!
3. OK, the party food is ready. Now, do you need anything else?
   a That's really nice of you, but I can manage now.
   b May I help you?
   c No, of course not.

7 **In pairs, use one of the questions from Exercise 6 to start your own dialogue. Use your own ideas to continue.**

DICTATION

8 **1.24 Listen. Then listen again and write down what you hear.**

SELF-ASSESSMENT Think about this unit. What did you learn? What do you need help with? **WORKBOOK** p. 14

BBC

CULTURE

Would you cross a desert?

Endurance tests: the most challenging races in the world

You're stressed and anxious, you have problems sleeping. What you need is a challenge. There has never been a better time, but which one to go for? Traditional marathons and triathlons are still popular but newer events have now appeared. They are held on difficult terrain and represent a greater challenge to participants. They are popular in the USA and are very competitive.

The first long-distance triathlon was the Ironman. It started in Hawaii, on Waikiki beach, in the 1970s and there are now forty countries across the world which hold Ironman events. An Ironman is the hardest one-day endurance test in the world. Participants must complete a 3.86-km swim, a 180-km bike ride and run a whole marathon – and no stopping is allowed! The World Championships are held in Hawaii every year. The run in Hawaii is particularly difficult because you have to cross a desert!

Other tough races include the Trans-Rockies. These are six separate contests which take place in different locations in the Rocky Mountains. You can do a twenty-four-hour bike race along Canada's highest peaks – but don't try it if you suffer from vertigo! Alternatively, head for New Mexico, where there is a ride that lasts three days through the desert – just try cycling through sand dunes!

As for the traditional marathon, you can still take part in the world's biggest, in New York. However, if you really want to push yourself, try the World Marathon Challenge. This is seven marathons, in seven days, on seven different continents! It's called The World Marathon Challenge for a reason! For many people, this is the challenge of a lifetime. Participants have to run 295 km, spend fifty-nine hours in the air and fly approximately 38,000 km from the Antarctic Circle to Sydney, Australia. All at your own risk!

GLOSSARY

terrain (n) a particular type of land
competitive (adj) determined to be more successful than other people
endurance (n) when you can continue to do sth difficult for a long time
tough (adj) difficult
peak (n) the top of a mountain

EXPLORE

1 In pairs, discuss the questions.

1 Would you like to take part in a marathon? Why / Why not?
2 Why do you think people run marathons, take part in extreme triathlons, cross deserts or climb the highest mountains?

2 Read the article and answer the questions.

1 What is the difference between the new events and the traditional ones?
2 Why is the Ironman Triathlon famous?
3 What makes the Ironman World Championship particularly difficult?
4 In which two countries do the Trans-Rockies events take place?
5 Why is the New York Marathon special?
6 What is the ultimate challenge race? Why?

3 In pairs, discuss the questions.

1 Which of these challenges would you like to take? Why?
2 How do you think people prepare for these types of events?

EXPLORE MORE

4 1.5 Watch Part 1 of a documentary about two men on an adventure. Answer the questions.

1 What kind of landscape can you see? Where is it?
2 What are the two men doing?
3 What problems do you think the men will have?

5 1.5 Watch the video again. Choose the correct option.

1 The desert of the Empty Quarter is special because it's the *hottest* / *most remote* place on earth.
2 Ben and James *have arguments* / *want to give up*.
3 They have been on many trips but this is the *best* / *most difficult* one.

6 1.6 Watch Part 2 of the video and answer the questions.

1 What other places have Ben and James travelled to?
2 Which country do they travel through on this trip?
3 What is their destination? What will they find there?

7 1.6 Watch the video again. Match the numbers below with what they refer to (1–6).

1940s eight 250 forty-seven ten eleven

1 original journey time in days ....
2 maximum temperature in the desert in Celsius ....
3 litres of water drunk per day ....
4 journey across desert in km ....
5 actual journey time in days ....
6 decade of Thesiger's expedition ....

8 Choose the best summary of the programme.

1 Ben and James recover their friendship by taking on an almost impossible journey.
2 Ben and James are the first people to discover the most remote place on earth.
3 Ben and James' final journey is the hardest they have ever done together.

9 What's your opinion of Ben and James' journey? Do you think an extreme experience like this can help save a friendship? Why? / Why not? Discuss in pairs or small groups.

YOU EXPLORE

10 CULTURE PROJECT In groups, prepare a digital presentation about a famous expedition from your country.

1 Use the internet to research the expedition.
2 Write a short script to describe the journey. Choose images or videos that you would like to use.
3 Share your presentation with the class.

2

What a waste!

VOCABULARY
Pollution | Protecting and damaging the environment | Compound nouns: the environment | Elections and campaigns

GRAMMAR
Past Perfect | *used to*

Grammar: Watch where you're running!

Speaking: Trash to treasure

BBC **Culture:** A power crisis

Workbook p. 29

BBC VOX POPS

CLIL 1 > p. 138

2.1 VOCABULARY Protecting the environment

I can talk about pollution and the environment.

1 CLASS VOTE **What do you do with the items below when you don't need them anymore?**

> empty pizza boxes old clothes old mobile phones
> plastic water bottles school textbooks

I throw them away. I recycle them.

2 **Study the Vocabulary A box. Find two things that are not in the poster.**

Vocabulary A	**Pollution**
bin endangered animal factory litter oil petrol plants rubbish smoke traffic	

3 **In pairs, look at the poster again. What causes the types of pollution below?**

> air pollution land pollution water pollution

Factories cause air pollution.

4 I KNOW! **Work in pairs. How many more words can you find which are related to pollution and the natural world? You get one point for every word! After three minutes, compare your results with another pair.**
ocean, skyscraper, …

5 1.25 **Listen to part of a radio programme about the rubbish route. Answer the questions.**

1 Where does the rubbish route start?
2 What containers are the food and the drink in?
3 How do the goods get to the shops?
4 What do people in the city want to escape from?
5 Why can't people use the bins in parks?

6 1.26 **WORD FRIENDS** Complete the Word Friends box with the words below. Listen and check.

aluminium cans energy parks plants

Word Friends	
recycle/throw away:	plastic bags, rubbish, [1] ________
protect/damage:	the planet, the environment, [2] ________
save/waste:	water, electricity, money, [3] ________
pollute/clean up:	the air, the ocean, rivers, beaches, [4] ________

7 In Exercise 5, you listened to the first part of the rubbish route. In pairs, finish the description. Use the poster and the Word Friends box to help you.

8 1.27 Read the quiz. Choose the correct option. Listen and check.

True or false?

"Does the Tooth Fairy *recycle* the teeth?"

- Some countries [1]*recycle / protect* strange rubbish, including false teeth!
- Recycling one aluminium can can [2]*save / pollute* enough energy to run a TV for three days.
- We [3]*clean up / throw away* enough cans to reach the moon and back twenty times!
- Acid rain [4]*recycles / damages* trees and plants, but not buildings.
- Sweden is working hard to [5]*protect / pollute* the environment and now recycles sixty-nine percent of its rubbish.
- Running the water when you're brushing your teeth can [6]*save / waste* around 5,000 litres of water a year.
- Plastic from ships [7]*pollutes / cleans up* the ocean. In 2010 a ship lost 28,000 rubber ducks. People are still finding the ducks today!

9 1.28 In pairs, do the quiz in Exercise 8. Listen and check.

10 1.29 Study the Vocabulary B box. Match words 1–7 with words a–g to make compound nouns. Listen and check.

Vocabulary B	Compound nouns
1 traffic	**a** bank
2 bottle	**b** energy
3 petrol	**c** centre
4 public	**d** transport
5 renewable	**e** change
6 recycling	**f** station
7 climate	**g** jam

11 1.30 Complete the blog post with the correct form of compound nouns from the Vocabulary B box. Listen and check.

Is it cool to be GREEN?

Definitely! We need to protect our planet for our future. That's why I always travel on [1]*public transport*. Too many people drive, so there are always [2] ________ in the city centre.

At my school we recycle as much as we can. We don't use [3] ________ such as sun or wind power, but our head teacher has plans for solar panels on the roof. Some people joke that they like warmer weather, but I tell them that [4] ________ is really not good. Rising ocean levels cause floods that can destroy houses and farms. The oceans are also getting polluted with plastic, so I never use plastic bags. In fact, I make my own bags! Next to my school there's a [5] ________ where we put soft drink bottles, but you can also use the bins for recycling cans, paper and clothes. There's a larger [6] ________ outside the city, where we can take our old TVs, furniture, books and even bicycles. You can find loads of cool things there.

12 [VOX POPS ▶ 2.1] **And YOU**

How green are you? Are your town and school green? In groups, take it in turns to talk about your ideas.

I always try to save water. For example, I take a quick shower and I rarely take a bath.

My town's got a huge recycling centre and they collect rubbish from your house.

At my school we recycle our pens!

2.2 GRAMMAR Past Perfect

I can talk about past events using the Past Perfect.

1 CLASS VOTE Which of the things below do *not* produce energy?

jellyfish milk natural gas sugar sun wind

2 Read the blog post quickly. Answer the questions.

1 How much do elephants eat?
2 How can animal waste help the zoo?

New power for the zoo | Elephant energy

Did you know that you can heat a building with animal waste? At school, I heard about a local zoo that had tried it, so I went to see for myself. When I got there, the zoo-keeper had just given the elephants some food. He told us that they've got huge appetites and can eat 100 kilos of fruit and vegetables every day! Over the previous week, he had collected a container of waste from all the plant-eating animals in the zoo. I hadn't realised what a mountain of animal waste looked like!

The mixture of animal waste and water produces a biogas. This goes into an engine that works on gas and produces electricity. So, had this idea really helped the zoo? Absolutely! Before they started using the waste, the zoo had found it difficult to control how much they spent on electricity. Now they can keep the animals warm and save money too!

3 Study the Grammar box. Find more examples of the Past Perfect in the blog post.

Grammar Past Perfect

Past Perfect
Max had collected the litter.
I hadn't realised how big it was.
Had they helped? Yes, they had./No, they hadn't.

Past Perfect and Past Simple
When we saw them, the animals had already eaten.
She'd given the lion some food before the visitors arrived.
They left the zoo after they'd had lunch.

Time expressions
when, before, after, just, already, by the time

GRAMMAR TIME > PAGE 119

4 Complete the sentences with the Past Perfect form of the verbs in brackets.

1 The visitors *had given* (give) the animals the wrong food and the next day they were sick.
2 For her project, Maria used photos of the animals that she ______ (take) at the zoo.
3 We ______ (not realise) how useful animal waste was until we started saving money.
4 They ______ (not feed) the animals when I got there.
5 ______ you ______ (hear) about this type of energy before you visited the zoo?

5 Read the sentences. Underline the action that happened first.

1 The lions were thirsty because nobody had given them any water.
2 The workers had left the factory before the fire started.
3 After the party had finished, we cleaned up the park.
4 Al realised that the bottle bank had moved to another place.
5 I couldn't recycle my old mobile because I'd given it to a friend.
6 The zoo-keeper had just fed the elephants when we arrived.
7 I wanted to recycle the empty cans, but Sarah had thrown them away.

6 And YOU In pairs, think about your country or the area where you live.

- What types of energy do people use?
- Do people use any alternative sources of energy? Use the words below to help you.

electricity gas solar energy solar panels wind farms

It's very sunny in Spain and we use solar energy a lot. People often have solar panels on the roof …

2.3 READING and VOCABULARY Find out about a teen activist

I can understand the main points and identify specific detail in an article.

1 CLASS VOTE **Have you ever been to an event to help raise awareness of environmental problems?**

2 1.31 **Read the article quickly. Match headings a–c with paragraphs 1–3.**

a At one with nature
b The power of music
c A different type of summer

3 **Read the article again. Choose the correct answers.**

1 What surprised the people in the United Nations most about Xiuhtezcatl?
  a He was very young.
  b His hairstyle and clothes were unusual.
  c He wasn't like a normal teenager.
  d He could speak several languages.
2 Xiuhtezcatl's experience in the forest
  a taught him about the Mashika.
  b made him want to work outdoors.
  c showed him a connection to the world.
  d helped him learn Nahuatl.
3 How did the documentary change Xiuhtezcatl?
  a He wants to act to protect the environment.
  b He'll learn more about Earth Guardians.
  c He felt he was different from other young people.
  d He'll join his mum's organisation.
4 How does Xiuhtezcatl feel about his life at the moment?
  a He's not sure he wants to have these amazing adventures.
  b He accepts he's busy, but hopes he can make a difference.
  c He'd like to have more time to perform at events and festivals.
  d He thinks working for the environment takes up too much time.

4 **Look at the highlighted words in the text. Check your understanding. Use a dictionary if necessary. Write a sentence for each word.**

1 ______________________

School's nearly out and for most teens it's a chance to hang out with friends and enjoy the summer vacation. But if you're a sixteen-year-old eco hip-hop artist, it's a busy time of international travel and public speaking. Xiuhtezcatl (roughly pronounced *shoo-tez-cat*) Martinez became known around the world in 2015, when he gave a talk about climate change to the United Nations General Assembly in New York. It wasn't his long hair and formal suit that got him noticed, but the fact that he started his talk in three different languages: English, Spanish and Nahuatl, the language of the Mexican Mashika or Aztec community.

2 ______________________

His passion for the environment comes from the time that Xiuhtezcatl spent in the forest with his dad, where he felt he was 'a big part of this world'. He's had his name since he was six. He got it from older members of the Mashika community and it means 'turquoise mirror' in the Nahuatl language. The community has a strong belief that we are all connected to the world we live in and must protect it and the animals that live in it. He shares this passion with his mom, who set up Earth Guardians, an organisation that educates young people and encourages them to protect the environment. However, it was after he'd watched a nature documentary that Xiuhtezcatl decided he could make a difference now.

3 ______________________

So where does hip-hop come into all of this? After a rap performance at school with his younger brother, Xiuhtezcatl realised that their lyrics could make people wake up to the problems of pollution and waste. They both now perform at events and festivals around the world. His mom is happy her son is having 'these amazing adventures' but worries all this is taking up a lot of his time. Xiuhtezcatl admits it's intense but is convinced he's doing the right thing.

2.4 GRAMMAR *used to*

I can talk about repeated past actions that no longer happen.

VIDEO **WATCH WHERE YOU'RE RUNNING!**

Skye: Ouch!

Park keeper: Are you OK, love?

Skye: Yeah, I'm fine. I tripped over that can.

Park keeper: Come and sit down for a minute. Oh, there's so much litter here these days. It used to be such a lovely park and look at it now – rubbish everywhere. Do you run here often?

Skye: No, this is my first time. I only moved back to this area last month. I used to live here though.

Park keeper: So did you use to come here when you were little?

Skye: Yes, I did – all the time. My mum and gran used to bring me here. I remember I had my fifth birthday party in this park – just by those trees. You're right. It didn't use to be this dirty.

Park keeper: Well, we used to have a team of people who cleaned up the park. Now it's only me – and it's too much for one person. It's a shame, really. Anyway, I should get back to work. Now, are you sure you're OK?

Skye: Yes, fine, thank you.

OUT of class

Ouch! *It's a shame, really.*

1 CLASS VOTE **Do you think it's important for a town or city to have a park? Why? / Why not?**

Yes, I think it's very important because …

2 2.2 1.32 **Watch or listen. Why does Skye trip up when she's jogging in the park?**

3 Study the Grammar box. Find more examples of *used to* in the dialogue.

Grammar *used to*

The river used to be clean.
We didn't use to find rubbish on the beach.
Did you use to play here? Yes, I did./No, I didn't.
Where did you use to live?

GRAMMAR TIME > PAGE 119

4 Complete the sentences with the correct form of *used to* and the verbs in brackets.

1 I *used to love* (love) cycling, but I don't have a bike now.
2 We ______ (not recycle) our rubbish.
3 My dad ______ (drive) me to school.
4 He ______ (drop) litter on the floor, but now he always puts it in the bin.
5 When my mum was little, she ______ (not watch) much television.

5 Complete the questions with the correct form of *used to* and the verbs in brackets. In pairs, ask and answer the questions.

1 *Did* Skye *use to live* (live) near the park?
2 ______ she ______ (visit) the park often?
3 ______ the park ______ (be) dirty?
4 ______ a team of people ______ (clean) the park in the past?

6 1.33 **Complete the dialogue with the correct form of *used to* and the verbs in brackets. Listen and check.**

Jo: Gran, you used to live in London when you were little. Was it very different?

Gran: Well, there [1]*didn't use to be* (not be) so many cars, that's for sure!

Jo: [2]______ you ______ (walk) everywhere?

Gran: No, there [3]______ (be) more buses and the underground [4]______ (not be) so expensive! And back then, London [5]______ (not have) so many swimming pools and shopping centres. I think you have a lot more fun now!

7 In pairs, complete the sentences about your town. **And YOU**

My town used to be … It didn't use to have …
There used to be … We didn't use to …

2.5 LISTENING and VOCABULARY Protecting the environment

I can identify specific detail in short conversations and talk about elections and campaigns.

1 **CLASS VOTE** **Do you think student councils are a good idea? What subjects do you think are important for students to discuss?**

2 **1.34 Listen to the dialogue. Answer the questions.**

1 Where are the people?
2 What are they doing?
3 What is the new school councillor going to do?

3 **Complete the sentences with the correct form of the phrases below.**

> become a member (of)
> hold an election
> ~~join a campaign~~
> organise an event
> sign up (to do sth)
> vote for (sth/sb)

1 I *joined a campaign* yesterday; the aim is to get more people to recycle their rubbish.
2 David has just ________ a group that protects local wildlife.
3 Please ________ to help clean up the beach. There's a pen and a list on the table over there.
4 Yesterday we ________ at our school for a new head boy and head girl.
5 I ________ my friend Jane because I think she'll be a great head girl.
6 Last month my brother ________ at school, called Trash to Treasure. The idea was that everyone made something from a piece of rubbish.

4 **1.35 Listen to four dialogues. Choose the correct answers.**

1 What is the date of the student election?

2 What is the boy going to do?

3 What did Mark's dad use to recycle when he was a boy?

4 What kind of campaign has Sarah joined?

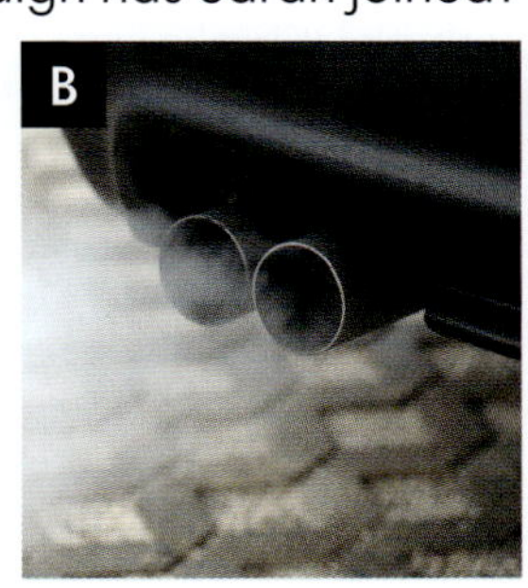

And YOU

5 **Imagine there will be student elections in your school. In pairs, write an election leaflet explaining what you would do if you became student councillors. Present your election leaflet to the class. Vote and choose the best candidates for student councillor.**

As student councillors, we would plant more trees and flowers around the school. We would also ask for more after-school sports clubs. In addition, we would …

2.6 SPEAKING Agreeing and disagreeing

I can agree and disagree with other people's point of view.

VIDEO TRASH TO TREASURE

Nina: What are you doing in your garage?

Skye: Actually, you guys can help me. I'm taking part in a Trash to Treasure competition. The idea is to make something new out of rubbish.

Nina: I think that's a great idea!

Dan: Really? I don't agree. Isn't rubbish just rubbish?

Nina: That's not always true.

Skye: Anyway, I want to make a chair out of these bottles. So, we need to cut the tops off the bottles and fit them inside each other. Like this. Then I think we should tie them together with some string.

Jay: I'm not sure about that. I think the string will come loose.

Skye: Mmm … Maybe you're right. I've got some strong sticky tape. OK, let's get started!

Some time later:

Skye: So what do you think? It looks like a chair to me!

Nina: Absolutely! Go on, Dan. Try it out!

Dan: Who, me?

Nina: Oh no! The chair's collapsed!

Jay: I think our design needs a bit more work!

Dan: Yeah, you can say that again!

OUT of class

Let's get started!
Try it out!
You can say that again!

1 CLASS VOTE **Do you always share the same opinions with your friends and family? What kind of things do you disagree about?**

I don't always agree with my friends. Sometimes …

2 2.3 1.36 **Watch or listen and answer the questions.**

1 Why is Skye making a chair? What material is she using?
2 Which friend thinks it isn't a good idea? Why?
3 What else could you make from plastic bottles?

3 Study the Speaking box. Find more examples of agreeing and disagreeing phrases in the dialogue.

Speaking Agreeing and disagreeing

Agreeing	Disagreeing
I think that's a good/great idea.	I don't agree.
Maybe you're right.	True, but ...
I think so too.	That's not always true.
I totally agree.	I don't think so.
Absolutely!	I don't think we should ...
You can say that again!	I'm not sure about that.
I suppose/guess so.	I totally disagree.

4 Complete the dialogues with phrases from the Speaking box.

1

A: I think if you care about the environment, you shouldn't use plastic bags at all.

B: Maybe you're [1]*right*, but sometimes you need them. For example, we use them in our kitchen bin.

A: I think that's [2]________, but then you should reuse them each time.

B: I'm not [3]________ about that. They'd stink!

2

A: My mum has to fly a lot because of her job.

B: I [4]________ think people should travel by plane. It causes too much pollution.

A: I guess [5]________, but some people need to travel to other countries for work.

B: That's not always [6]________. You can have Skype meetings instead.

5 1.37 **Listen to five people talking about recycling and reusing things. Respond to each statement with a phrase from the Speaking box. Give reasons.**

And YOU

6 [VOX POPS 2.4] **In pairs, discuss one of these statements.**

- People spend too much money on protecting animals. They should spend it on helping people instead.
- Everyone should use public transport.
- It's very easy to save energy, but not water.

2.7 ENGLISH IN USE Question tags

I can use question tags to check information.

Girl: You're not throwing that bottle away, are you, Jake? You can recycle it.
Boy: Oh yeah, I forgot.

Girl: You didn't leave the TV on, did you? It's a waste of electricity.
Boy: Oh yeah, sorry. I forgot.

Girl: You know the party starts in half an hour, don't you? And you really need a shower! Did you forget?
Boy: No. I'm saving water!

1 **Read the cartoon. Why is Jake's sister annoyed with him?**

2 **Study the Language box. Find more examples of question tags in the cartoon.**

Language **Question tags**

We form question tags with the auxiliary/modal verb and the pronoun. If the statement is positive, we use a negative question tag. If it's negative, we use a positive question tag.

Positive statement + negative question tag

You're William, aren't you?
We can recycle this box, can't we?

Negative statement + positive question tag

The school hasn't got a bottle bank, has it?
They'll help us pick up the litter, won't they?

With the Present Simple and Past Simple of most verbs, we use *do/don't*, *does/doesn't* and *did/didn't*.

Her dad works at the petrol station, doesn't he?
You didn't remember to switch off the lights, did you?

3 **Complete the questions with question tags.**

1 Jessica doesn't recycle her clothes, *does she*?
2 We're all wasting too much energy, ________?
3 You can't recycle all kinds of plastic, ________?
4 Most cars use unleaded petrol, ________?
5 This town hasn't got very a good public transport system, ________?
6 Tim wrote an essay about recycling, ________?
7 You didn't throw away those bottles, ________?
8 Anna will help clean up the beach, ________?

4 **Complete the text with question tags.**

Most homes have got bins for recycling glass, paper and plastic, [1] *haven't they*? But what about e-waste? I'm sure your house is full of electronic gadgets, [2] ________? What happens to these products when we no longer want them? You probably didn't recycle your last mobile phone, [3] ________? According to a survey, only ten percent of people recycle their mobile phones. You can imagine how much e-waste that creates, [4] ________? In fact, for the first time ever, there are more mobile internet gadgets in the world than people! That isn't good news for the environment, [5] ________? Fortunately, there are many companies that recycle e-waste. So next time you get a new smartphone or video game, you'll know what to do with your e-waste, [6] ________? Recycle it, don't bin it!

5 **What do you do with your e-waste? How do you think we could get more people to recycle their e-waste?**

And YOU

WORDLIST Pollution | Protecting and damaging the environment | Elections and campaigns

acid rain /ˈæsɪd reɪn/
air pollution /eə pəˈluːʃən/
aluminium /ˌæləˈmɪniəm/
appetite /ˈæpətaɪt/
awareness /əˈweənəs/
bin /bɪn/
biogas /ˈbaɪəʊˌgæs/
bottle bank /ˈbɒtl bæŋk/
can /kæn/
candidate /ˈkændədət/
climate change /ˈklaɪmət tʃeɪndʒ/
collapse /kəˈlæps/
community /kəˈmjuːnɪti/
connection /kəˈnekʃn/
container /kənˈteɪnə/
councillor /ˈkaʊnsələ/
design /dɪˈzaɪn/
Earth /ɜːθ/
electricity /ɪˌlekˈtrɪsəti/
encourage /ɪnˈkʌrɪdʒ/
endangered /ɪnˈdeɪndʒərd/
engine /ˈendʒɪn/
environment /ɪnˈvaɪrənmənt/
environmental /ɪnˌvaɪrənˈmentl/
escape /ɪˈskeɪp/
e-waste /iː weɪst/
factory /ˈfæktəri/
false teeth /fɔːls tiːθ/
fit /fɪt/
flood /flʌd/
formal /ˈfɔːməl/
gadget /ˈgædʒɪt/
green /griːn/
guardian /ˈgɑːdiən/
head boy /hed bɔɪ/
head girl /hed gɜːl/
heat /hiːt/
intense /ɪnˈtens/
jellyfish /ˈdʒelifɪʃ/
land pollution /lænd pəˈluːʃən/
leaflet /ˈliːflət/
litter /ˈlɪtər/
loose /luːs/
lyrics /ˈlɪrɪks/
natural gas /ˈnætʃərəl gæs/
oil /ɔɪl/
organisation /ˌɔːgənaɪˈzeɪʃən/
outdoors /ˌaʊtˈdɔːz/
petrol /ˈpetrəl/
petrol station /ˈpetrəl ˈsteɪʃən/
plant /plɑːnt/
pollution /pəˈluːʃən/
public transport /ˈpʌblɪk ˈtrænspɔːt/
recycling centre /riːˈsaɪklɪŋ ˈsentə/
renewable energy /rɪˈnjuːəbəl ˈenədʒi/
re-use /ˌriːˈjuːz/
rubbish /ˈrʌbɪʃ/
set up /set ˈʌp/
smoke /sməʊk/
solar energy /ˈsəʊlə ˈenədʒi/
solar panel /ˈsəʊlə ˈpænəlz/
sticky tape /ˈstɪki teɪp/
stink /stɪŋk/
string /strɪŋ/
student council /ˈstjuːdənt ˈkaʊnsəl/
tie (sth) together /taɪ təˈgeðə/
traffic /ˈtræfɪk/
traffic jam /ˈtræfɪk dʒæm/
trash /træʃ/
treasure /ˈtreʒə/
trip over /trɪp ˈəʊvə/
turquoise /ˈtɜːkwɔɪz/
United Nations /juːˈnaɪtɪd neɪʃnz/
unleaded /ʌnˈledəd/
vegetarian /ˌvedʒəˈteəriən/
waste /weɪst/
water pollution /ˈwɔːtə pəˈluːʃən/
wildlife /ˈwaɪldlaɪf/
wind farm /wɪnd fɑːm/

WORD FRIENDS

clean up rivers/beaches/parks
damage the environment
pollute the air/the ocean
protect the planet
recycle plastic bags/aluminium cans
save electricity/energy
throw away rubbish
waste water/money
become a member (of)
hold an election
join a campaign
organise an event
sign up to (do sth)
vote for (sth/sb)

VOCABULARY IN ACTION

1 Use the wordlist to find:

1 five types of energy *solar energy, …*
2 three types of pollution *air pollution, …*
3 four words that describe a person *candidate, …*
4 two words that describe a group of people *community, …*

2 Complete the sentences with the verbs from Word Friends.

1 We can ________ energy if we turn off the lights when we go out.
2 The school is going to ________ an election for a new head boy.
3 The chemical waste from a factory can ________ the environment.
4 When I leave school, I want to ________ a member of an environmental group.
5 We must ________ the beach so that the turtles won't die.
6 I would ________ for the person who wants to stop climate change.

3 In pairs, choose two or three words each from the wordlist and write sentences. What's the longest sentence you can make?

The smoke from the factories is polluting the air.

4 1.38 PRONUNCIATION Listen to the intonation in the question tags.

You're in the nature club, aren't you?
When you want to check information, your voice goes up. It's a real question.

You're in the nature club, aren't you?
When you probably know the answer and expect the other person to agree, your voice goes down.

5 1.39 In pairs, practise saying these questions. Listen and check.

1 You enjoy wildlife, don't you?
2 You aren't a member, are you?

Revision

VOCABULARY

1 Write the correct word for each definition.

1 To keep someone or something safe. p*rotect*
2 It's black or grey and is produced when something burns. s _ _ _ _
3 A building where things are produced in large quantities. f _ _ _ _ _ _
4 To make air, water, etc. dirty. p _ _ _ _ _ _
5 A long line of vehicles on the road that can't move. t _ _ _ _ _ _ j _ _
6 To use more of something than you need or than is useful. w _ _ _ _

2 Complete the sentences with the words and phrases below.

endangered animal public transport recycling centre rubbish ~~throw away~~

1 Do you usually ***throw away*** your old clothes?
2 Do you know where the nearest ______ is?
3 Do you think people should use ______ instead of their own cars?
4 If you see ______ in the street, do you pick it up?
5 Which ______ would you help protect?

3 In pairs, ask and answer the questions in Exercise 2.

GRAMMAR

4 Complete the diary entry with the Past Perfect form of the verbs below.

cause choose forget not arrive not have ~~plan~~

Thursday was our school trip. I was excited because our teacher [1]***had planned*** a day at a wind farm. She [2]______ the biggest wind farm in Scotland with more than 200 wind turbines. But when we got to school in the morning, the bus [3]______ and we had to wait for ages. We heard that an accident in the town centre [4]______ a huge traffic jam. When it finally came, I was starving because I [5]______ my packed lunch. It was a really long journey and when we got to the farm, the wind turbines weren't moving. The farm [6]______ any wind that week!

5 Complete the sentences with the correct form of *used to*.

1 The factories ***used to*** pollute the air, but they're cleaner now.
2 Oliver ______ have any hobbies, but now he recycles furniture.
3 ______ your friend ______ be a member of the Teen Action group?
4 The school ______ throw away a lot of paper, but now it recycles it.
5 ______ you ______ collect things on the beach when you were little?
6 The lake in the park ______ have so much litter in it, did it?

6 Match sentences 1–6 with question tags a–f.

1 You recycle everything,
2 The smoke smells bad,
3 It's a long traffic jam,
4 The campaign will help,
5 You don't want to waste it,
6 The oil polluted the river,

a do you?
b won't it?
c don't you?
d didn't it?
e isn't it?
f doesn't it?

SPEAKING

7 In pairs, role-play the situations.

1 A: Tell your friend about an idea to recycle some old jeans. Say why you think it's a good idea.
B: Say if you agree or disagree with your friend's idea.

2 B: Tell your friend about an event you are organising to make people more aware of the litter in your local park. Say why you think it's a good idea.
A: Say if you agree or disagree with your friend's idea.

DICTATION

8 1.40 Listen. Then listen again and write down what you hear.

SELF-ASSESSMENT Think about this unit. What did you learn? What do you need help with? **WORKBOOK** p. 26

BBC CULTURE

When will the lights go out?

Alternative energies

Imagine life without electricity! What effect would that have on the typical British family? Well, there would be no hot water for showers in the morning or, more importantly, the traditional cup of tea! Most families use kettles for this – electric water boilers that sit in every British kitchen. Then, of course, you wouldn't be able to charge your phone, tablet or laptop. Now that's serious! And when you left the house, there wouldn't be any traffic lights, cash machines or supermarkets.

You might think that is just a horror story, but the lights might go out sooner than we think if we don't act soon and move to renewable energy. These are forms of energy which protect the environment as they do not produce carbon dioxide emissions that lead to climate change. They are often cheaper because the energy is generated from 100 percent natural resources – so they can never run out like coal!

So what forms of renewable energy are there? Electricity can also be provided by the wind (wind power), the sun (solar power), the sea (tidal/wave power) and even by volcanoes (geothermal power). The type of energy a country uses depends a lot on geography. Sunny Spain has more solar power than the UK and volcanic Iceland has much more geothermal power.

In the UK, wind power is one of the most popular forms of renewable energy. It used to represent only a fraction of the country's energy supply but now it provides a mighty eleven percent. In fact, Britain currently stands at number six in the world's wind power producers, with over 7,000 onshore wind turbines. And now there are almost 5,000 turbines offshore as well (that's in the middle of the sea!), making it the world leader. Why not visit the largest offshore wind farm in the world at the mouth of the River Thames?

GLOSSARY
emissions (n) gas that goes into the air
run out (v) if sth runs out, there is no more of it left
wind turbine (n) a machine that produces electricity from the wind
onshore (adj) on the land, not in the sea

EXPLORE

1 **Look at the photo. In pairs, discuss the questions.**

1 What can you see in the photo? What form of energy does it produce?
2 Is this form of energy popular in your country? Why? / Why not?
3 Why is this form of energy better than traditional forms such as coal?
4 What other forms of energy can you think of?

2 **Read the article and check your answers to Exercise 1.**

3 **In pairs, discuss the questions.**

1 What did you find out about wind power that you hadn't heard before?
2 Where do you think they could build wind farms in your country? Why?

EXPLORE MORE

A

B

C

4 **You are going to watch part of a BBC documentary about electricity. Match photos A–C with descriptions 1–3.**

1 ☐ a place where electric power is generated by coal, gas, wind, etc.
2 ☐ a screen at the National Grid which shows supply and demand of electricity
3 ☐ the place which controls the UK's energy consumption

5 **2.5 Watch Part 1 of the video and check your answers to Exercise 4.**

6 **2.5 Watch the video again. Choose the correct option.**

1 The 'nightmare scenario' is that future demand for electricity will be *too high / not high enough*.
2 *250 / 25* people run the National Grid.
3 There are more than *300 / 3,000* power stations across the UK.
4 The demand is high today because it is *winter / night time*.

7 **2.6 Watch Part 2 of the video and complete the summary with the words below.**

billion coal lives needs power renewable stations

In winter, Britain uses on average fifty gigawatts (GW) of electricity – that's fifty [1]______ watts! Nine nuclear power [2]______ provide seven GW and [3]______ power stations generate around twenty-five GW. [4]______ energy power stations provide around ten GW. At the moment the grid has enough [5]______ to supply all our [6]______ but that will soon change. As our nuclear stations reach the end of their [7]______, almost all will need to be switched off.

8 **What is the power crisis described in the video? Do you think that your country is going through a similar crisis? Why? / Why not? How can you save energy in your daily life? Discuss in pairs.**

YOU EXPLORE

9 CULTURE PROJECT **In groups, prepare a presentation about the electricity supply in your country.**

1 Use the internet to research the different forms of power used (what percentage is solar, gas, coal, wind, nuclear, etc.).
2 Write a short script to describe your research. Choose images or videos that you would like to use.
3 Share your presentation with the class.

3

Style challenge!

VOCABULARY
Clothes and accessories | Adjectives to describe clothes and accessories | *have*, *be*, *wear* | Parts of clothes and shoes | Descriptive adjectives

GRAMMAR
Present Perfect Continuous | Present Perfect Simple and Continuous

Grammar: Stage success!

Speaking: Where are my trousers?

BBC Culture: An unlikely fashion icon

Workbook p. 41

BBC VOX POPS

EXAM TIME 1 > p. 127
CLIL 2 > p. 139

3.1 VOCABULARY Clothes and appearance

I can describe clothes, accessories and appearance.

1 CLASS VOTE Where do you usually buy clothes? Why?

at a market | in a second-hand shop | in a shopping mall | online | other?

2 2.01 Study the Vocabulary A box. Find the items in the website photos A–G above. Listen and check.

Vocabulary A Clothes and accessories

bracelet boots earrings gloves hoodie leggings necklace pullover raincoat sandals scarf suit tights tracksuit wellies

3 2.02 Listen to four people talking about clothes and accessories from the website. Match speakers 1–4 with items of clothing from the Vocabulary A box.

1 ______ 2 ______ 3 ______ 4 ______

4 I KNOW! What clothes or accessories from the Vocabulary A box would you expect to find in these sections of the website? Can you add any more?

Street I.D. Fashion

BASICS | ACTIVE | PARTY | ACCESSORIES

5 2.03 Study the Vocabulary B box. Write the adjectives in the correct columns in the table below. Listen and check.

Vocabulary B Adjectives to describe clothes and accessories

awesome baggy black-and-white checked cotton denim fashionable flowery leather old-fashioned plain polka-dot scruffy skinny smart striped tight woollen worn-out

Use adjectives in this order:
opinion/general – size/fit – colour – pattern – material
She loves her worn-out, plain, leather jacket.
He's wearing an awesome, red, checked, cotton shirt.

General appearance	Opinion	Size/Fit
	awesome	
Colour	**Pattern**	**Material**

6 Choose three items from the website on page 34. Describe them using as many adjectives as possible. Remember to use the correct order.

There's a smart, blue-and-red, striped tie.

7 2.04 WORD FRIENDS Complete the phrases with *be*, *have* or *wear*. Listen and check.

Word Friends

_______ a pale complexion, a piercing, dyed hair, freckles, painted nails, pierced ears
_______ good-looking, in his/her thirties, slim, tanned
_______ a wig, glasses, jewellery

8 2.05 Complete the sentences with words and phrases from the Word Friends box. Listen and check.

1 Sarah *is tanned* after her holiday in Italy.
2 The boy's brother _______ two _______.
3 The actor _______ really _______.
4 My friend _______ _______ all over her nose.
5 Her older sister always _______ _______.

9 I KNOW! Can you think of any other uses of *have*, *be* or *wear* to describe appearance?

have brown hair, be tall, wear a hat, …

10 In pairs, describe people you know.

My brother is slim, has short, brown hair and a pale complexion.

11 2.06 Read the article. Choose the correct option. Listen and check.

Dress to impress! (for guys)

Do you always wear the same old baggy [1]*sunglasses* / *(jeans)*, smelly trainers and a [2]*smart* / *worn-out* T-shirt? Then you need to read these top tips!

- **Choose a style:** What style do you like? Skater: trainers, jeans, hats and accessories. Hipster: checked [3]*freckles* / *shirts*, skinny jeans, big glasses and scarves. Classy: suits, shirts and [4]*smart* / *scruffy* shoes.
- **Do your research:** Check which shops sell the style of clothes you want to buy.
- **Take your friends shopping:** A second opinion is always a good idea and friends can encourage you to try new styles.
- **Learn what colours suit you:** If you [5]*have* / *are* a pale complexion, you need to wear strong colours. If you [6]*wear* / *are* tanned, however, you can usually wear pale colours.
- **Buy clothes that fit:** Size is so important! You don't want clothes that are too tight or too [7]*skinny* / *baggy*. Remember sizes are not always the same in different shops. Always try on clothes before you buy them.
- **Accessorise:** Accessories aren't just for girls! A cool pair of sunglasses, a good belt or some [8]*baggy* / *leather* bracelets can make an outfit, and the right [9]*denim* / *hat* could save you when your hair's a mess! Lots of guys [10]*wear* / *have* piercings now too!

12 In pairs, ask and answer the questions. **And YOU**

1 Which advice in the text do you agree/disagree with? Why?
2 Do you think the same advice is true for girls too? Why? / Why not?
3 How important are clothes and appearance for you?

3.2 GRAMMAR Present Perfect Continuous

I can talk about things that started in the past and have continued until now.

VIDEO STAGE SUCCESS!

Jay: Hi, everybody. As you all know, we've been working for a long time to raise money for the school trip. And here it is, the Belmont Academy Fashion Show.

Skye: That was brilliant, Dan! You've been practising! Now, quick. Go and put this on.

Dan: What about the other hat?

Skye: I can't find it.

Dan: Hurry up, Skye! I'm back on in a minute.

Skye (on the phone): Tommo? Where are you? Have you got the kayak for the final scene? Great! Now, just get here as soon as you can!

Jay: And now it's time for Nina!

Skye: Tommo? At last! We've been waiting for you for ages. Dan's been doing really well.

Tommo: Listen, I've been thinking. You can use my kayak, but … do I have to go on stage?

Skye: But we've been waiting for you, Tommo. Come on!

Tommo: I just feel really nervous.

Dan: You'll be great. Just put on these sports clothes and imagine you're going out in your kayak. Forget about everybody else.

Jay: And now the moment you've all been waiting for. Please give a big cheer for Tommo!

OUT of class

Hurry up! I've been thinking.
At last! You'll be great.

1 CLASS VOTE **Would you like to be in a fashion show at your school? Why? / Why not?**

I would love to be in a fashion show because …

2 3.1 2.07 **Watch or listen. Why are they organising a fashion show?**

3 Study the Grammar box. Find more examples of the Present Perfect Continuous in the dialogue.

Grammar — Present Perfect Continuous

I've been working hard.
She hasn't been practising much.
How long have you been waiting?

Time expressions

all day/night
We've been working all day.

since last Friday/October/Saturday/I woke up
They've been waiting here since one o'clock.

for two hours/three years/a long time/ages
She's been doing her homework for three hours.

GRAMMAR TIME > PAGE 120

4 Complete the advert with the Present Perfect Continuous form of the verbs in brackets.

[1] *Have* you *been looking* (look) for something new to wear? [2] ______ you ______ (think) of buying a fashionable polka dot dress but couldn't find one? At Awesome we [3] ______ (make) clothes the way you want them since we started. Our designers [4] ______ (listen) to your ideas and our expert shoppers [5] ______ (collect) the best fashions. So, if you [6] ______ (save) for something super cool, check out our new collection.

5 Complete the sentences with *for* or *since*.

1 I've been saving up *for* ages to buy this fantastic jacket!
2 Has Liam been making his own clothes ______ a long time?
3 Emma has been practising for the show ______ October.
4 Jake hasn't been taking any selfies ______ his mum cut his hair!

6 In pairs, tell each other four things using the Present Perfect Continuous and these verbs.

help look for practise save up think about

I've been saving up for some new trainers.

3.3 READING and VOCABULARY A bad hair day

I can identify specific detail in a text and talk about the main ideas.

1 CLASS VOTE **Do you like going to the hairdresser's? Why? / Why not?**

2 Read the comments people made after a visit to the hairdresser's. In pairs, discuss how they're feeling.

1 It cost a lot of money and it doesn't look any different.

2 The colour is really awesome. I can't wait to show my friends.

3 It's incredibly short. I don't know if I like it.

4 It's awful – my ears look too big.

3 Look at the title of the article and the photo. What do you think it will be about?

4 Read the first paragraph. In pairs, answer the questions.

1 What problems do James and Georgia have?
2 Do you agree that boys and girls have similar hair problems?

5 2.08 **Now read the whole article. Mark the sentences T (true) or F (false).**

1 ☐ The teenagers in the survey were between twelve and sixteen years old.
2 ☐ Most teens are generally happy with how their hair looks.
3 ☐ Wigs in ancient Egypt were attractive and practical.
4 ☐ Egyptians copied Cleopatra's hairstyles to be fashionable.
5 ☐ Copying a hairstyle from the internet might not always be successful.
6 ☐ The author thinks your hairstyle should express your personality.

6 Look at the highlighted words in the text. Check your understanding. Use a dictionary if necessary.

7 Work in pairs. What is the main idea in each paragraph? Write one sentence that summarises the whole text.

Are you having a bad hair day?

Do you usually wake up, take one look at your hair and run for the shower? In a recent survey by Teensnet of 2,000 teenagers aged around sixteen years old, eight out of ten said they weren't happy with their appearance and it's their hairstyle that's been causing most of their problems. 'Since the age of twelve, I haven't left the house without checking my hair a million times in the mirror,' says James. His friend Georgia has been going to the same hairdresser since she was little, but says that she never has her hair cut if she's got school the next day. 'I worry that it won't look right,' she says. These are problems that many teens have – and yes, it's boys and girls.

Hair worries are not a modern thing. Men and women have been trying different styles for thousands of years. You can cut it, straighten it, gel it and colour it. The ancient Egyptians thought that hair was very important and created beautiful hairstyles with hair extensions and beads. Men and women cut off their hair then dyed it and made fashionable wigs that looked good and also protected their heads from the sun. Historians say that Queen Cleopatra used different styles to show her power and fame. Paintings from that time show that Egyptians copied her styles – perhaps because they wanted to appear powerful too.

Today we still try to copy others. Celebrities, especially football players and pop stars, have been influencing our appearance for a long time. A photo of a famous person with the 'perfect' hairstyle can go viral and suddenly lots of people try to copy it. However, if the style doesn't suit the shape of your face or your complexion, it can be a disaster. How many times have you looked at a photo of yourself and thought 'Oh no, why did I think rainbow-coloured hair was a good idea?' So, yes, hair is important because it makes us feel good about ourselves. But maybe it's time to forget what other people look like and choose a style that reflects our true selves.

8 Cover the text and take it in turns to tell each other what it's about.

Lots of teenagers aren't happy with their appearance ...

And YOU

9 In pairs, ask and answer the questions.

1 Who influences your hairstyle? Your parents? Your friends? Your favourite pop stars or sports heroes? Your hairdresser?
2 Have you ever tried to copy a hairstyle or do you know somebody who's copied a hairstyle? What was it like?

3.4 GRAMMAR Present Perfect Simple and Continuous

I can understand the difference between the Present Perfect Simple and Continuous.

1 CLASS VOTE Have you ever made your own clothes or accessories? What are the advantages and disadvantages of making your own things?

2 Read the blog post and the comments. What does the girl make that everyone wants? Why do her friends want them?

Kelly's blog

Everyone wants one!

Last month it was my best friend Rachel's birthday and I made her a case for her tablet. Since Rachel's birthday, lots of people have been asking me to make more and so I've been very busy. I've been creating lots of new designs and have made tablet cases for eight people in my class at school. I think people like them because they're different. They like the fact that you can't buy them in the shops. I've been taking photos of all the cases I've made. I've uploaded some photos here so you can tell me what you think!

Cara: I've been looking for a cool case for my tablet for ages and I haven't seen anything I like. These are awesome! I'm going to try making one. Thanks, Kelly!

Nathan: I've been reading your blog for ages and I've found it really useful. Your ideas are great and my friends love them.

3 Study the Grammar box. Find more examples of the Present Perfect Simple and Continuous in the blog post and comments.

> **Grammar** Present Perfect Simple and Continuous
>
> **Present Perfect Simple**
> They've made a lot of jewellery. (focus on result)
> She hasn't bought a new skirt. (focus on result)
>
> **Present Perfect Continuous**
> She's been looking for a new skirt for ages. (focus on activity)
> They've been taking photos of the jewellery. (focus on unfinished action)
>
> **Time expressions**
> for
> I've been waiting for her email for a week.
> since
> I've known Jessica since October.
>
> **Be careful!**
> With state verbs (*know, understand,* etc.) you can only use the Present Perfect Simple.
>
> GRAMMAR TIME > PAGE 120

4 2.09 Choose the correct option. Listen and check.

1. Here you are. *I've made* / *I've been making* you a necklace. Do you like it?
2. *I've been being* / *I've been* interested in fashion since I was about twelve.
3. I'm really tired. *I've shopped* / *I've been shopping* all morning.
4. I don't know what to wear for the party. *I've tried* / *I've been trying* on five different dresses and I don't like any of them!
5. *I've been wearing* / *I've worn* these shoes all evening and my feet really hurt!

5 Write questions using the Present Perfect Simple or Continuous. In pairs, ask and answer the questions.

1. how long / you / have / your mobile phone / ?
2. how long / you / learn / English / ?
3. how long / you / know / your best friend / ?
4. how long / your favourite clothes shop / be / open / ?

A: How long have you had your mobile phone?
B: I've had it for two years.

6 [VOX POPS 3.2] Do you know anybody who's good at making things? What do they make, how long have they been doing it and what have they made? Write a few sentences.

And YOU

3.5 LISTENING and VOCABULARY The National Museum of Fashion

I can identify specific detail in a conversation and talk about unusual clothes.

1 CLASS VOTE **Do you think we can learn about life in the past by looking at old clothes and accessories? Why? / Why not?**

2 2.10 **Label the photos with words from the Vocabulary box. Listen and check.**

Vocabulary	**Parts of clothes and shoes**
button collar heel hood laces pocket sleeve sole zip	

1 ______
2 ______
3 ______
4 ______
5 ______
6 ______
7 ______
8 ______
9 ______

3 2.11 **Choose the correct option. Listen and check.**

1 I left my money in my coat *pocket* / *collar*.
2 There's a hole in the *sole* / *button* of my shoe. When it rains, my toes get wet!
3 This *zip* / *collar* is really uncomfortable. It's too tight around my neck.
4 I can't walk in these shoes – the *heel* / *hood* is broken.
5 I can't take my jeans off! The *zip* / *sole* is stuck!
6 It takes a long time to put my new boots on. They have long *laces* / *sleeves*.
7 I always leave the top *heel* / *button* open on my shirt.
8 My arms get hot in the summer, so I like to wear *short sleeves* / *a short pocket*.

4 **Look at the photos. What do you think these objects are?**

The National Museum of Fashion

Take a fascinating journey through the different ages of fashion!

☐ A

☐ B

☐ C

5 2.12 **Listen to a conversation between a radio presenter, Ryan, and a reporter, Sylvia, about the National Museum of Fashion. Put photos A–C in the order you hear about them.**

6 2.12 **Listen again. Choose the correct answers.**

1 Sylvia says the museum
  a is mostly about modern fashion.
  b shows only clothes from the past.
  c has both old and modern clothes.
2 'Chopines' were
  a fifteen centimetres high.
  b only popular in Venice.
  c in fashion between the fifteenth and seventeenth centuries.
3 Who wore very tall chopines?
  a both men and women
  b women who loved fashion
  c women who wanted to show their social status
4 A 'ruff' is a type of collar that was popular
  a before the fourteenth century.
  b in the sixteenth and seventeenth centuries.
  c after the seventeenth century.
5 A story says that Napoleon put buttons on his soldiers' sleeves
  a to help keep the uniforms cleaner.
  b in order for the soldiers to look smarter.
  c to make the uniforms more comfortable.

7 [VOX POPS ▶ 3.3] **In pairs, describe the most unusual item of clothing you've ever seen. Take it in turns to ask and answer these questions.**

And YOU

- What was it?
- Where did you see it?
- What did it look like?
- Did you like it? Why? / Why not?

3.6 SPEAKING Giving compliments

I can give and respond to compliments.

VIDEO WHERE ARE MY TROUSERS?

Jay: Phew! I'm so glad that's over. I've been worrying about it all week. I hate being on stage.
Tommo: But you look great in that suit. I was a disaster!
Jay: No, you weren't, Tommo. Your kayak idea was awesome!
Tommo: Oh, thanks. You've made my day. Now, where are my trousers?
Skye: Tommo, those shorts are so cool. You did really well.
Tommo: Really? But Dan and Nina were brilliant. I love their style.
Skye: Dan's being really moody.
...
Nina: Dan, stop being stupid. You were brilliant! Let's get a drink.
Dan: No, I'm going now.
Tommo: Dan, what's up? Don't go.
Skye: They're always together now.
Tommo: Are you jealous, Skye?
Skye: No! It's just that you're always so nice, Tommo, but Dan's a bit of a big head.
Tommo: Skye! That's not like you. What's the matter?
Skye: I miss my old school.
Tommo: You'll be fine. Hang on! Where are my trousers? Dan!

Dan's a bit of big head.
That's not like you.

OUT of class

1 CLASS VOTE **Do you usually comment when a friend is wearing new clothes or has a different hairstyle? Why? / Why not?**

If a friend of mine has a new hairstyle, …

2 3.4 2.13 **Watch or listen and answer the questions.**

1 How does Jay feel after the show?
2 Why do you think Dan is angry?

3 Study the Speaking box. Find more examples of giving and responding to compliments in the dialogue.

Speaking Giving compliments

Complimenting appearance
You look good/great in that suit/in pink/in that colour.
What a nice T-shirt!
Your clothes are awesome.
That jacket is cool.
You've got amazing hair/a nice smile.
I like your style.
You've got great taste in clothes.
It really suits you.

Complimenting actions
You are/were brilliant/fantastic!
You did really well.
You're always so kind/helpful.

Responding to compliments
Thanks. You've made my day.
That's really nice of you.
You've made me feel really good.
Really?/Are you sure?/Do you really think so?

4 2.14 **Order the dialogues. Listen and check.**

1 [ ] Yes, it suits you.
[ ] You look good in blue.
[ ] Yes, I got it yesterday, but I'm not sure about the colour.
[1] That jacket is awesome! Is it new?
[ ] Are you sure?

2 [ ] Really? I was very nervous.
[ ] Thanks. You've made my day.
[1] That was a great show. You were brilliant.
[ ] Honestly – you did really well.

And YOU

5 In pairs, read the compliments. Are they about appearance or actions? Take it in turns to choose one and say it to your partner. Your partner responds. How long can you keep the conversation going?

I love your hair.
You look good in that hat.
You've got a nice smile.
Your clothes are really cool.
You were brilliant in class today.
You're always nice to people.

3.7 WRITING An email describing appearance

I can write an email describing people's clothes and appearance.

1 CLASS VOTE **Look at these ideas for fancy-dress party themes. Which one is your favourite? What other themes can you think of?**

- James Bond
- Star Wars
- Wild West
- celebrities
- animals
- beach party

2 **Read Skye's email about her fancy-dress birthday party. What is the theme?**

Hi Alisha,

I haven't heard from you for ages. What have you been doing? I've been planning a fancy-dress party for my birthday next month and I'd love you to come.

The theme of my party is the 1980s, so you'll have to dress up! At that time girls used to wear short leggings under a mini skirt or polka-dot dresses with coloured necklaces and plastic bracelets, and the guys wore baggy trousers and jackets in bright colours. I've found an amazing outfit! I'm going to wear a checked dress with pink and red striped tights, a bright green wig and huge earrings!

By the way, I've made friends with an interesting girl from Colombia called Nina. She's pretty and really trendy and was in the school fashion show we had recently. She's also friendly and fun to be with and she's really into hip-hop music. We enjoy talking about the latest songs. Sometimes she has cool hair extensions or she wears crazy hats. I hope you can come to the party so that you can meet her. Anyway, let me know if you can make it.

Bye for now,

Skye

3 **Complete the Vocabulary box with adjectives from Skye's email. Can you add any other words?**

Vocabulary Descriptive adjectives

Clothes
short, mini, ______, ______, ______, ______, ______, ______

Accessories
coloured, plastic, ______, ______, ______, ______, ______

Appearance
pretty, ______

Personality
interesting, ______, ______

4 **Skye wants two friends who don't know each other to meet at her party. In pairs, discuss if this is a good idea. Give reasons.**

5 **Look at the words in bold and match sentences 1–2 with descriptions a–b. Find more examples in Skye's email.**

1 We've having the party in the summer **so that** everybody can come.
2 The guests will be hungry, **so** I'm making lots of food.

a shows the purpose of an action
b shows the result of an action

6 **Study the Writing box. Which phrases can you find in Skye's email?**

Writing An email describing appearance

Starting your email
I haven't heard from you for ages.
What have you been doing/up to?
Sorry I didn't write sooner, but I've been busy.
I've got some great news!

Describing clothes and appearance
I'm going to wear short leggings/baggy trousers.
I'm going to have a ponytail/a crazy hairstyle.
She's/He's stunning/cool/handsome/pretty.

Giving more information
By the way, ...
I also wanted to tell you about ...

Ending your email
Anyway, let me know if you can come/make it.
Write back soon.
Cheers./Bye for now./Speak soon.

Writing Time

7 **Write an email to a friend about a fancy-dress party. Follow the instructions below.**

1 Say what the theme is.
2 Describe what you're going to wear.
3 Your cousin is going to the party. Describe him/her and say why you would like your friend to meet him/her.

TIP

Use descriptive adjectives to make your writing more lively and interesting.

WORDLIST Clothes and accessories | Adjectives to describe clothes and accessories | Parts of clothes and shoes | Descriptive adjectives

accessories /əkˈsesəris/
active /ˈæktɪv/
appearance /əˈpɪərəns/
awesome /ˈɔːsəm/
baggy /ˈbæɡi/
basics /ˈbeɪsɪks/
bead /biːd/
belt /belt/
black-and-white /ˌblæk ən ˈwaɪt /
boots /buːts/
bracelet /ˈbreɪslət/
button /ˈbʌtn/
case /keɪs/
cause /kɔːz/
checked /tʃekt/
classy /ˈklɑːsi/
clothing /ˈkləʊðɪŋ/
collar /ˈkɒlə/
collection /kəˈlekʃən/
compliment /ˈkɒmplɪmənt/
cotton /ˈkɒtn/
denim /ˈdenɪm/
design /dɪˈzaɪn/
designer /dɪˈzaɪnə/
dress /dres/
dress up /dres ʌp/
earring /ˈɪə rɪŋ/
extension /ɪkˈstenʃən/
fancy-dress /ˈfænsi dres/
fashion show /ˈfæʃən ʃəʊ/
fashionable /ˈfæʃənəbəl/
fit /fɪt/
flowery /ˈflaʊəri/
friendly /ˈfrendli/
gel /dʒel/
gloves /ɡlʌvz/
go viral /ɡəʊ ˈvaɪərəl/
hairdresser /ˈheə ˌdres əz/
hairstyle /ˈheəstaɪl/
handsome /ˈhænsm/
heel /hiːl/
hipster /ˈhɪpstə/
hood /hʊd/
hoodie /ˈhʊdi/
huge /hjuːdʒ/
impress /ɪmˈpres/
influence /ˈɪnfluəns/
jealous /ˈdʒeləs/
jewellery /ˈdʒuːəlri/
laces /ˈleɪsɪz/
leather /ˈleðə/
leggings /ˈleɡɪŋz/
market /ˈmɑːkət/
material /məˈtɪəriəl/
mini /ˈmɪni/
nail varnish /neɪl ˈvɑːnɪʃ/
necklace /ˈnekləs/
old-fashioned /ˌəʊld ˈfæʃənd/
outfit /ˈaʊtfɪt/
pair /peə/
pale /peɪl/
pattern /ˈpætən/
plain /pleɪn/
plastic /ˈplæstɪk/
pocket /ˈpɒkət/
polka-dot /ˈpɒlkə dɒt/
ponytail /ˈpəʊniˌteɪl/
pretty /ˈprɪti/
protect /prəˈtekt/
pullover /ˈpʊlˌəʊvə/
raincoat /ˈreɪnkəʊt/
reflect /rɪˈflekt/
sale /seɪl /
sandals /ˈsændəlz/
scarf /skɑːf/
scene /siːn/
scruffy /ˈskrʌfi/
second-hand /ˌsekəndˈhænd/
shopping mall /ˈʃɒpɪŋ mɔːl/
shorts /ʃɔːts/
skater /ˈskeɪtə/
skinny /ˈskɪni/
sleeve /sliːv/
smart /smɑːt/
smelly /ˈsmeli/
social status /səʊʃl steɪtəs/
sole /səʊ/
stage /steɪdʒ/
straighten /ˈstreɪtn/
striped /straɪpt/
stunning /ˈstʌnɪŋ/
style /staɪl/
suit /suːt/
survey /ˈsɜːveɪ/
taste /teɪst/
theme /θiːm/
tight /taɪt/
tights / taɪts/
tip /tɪp/
tracksuit /ˈtræksuːt/
trendy /trendi/
trousers /ˈtraʊzəz/
try on /traɪ ɒn/
uncomfortable /ʌnˈkʌmftəbəl/
uniform /ˈjuːnɪfɔːm/
wellies /ˈweliz/
wig /wɪɡ/
woollen /wʊlən/
worn-out /ˌwɔːn ˈaʊt/
zip /zɪp/

WORD FRIENDS

be good-looking/in your thirties/slim/tanned
have a pale complexion/a piercing/dyed hair/freckles/painted nails/pierced ears
wear a wig/glasses/jewellery

VOCABULARY IN ACTION

1 Use the wordlist to find:

1 three things you wear on your feet *boots, …*
2 five things that are part of a jacket *hood, …*
3 three words to describe the size of a piece of clothing *baggy, …*
4 four words to describe the material something is made of *woollen, …*
5 four different kinds of patterns *striped, …*

2 Complete the sentences with words or phrases from Word Friends.

1 Jo always has *painted nails* . She usually does them in a colour to match her clothes.
2 I wore a curly pink ________ to the party.
3 My mum wears ________ for reading, but she doesn't need them all the time.
4 My sister has ________ and she always wears really big earrings.
5 It was really sunny at the tennis match yesterday. My face and arms are ________ , but the rest of me is white!
6 My brother doesn't wear any ________ . He doesn't like rings or necklaces.

3 2.15 PRONUNCIATION Listen to the questions and answers. When is the pronunciation of 'a' in *have* and *haven't* weak (/ə/) and when is it strong (/æ/)? In pairs, practise the dialogues.

1 A: Have you been waiting here for long?
B: Yes, I have.
2 A: Have you ever dyed your hair red?
B: No, I haven't.

Revision

VOCABULARY

1 **Write the correct word for each definition.**

1. A piece of jewellery you wear around your wrist. **b** *r a c e l e t*
2. The bottom part of a shoe that touches the ground. **s** _ _ _
3. These keep your hands warm. **g** _ _ _ _ _
4. A top and trousers that you usually wear for doing exercise. **t** _ _ _ _ _ _ _ _
5. Untidy and not smart. **s** _ _ _ _ _ _
6. Very light in colour. **p** _ _ _

2 **Complete the sentences with the words below.**

> ~~appearance~~ dyed earrings glasses heels second-hand

1. I think some people spend too much time and money on their *appearance*.
2. Jewellery such as ______ always looks better on women than on men.
3. I love buying cheap ______ clothes. I think new clothes are a waste of money.
4. I don't know why women wear high ______. They look so uncomfortable!
5. I think people who wear ______ look more intelligent.
6. I believe people who have ______ hair are often more creative.

3 **Work in pairs. Do you agree with the sentences in Exercise 2? Why? / Why not?**

GRAMMAR

4 **Complete the sentences with *for* or *since*.**

1. She's been wearing that jacket *for* years – it looks really scruffy now!
2. I've had pierced ears ______ I was ten.
3. He's tried on five different pairs of trainers ______ we came into this shop!
4. Laura has had dyed red hair ______ about a year.
5. They've been looking round the fashion exhibition ______ hours.
6. I've had this bracelet ______ my birthday. It was a present from my mum.
7. My brother hasn't had a party ______ he finished school five years ago.
8. I've been wearing these boots ______ twelve hours. My feet hurt!

5 2.16 **Complete the article with the Present Perfect Simple or Continuous form of the verbs in brackets. Listen and check.**

Fashion weekly – fashion you can eat?

For the last few days, designers [1]*have been preparing* (prepare) for today's fashion show. So what's different about this show? Well, the designers [2]______ (make) all the outfits out of chocolate. Yes, that's right – chocolate! It's the first chocolate fashion show in this city and people [3]______ (queue) all morning to buy tickets. One fashion fan told me, 'I [4]______ (be) to lots of fashion shows, but I [5]______ (never/see) clothes made out of chocolate! I can't wait!' Of course, chocolate melts when it gets warm and the organisers [6]______ (put) the air conditioning on cold, so if you're planning to come to the show, wear a hat and scarf!

6 **In pairs, ask and answer questions about your day. Use the Present Perfect Simple and Continuous.**

What have you been doing this morning?
Who have you seen this morning?
Have you eaten breakfast?

SPEAKING

7 **In pairs, role-play the situations.**

1

A: Tell your friend that you are not sure about your new haircut.

B: You like your friend's new haircut. Give him/her a compliment about their appearance.

2

B: You have entered a design competition. Tell your friend you are worried that your fashion designs aren't good enough.

A: You think your friend is good at designing clothes. Give him/her a compliment about the designs.

DICTATION

8 2.17 **Listen. Then listen again and write down what you hear.**

BBC

CULTURE

Who is the queen of fashion?

The Queen of fashion

It's hard to imagine that the royal look could be a fashion icon in the UK but that's exactly what it has become in recent years.

The Queen's headscarf, Burberry check or tartan skirt might seem old-fashioned, but when they are reinvented by famous designers such as Dolce & Gabbana, these country clothes take on a very trendy look. Changing the position of a sleeve or a pocket can give them a modern touch. The royal tartan check was even used in punk fashion as a statement of rebellion. Yes, rock stars wore kilts!

But the Queen's Barbour jacket is perhaps the most distinctive of all her garments. Dating from the 1890s, Barbours were originally made for country people and sailors who needed hard-wearing, waterproof clothes. But now they are equally popular with farmers, 'fashionistas' and film stars – both male and female. One of the latest stars to wear one was actor Daniel Craig in the James Bond films. Helen Mirren also wore one in her role as – yes, you guessed it – the Queen!

However, the real queen of royal fashion these days is Kate Middleton, or Catherine, the Duchess of Cambridge, Prince William's wife. Unlike Princess Diana, who wore royal tiaras and her hair short, Kate prefers the more informal trend for long hair. She also dresses in a more extravagant but affordable way. In fact, her look is a careful combination of designer fashion with everyday clothes that can be bought anywhere in the UK.

Her influence is so great that it's become known as 'the Kate effect'. As soon as she wears a particular dress that is available on the high street, the same garment sells out in no time. In this way, she has made some British clothes brands more popular. Now, thanks to Kate, everyone can feel like a queen for the day!

GLOSSARY
distinctive (adj) easy to recognise because of being different or special
kilt (n) a type of skirt made of tartan, often worn by Scottish men
garment (n) a piece of clothing
waterproof (adj) not allowing water to go through
affordable (adj) not expensive

EXPLORE

1 In pairs, discuss the questions.

1 Who can you see in the photo?
2 Would you say the look is modern or old-fashioned? Why?
3 Do you follow fashion? Why? / Why not?

2 Read the text and choose the correct option.

1 The writer believes it's *strange* / *normal* that the Queen is a fashion icon.
2 In the past the Barbour jacket was only used as a *working garment* / *fashion item*.
3 Barbour jackets are worn by *men only* / *both sexes*.
4 Kate Middleton *rejects high street fashion labels* / *wears clothes anyone can afford*.
5 'The Kate effect' describes the fact that people *buy* / *copy* the same clothes Kate Middleton has worn.

3 In pairs, discuss the questions.

1 Are celebrities like Kate Middleton considered fashionable where you live? Why? / Why not?
2 Are you influenced by how famous people dress? If so, who?

EXPLORE MORE

4 3.5 Watch Part 1 of a documentary about British fashion. Answer the questions.

1 What clothes and fashion items can you see?
2 What are the differences and similarities between them?

5 3.5 Watch the video again. Mark the sentences T (true) or F (false). Correct the false sentences.

1 ☐ Designers think British style is weird and wonderful.
2 ☐ The Queen is a typical fashion icon.
3 ☐ British style is great because it is practical.
4 ☐ British clothes are not well-known.
5 ☐ British clothing is designed to protect us.

6 Check your memory. Tick the clothes and fashion accessories that you saw in the video.

☐ suit	☐ leather bag
☐ tie	☐ belt
☐ cap	☐ tracksuit
☐ buttons	☐ tights
☐ riding boots	☐ sandals
☐ gloves	☐ swimsuit
☐ zip	☐ necklace
☐ hoodie	☐ umbrella

7 3.5 Watch the video again and check your answers to Exercise 6.

8 3.6 Watch Part 2 of the video about the Barbour jacket. Answer the questions.

1 What is James Percy's job at Barbour?
2 How long have Barbour been making their wax jackets?
3 What happened to sales of Barbour jackets in the USA after the premiere of the film *The Queen*?
4 How do Europeans like their Barbour jackets?
5 How do British people prefer them?
6 Which taste do you think James shares – the European or the British? Why?

9 Do you like any of the clothes from the two clips? Would you wear any of them? Give reasons. What clothes are popular where you live? Do they normally look old or new? Discuss in pairs or small groups.

YOU EXPLORE

10 CULTURE PROJECT In small groups, prepare a presentation about clothes and fashion in your town.

1 Discuss popular fashion styles where you live and why they are in fashion at the moment.
2 Write a short script to describe your ideas. Choose images or videos that you would like to use.
3 Share your presentation with the class.

4

Team work

VOCABULARY
Jobs | Finding and losing a job | Working conditions | Success at work

GRAMMAR
Talking about the future | Future Continuous

Grammar: Exciting news

Speaking: A tough day!

BBC Culture: The contest

Workbook p. 53

BBC VOX POPS

My world

A

Lisa: It's great to have hands-on experience. I didn't …

CLICK FOR MORE

B

Alex: I've really enjoyed it and it looks good on my CV! It was …

CLICK FOR MORE

C

Jack: It's helped me decide what I want to do in the future and it's given …

CLICK FOR MORE

D

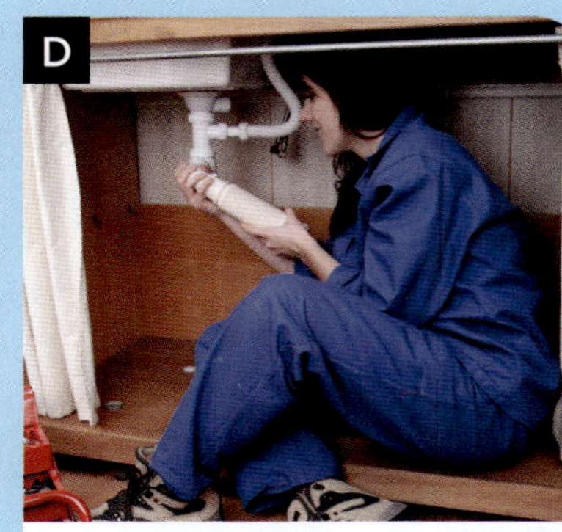

Ella: It was more interesting than I expected. I learned so much …

CLICK FOR MORE

4.1 VOCABULARY Work and jobs

I can talk about jobs and work experience.

1 CLASS VOTE **What are the most important factors in a job? Order the factors below (1 = very important, 5 = not important). Can you think of any other things which are important?**

holidays hours money people place of work

2 2.18 **Study the Vocabulary A box. Find some of the jobs in the photos. Listen and check.**

Vocabulary A Jobs

cleaner cook engineer interpreter librarian lifeguard manager painter plumber psychologist scientist writer

Compound nouns

app designer computer programmer dentist's assistant fashion designer film director flight attendant lorry driver music critic travel agent veterinary assistant

3 2.19 **Listen to six students talking about doing work experience. What jobs do they refer to?**

1 ______ 4 ______
2 ______ 5 ______
3 ______ 6 ______

4 **I KNOW!** Work in pairs. How many more jobs can you add to the Vocabulary A box?

5 In pairs, take it in turns to describe a job for your partner to guess.

I help people understand each other when they don't speak the same language.

6 2.20 **WORD FRIENDS** Complete the Word Friends box with the verbs below. Listen and check.

apply earn get (x2) meet quit sign ~~write~~

Word Friends

look for a job	**gain** work experience
write a CV	______ a promotion
______ **for** a job	**get** fired
have an interview	**give up**/______ work
have training	**be** unemployed
______ a contract	**get** unemployment benefits
______ your colleagues	**be** retired
be part of a team	______ a pension
______ a salary/a wage	

7 Complete the sentences with verbs from the Word Friends box. In pairs, discuss the questions.

1 Do you think it's important to be 100 percent honest when you *write* your CV?
2 How do most people feel when they ______ an interview? Why?
3 Do you like to ______ part of a team or do you prefer to work alone? Why?
4 Do you think it's important to ______ some work experience before you leave school?
5 Can you think of some reasons why people ______ fired from their job?
6 At what age do people ______ a pension in your country? Do you think this is the right age?

8 2.21 Study the Vocabulary B box. Complete the article with the words and phrases below. Listen and check.

company flexible overtime
hourly rate ~~part-time~~ paid holiday

Vocabulary B **Working conditions**

It's a full-time/part-time/temporary/permanent/summer job.
I work in a big company/in a small firm.
It's well-paid/badly-paid.
The hourly rate is ...
We work shifts/flexible hours/nine to five.
We often work overtime.
You can get a bonus/a pay rise.
You have paid holidays.

Could you be a teen trep?

Lots of young people I know are starting to get [1]*part-time* and full-time jobs. They work a lot of [2] ______, so they are too tired to go out. The [3] ______ for their jobs is low – for example, my friend, who is a waiter, earns £4.50 an hour. When they complain, I want to say, 'Why don't you start your own [4] ______ then?' I'm a teen 'trep' – that's short for 'entrepreneur'. I create online games. OK, so I don't get any [5] ______ and I usually save money during the year so I can take a break in the summer. On the other hand, the hours are [6] ______ and there's lots of freedom. So what makes a successful trep? First of all, you need to think outside the box. You'll also need people skills and good problem solving skills. If this sounds like you, why not be the next teen trep?

9 Answer the questions.

1 What's a teen trep? What are the advantages and disadvantages of starting your own company?
2 What skills do you need to be a young trep?
3 What do you think the phrase *think outside the box* means?

10 [VOX POPS 4.1] In pairs, discuss the questions. **And YOU**

1 In your opinion, which jobs should be better paid? Why?
2 What job would you like to do? What job wouldn't you want to do? Why?

4.2 GRAMMAR Talking about the future

I can use different forms to talk about future events.

1 CLASS VOTE **What are the advantages and disadvantages of an open air cinema? Do you think it would be fun to work in one?**

2 **Read the email. What are Dimitris' plans?**

Hi Matt,

What are you going to do in the summer? I'm going to Greece. My uncle is starting an open air cinema this summer and I'm going to help sell tickets. My uncle lives next to the sea, so I'll be able to swim every day. I'll probably spend my mornings on the beach with my cousins and then I'll work with my uncle in the evenings.

My flight is on the day after we finish school and I fly back to the UK on 30 August. I'm going to miss hanging out with my friends, but I won't miss the British weather! I'll send you a postcard from Greece! ☺

Bye for now,
Dimitris

3 **Study the Grammar box. Find more examples of these forms in the email.**

Grammar **Talking about the future**

will
I'll get you some water – you look thirsty. (spontaneous decision)
They won't find this kind of work difficult. (prediction)

be going to
I'm not going to work full-time. (plan)
The job's going to be interesting. (prediction based on facts)

Present Continuous
Sam and Chloe are arriving at two o'clock. (arrangement)

Present Simple
The train leaves in twenty minutes. (timetable)

Look at the future forms of *can* and *must*.
I can save some money. → I'll be able to save some money.
I must be back at two. → I'll have to be back at two.

GRAMMAR TIME > PAGE 121

4 **Complete the second sentence so that it means the same as the first one. Use no more than three words.**

1 Julia and Zara have arranged to visit their friend at the weekend.
Julia and Zara *are visiting* their friend at the weekend.
2 They're expecting to be well-paid.
They think ______ well-paid.
3 The boat is timetabled to leave at 4 p.m. tomorrow.
The boat ______ at 4 p.m. tomorrow.
4 I'm planning to quit my job.
I ______ to leave my job.

5 🔊 **2.22** **Circle the correct option. Listen and check.**

Mark: Hi, Lara. Are you OK? You look worried!
Lara: I am! My interview at the bakery [1]*will be* / (*is*) in half an hour!
Mark: I didn't know you were looking for a job.
Lara: Yes. I [2]*'m going* / *'ll go* on holiday next month; it's all booked now, so I need to save some money!
Mark: Oh, I see. And where [3]*do you go* / *are you going?*
Lara: Ireland – I can't wait. My friend's grandparents have invited us, so we [4]*'re staying* / *'ll stay* at their house in Dublin.
Mark: Cool! [5]*Will you be able to* / *Are you able to* travel around Ireland a bit?
Lara: Yes, definitely. We plan to go to Cork, Galway and Limerick.
Mark: I hope you have a great time – and good luck with the interview!
Lara: Thanks!

And YOU

6 **Write two true sentences and one false one about your plans for the holidays. Use *be going to* for plans and the Present Continuous for arrangements. In pairs, ask and answer questions to find out the information that is not true.**

4.3 READING and VOCABULARY Summer jobs

I can find specific detail in short texts.

1 CLASS VOTE Do you think summer jobs are a good idea? Why? / Why not?

2 2.23 Read the ads quickly. What jobs are advertised?

A

Train on the job

Are you a strong swimmer, a good communicator and would like a challenge? We are looking for lifeguards for our busy summer season. No experience is necessary as you will get two weeks of training before you start the job. As well as being physically fit, you need to be available for work Mon–Fr, 7 a.m.–11 a.m.

For more information, please contact Kim Rogers on 07865542342.

B

Summer staff needed at City Souvenirs

We are looking for shop assistants for our busy gift shop. Applicants need to be reliable, friendly and enjoy speaking to customers. A second language is preferred as many of our customers are tourists from other countries. The positions are part-time and the hours will be mostly at weekends. Visit our website for more information.

C

Keystones: new vacancy

Keystones Italian restaurant has a part-time position available for a lunchtime kitchen assistant. The role includes preparing food and cleaning the kitchen. This is a great opportunity to gain experience and work with some great chefs. The hours are between 10 a.m. and 6 p.m., Thurs–Sun. Call Marco for more information on 07796472837.

D

Star summer job!

Little Stars Summer Camp is looking for activity leaders to organise activities for children aged 5–8. You will work as part of a team, and activities will include arts and crafts and sports. Working hours are between 1 p.m. and 5 p.m., Monday to Friday. So if you love working with children and have lots of energy, please write to: littlestars@pmail.co.uk.

3 Look at the highlighted words in the ads. Check your understanding. Use a dictionary if necessary.

4 2.24 Three young people are looking for summer jobs. Match the people with ads A–D.

Joe ☐

Joe likes being outdoors and is very sociable. He loves water sports and often takes his young cousins surfing. He enjoys learning new things. This summer he's having guitar lessons every morning.

Lola ☐

Lola usually does babysitting for some neighbours, but now she's looking for a completely different experience. She likes talking to people and is a fast learner. At the moment Lola is learning Chinese on Tuesday and Thursday afternoons and is quite fluent in it. She isn't very sporty, but she loves drawing.

Otto ☐

Otto is half German and half Scottish. He loves sport and he's part of a swimming club that meets every morning at 8 a.m. – also in the summer. He's quite shy and finds it difficult to talk to people he doesn't know. He likes working with his hands and is very neat and tidy.

5 And YOU Do you think you would be good at any of the summer jobs in the ads? Why? / Why not?

I think I would be a good lifeguard because I'm a strong swimmer and I'm quite brave!
I don't think I'd be a good activity leader because I'm not very patient with children.

4.4 GRAMMAR Future Continuous

I can talk about actions in progress in the future.

VIDEO EXCITING NEWS

Dan: Look – you've got a letter.
Skye: At last! I've been waiting for ages for this. It's from the vet. He says I can help in the surgery this summer.
Dan: Cool. What will you be doing?
Skye: Let me see. I'll be working in the office and I'll be doing simple day-to-day jobs with the vet.
Dan: Mmm … simple day-to-day jobs …
Skye: Yes, it'll be fun. I'll be working with different animals. I'll be looking after sick pets. And I'll be helping people who are worried about their pets.
Dan: But you haven't got any experience. You haven't even got a real pet. Well, except for Basil.
Skye: Do you mind? Basil *is* a real pet. And anyway, that's why I'm doing it, Dan. I need the experience. Just wait and see. In ten years I'll be working as a vet and I'll be enjoying it.
Dan: Yes, but until then you won't be helping them. You'll be cleaning up after them!

I've been waiting for ages!
Do you mind?
Just wait and see.
OUT of class

1 CLASS VOTE What do you think is a good age to do work experience?

2 4.2 2.25 Watch or listen and answer the questions.

1 What news does Skye receive?
2 What does Dan think about the news?

3 Study the Grammar box. Find more examples of the Future Continuous in the dialogue.

Grammar Future Continuous

She'll be helping in the office.
We won't be working outside.
Will you be working with animals? Yes, I will./No, I won't.
When will you be working there?

Time expressions
in five/ten/twenty years
I'll probably be working in a hospital in five years.
at 9 p.m./half past eight tonight
I'll be doing my homework at 7 p.m. tonight.
next summer/next year/in the future
I'll be working with animals next summer.

GRAMMAR TIME > PAGE 121

4 Complete the sentences about Dan and Skye with the Future Continuous form of the verbs in brackets.

1 Skye *will be doing* (do) a lot at the surgery.
2 ________ Dan ________ (work) with Skye in the summer?
3 The vet ________ (show) Skye how to look after sick animals.
4 Skye probably ________ (not earn) much money.
5 Skye ________ (visit) farms to learn about other animals.
6 Dan ________ (not see) much of Skye because she'll be busy.

5 Make questions in the Future Continuous. In pairs, ask and answer the questions.

1 you / work / in your own country / in the future / ?
2 what subjects / you / study / next year / ?
3 you / do / work experience / next summer / ?
4 your friends / go to university / after school / ?
5 you / celebrate / your birthday / soon / ?

A: Will you be working in your own country in the future?
B: No, I won't. I'll probably be working abroad.

And YOU

6 [VOX POPS 4.3] In pairs, complete the sentences to make them true for you. Use the Future Continuous.

Next summer …	After dinner this evening …
In five years …	At 11 p.m. tonight …
In fifty years …	This weekend …

In five years I will be studying Art …

4.5 LISTENING and VOCABULARY Success at work

I can understand specific detail in a conversation and talk about success at work.

1 CLASS VOTE **Have you ever won a prize? What was it? What was it for?**

2 2.26 **Study the Vocabulary box. Then write the correct word for each definition. Listen and check.**

Vocabulary	Success at work
award candidate career diploma employer speech	

1 a prize that you get for doing something well *award*
2 a job that you have trained for and have done for a long time ______
3 a formal talk to a group of people ______
4 a document that shows you have completed a course ______
5 someone who wants to be chosen for a job or a prize ______
6 a person or company that pays you to work ______

3 2.27 **Listen to the first part of a recording. Answer the questions.**

1 What type of event is taking place?
2 What's going to happen later in the evening?

4 **Look at the photos of Max and Hannah. What do you think their jobs are?**

5 2.28 **Listen to the second part of the recording. Were you right about Max's and Hannah's jobs?**

6 2.28 **Listen again. Mark the sentences *T* (true) or *F* (false).**

1 ☐ Max felt calm on the TV show.
2 ☐ Max got his diploma when he was seventeen.
3 ☐ Max and Hannah are both interested in sport.
4 ☐ Hannah designed the app after a family holiday.
5 ☐ Hannah's mum owns a sports shop.
6 ☐ Max thinks of his dad as a colleague.
7 ☐ Both Hannah and Max won an award.

7 **In pairs, compare and contrast Hannah's and Max's stories.**

Hannah is only fifteen and she's an app designer. Max is older and he's a personal trainer.

And YOU

8 **In pairs, think of a simple idea for a new business. Explain your idea to the rest of the class. Use these questions to help you.**

- What is the business?
- Why is the business a good idea?
- How many people are in the business?
- What's the future for your business?

Max

Hannah

4.6 SPEAKING Instructions and reminders

I can give instructions, remind somebody what to do and respond.

VIDEO A TOUGH DAY!

Annie: Thanks for coming, Tommo. My brother, Sam, usually works today, but he's off sick.
Tommo: No worries, Annie. I'm looking forward to it, but you'll have to talk me through it.
Annie: Oh, it's all very simple. First, show the customers to a table. Make sure the table is clean. Then give them a menu.
Tommo: That seems easy.
Annie: Yes, but be sure to give them time to read the menu.
Tommo: Of course. Then what?
Annie: After a few minutes go back to the table and take their order. Don't forget to write it down and always write the table number on the order.
Tommo: I hope I remember it all!
Annie: You need to be organised, Tommo. I'll be in the kitchen, so try to bring me the orders as soon as possible.
Tommo: No problem. Anything else?
Annie: Yes. Remember to be polite with all the customers.
Tommo: Sure.
Annie: Now, the last thing you need to do is put this apron on and enjoy it. Don't look so worried!

OUT of class

He's off sick. *It's all very simple.*

1 CLASS VOTE **Do you find it easy to remember instructions or do you often forget things?**

2 Look at the photo. What is Tommo doing?

3 4.4 2.29 **Watch or listen and answer the questions.**

1 Why does Annie want Tommo to help in the café?
2 How does Tommo feel about working there?
3 What does Tommo need to wear in the café?

4 Study the Speaking box. Find more examples of instructions and reminders in the dialogue.

Speaking Instructions and reminders

Giving instructions
First,/Firstly,/Second,/Secondly, wash the glasses.
Then put ice in the glasses.
Make sure they have a menu.
Be sure to smile.
After a few minutes,/After that,/Next, ...
The last thing you need to do is .../Finally, ...
Always/Never put your notebook down.
Try to/not to ...
You need to .../It's important to ...

Reminding
Don't forget to give them some water.
Remember to write it down.

Responding to instructions
That seems easy.
Of course./OK./Sure./No worries./No problem.
Then what?/Then what do I do?
I hope I remember it all!

5 2.30 **Complete the dialogue with words from the Speaking box. Listen and check.**

Jay: I've got an interview for a summer job at the museum, but I'm not sure how to prepare.
Nina: Well, [1]*first*, look at the website to find out a bit about the museum.
Jay: Of course. Then [2]________?
Nina: After [3]________, you need to decide what you're going to wear.
Jay: That [4]________ easy.
Nina: Hmm. It's [5]________ to wear something smart. That shirt's too scruffy!
Jay: No [6]________. Anything else?
Nina: [7]________ forget to check the time of the interview.
Jay: You're making me really nervous! I [8]________ I remember it all.

6 In pairs, choose a summer job. Take it in turns to tell each other how to prepare for an interview. And YOU

help in a children's activity camp help in a gift shop

A: Guess what! I've got an interview for ... How should I prepare?
B: Well, first ...

4.7 ENGLISH IN USE Verbs with prepositions

I can use a wide range of verbs that are followed by a preposition.

1

Dad: Listen, son. I don't want to argue about this, but if you want to succeed in life, you've got to be more active.
Son: Yes, Dad.

2

Dad: You can't always depend on others. To be honest, I worry about you.
Son: Shh, Dad! Can you just wait a minute?

3

Son: Dad! I've updated my CV. I've just applied for three summer jobs online and now I'm preparing for an interview. Now, what were you saying?

1 **Read the cartoon. Why is the father angry with his son?**

2 **Study the Language box. Which verbs are used in the cartoon?**

Language — Verbs with prepositions

complain/worry about
Stop worrying about your interview – you'll be fine.
apply/apologise/prepare for
I've applied for a job at the café.
believe/specialise/succeed in
Amy specialises in art classes for teens.
consist/smell of
The team consists of nurses and doctors.
concentrate/depend on
You must concentrate on your work.
compare/cope/deal with
I often deal with difficult customers.

Some verbs can be followed by either of two prepositions, with no change in meaning.
I always dream about/of food when I go to bed hungry.

Some verbs can be followed by either of two prepositions, but with a different meaning.
She always argues with her younger brother. (person)
We mustn't argue about the money. (subject)

3 **Choose the correct option.**

1 I can never concentrate *on / in* my homework when I listen to music.
2 Jessica should apologise *about / for* her behaviour.
3 Do you usually compare this year's results *from / with* last year's?
4 It smells *of / from* chocolate in here. Is somebody baking?
5 Our school specialises *with / in* the Science subjects.
6 I don't like to complain *about / for* things, but this food is terrible!

4 2.31 **Complete the text with the verbs below. There are two extra verbs. Listen and check.**

agree apply ~~depend~~ dreamed specialised succeed was concentrating worry

Are you ready for your dream job?

Using social media is a popular hobby. We all [1]*depend* on social networking to connect with other people, but did you know that digital skills can also help you when you [2]______ for a job? That's what happened to me! I was eighteen and I [3]______ on my studies when a friend asked me to help her with a social media campaign for a school election. I did it for fun, but a company which [4]______ in computers followed my campaign and offered me a job! Now I help the company to [5]______ in creating a positive online image! Once I [6]______ about the perfect job and now I've got it!

5 **In pairs, answer the questions.**

And YOU

1 What subjects would you like to specialise in at school?
2 What do you worry about?
3 When did you last complain about something?

WORDLIST Jobs | Working conditions | Success at work

app designer /æp dɪˈzaɪnə/
arts and crafts /ɑːts ənd krɑːfts/
available /əˈveɪləbəl/
award /əˈwɔːd/
badly-paid /ˈbædli peɪd/
bonus /ˈbəʊnəs/
business /ˈbɪznəs/
candidate /ˈkændɪdət/
career /kəˈrɪə/
cleaner /ˈkliːnə/
colleague /ˈkɒliːg/
communicator /kəˈmjuːnɪkeɪtə/
company /ˈkʌmpəni/
computer programmer /kəmˈpjuːtə ˈprəʊgræmə/
cook /kʊk/
CV /ˌsiː ˈviː/
day-to-day /ˌdeɪ tə ˈdeɪ /
dentist's assistant /dentɪsts əˈsɪstənt/
diploma /dɪˈpləʊmə/
employer /ɪmˈplɔɪə/
engineer /ˌendʒɪˈnɪə/
entrepreneur /ˌɒntrəprəˈnɜː/
experience /ɪkˈspɪəriəns/
fashion designer /ˈfæʃən dɪˈzaɪnə/
film director /fɪlm dəˈrektə/
firm /fɜːm/
flexible hours /fleksəbəl ˈaʊ‿əz/
flight attendant /flaɪt əˈtendənt/
full-time /ˌfʊl ˈtaɪm/
hands-on /hændz ɒn/
hourly rate /ˈaʊəli reɪt/
interpreter /ɪnˈtɜːprətə/
librarian /laɪˈbreəriən/
lifeguard /ˈlaɪfgɑːd/
lorry driver /ˈlɒri ˈdraɪvə/
manager /ˈmænɪdʒə/
music critic /ˈmjuːzɪk ˈkrɪtɪk/
neat /niːt/
opportunity /ˌɒpəˈtjuːnɪti/
overtime /ˈəʊvətaɪm/
paid holidays /peɪd ˈhɒlədeɪz/
painter /ˈpeɪntə/
part-time /ˌpɑːt ˈtaɪm/
pay rise /peɪ raɪz/
people skills /ˈpiːpəl skɪlz/
permanent /ˈpɜːmənənt/
physically fit /ˈfɪzɪkli fɪt/
plumber /ˈplʌmə/
position /pəˈzɪʃən/
problem solving skills /ˈprɒbləm ˈsɒlvɪŋ skɪlz/
proof /pruːf/
psychologist /saɪˈkɒlədʒɪst/
qualifications /ˌkwɒlɪfɪˈkeɪʃənz/
scientist /ˈsaɪəntɪst/
shift /ʃɪft/
sociable /ˈsəʊʃəbl/
speech /spiːtʃ/
staff /stɑːf/
summer job /sʌmə dʒɒb/
surgery /ˈsɜːrdʒəri/
temporary /ˈtempərəri/
travel agent /ˈtrævəl ˈeɪdʒənt/
vacancy /ˈveɪkənsi/
veterinary assistant /ˈvetərənəri əˈsɪstənt/
well-paid /ˌwel ˈpeɪd /
working hours /ˈwɜːkɪŋ ˈaʊ‿əz/

WORD FRIENDS

apply for a job
be/get fired
be part of a team
be retired
be unemployed
earn a salary/wage
gain work experience
get a pension
get a promotion
get unemployment benefit
have training
give up/quit work
have an interview
look for a job
meet your colleagues
sign a contract
write a CV

VOCABULARY IN ACTION

1 Use the wordlist to find:

1 four office jobs *manager, …*
2 five creative jobs *cook, …*
3 four jobs where your wear a uniform *flight attendant, …*
4 four words or phrases related to money *well-paid, …*
5 three phrases we use when we stop working *quit work, …*

2 Complete the sentences with verbs from Word Friends.

1 You should buy new clothes when you *have* an interview.
2 Don't ________ a contract until you have read every word.
3 If you ________ fired, it will be difficult to find another job.
4 When you ________ a CV, you should include your hobbies.
5 A person who works hard always ________ a promotion in the end.
6 If you are very shy, it can be difficult to ________ part of a team.

3 In pairs, decide if you think the sentences in Exercise 2 are true.

4 In pairs, choose three words/phrases each from the wordlist. Give them to your partner. Write two or three sentences with the words/phrases your partner gives you.

Nancy is a lorry driver. She loves her job and has just got a pay rise. She never wants to give up work.

5 2.32 PRONUNCIATION **Listen to three ways to pronounce the letter 'g'.**

/g/: colleague, ________, ________, ________, ________, ________

/dʒ/: manager, ________, ________, ________, ________, ________

silent: sign, ________, ________, ________

6 2.33 **Write the words below in the correct category in Exercise 5. One word goes in two categories. Listen and repeat.**

app designer campaign computer programmer
engineer foreign gift language lifeguard
organise psychologist travel agent wage

Revision

VOCABULARY

1 Write the correct word for each definition.

Someone who:

1 helps swimmers in danger at the beach is a **l** *i f e g u a r d*.
2 repairs water pipes, toilets, showers, etc. is a **p** _ _ _ _ _ _ _.
3 translates spoken words into another language is an **i** _ _ _ _ _ _ _ _ _ _.
4 works in a library is a **l** _ _ _ _ _ _ _ _.
5 looks after passengers on a plane is a **f** _ _ _ _ _ _ _ _ _ _ _ _ _ _ _.
6 studies how people's minds work is a **p** _ _ _ _ _ _ _ _ _ _ _.

2 Complete the email with the words below.

badly-paid get meet
overtime part-time ~~quit~~

Guess what! Mum's got a new job. She [1]*quit* her old job because it was [2]________ and she had to work [3]________ – sometimes she stayed in the office till 8 p.m. In her new job, she can work [4]________, which is good because she wants to have more time at home. There's also a good possibility that she will [5]________ a promotion if she works hard. Tomorrow she's going to [6]________ her new colleagues. I'm a bit worried because ... they're my teachers. Yes! Mum's going to work at my school!

GRAMMAR

3 Choose the correct option.

1 Don't worry. I *will help* / *help* you with your homework later.
2 Jack's decided that he *isn't going to work* / *isn't working* in his dad's company.
3 When I start my new job next week, I will *be able to* / *can* practise my English.
4 This evening Alice *helps* / *is helping* in her local theatre.
5 Let's wait here. The train *is going to leave* / *leaves* in ten minutes.
6 I've failed an exam, so I will *have to* / *must* take it again in the summer.

4 Complete the dialogues with the Future Continuous form of the verbs in brackets.

1 A: I've got an interview tomorrow.
B: Good luck! I *'ll be thinking* (think) of you!
2 A: What time will you be home tonight?
B: I'm not sure, but I ________ (not work) late again.
3 A: This time tomorrow you ________ (relax) after your first day at work.
B: No, I won't. I ________ (study). I've got my driving test on Friday!

5 Complete the sentences with prepositions.

1 Jack is always complaining *about* his job.
2 I have to cope ________ some really difficult customers.
3 You'll feel better if you apologise ________ your mistake.
4 Our workforce consists ________ European and Asian workers.
5 I don't want to argue ________ my boss.
6 Laura has finally succeeded ________ getting a place at Art School.

SPEAKING

6 2.34 Sam wants to be a teacher and is spending a day at a primary school doing work experience. Order the conversation. Listen and check.

Sam:	Thanks for having me. What should I do first?	*1*
Teacher:	After a few minutes, read the children a story.	__
Sam:	I hope I remember it all.	__
Teacher:	Then ask the children about the story. Be sure to listen to them.	__
Sam:	That seems easy. They love stories. Then what do I do?	__
Teacher:	First, say hello to the pupils and write your name on the board.	__
Sam:	Of course. Then what?	__
Teacher:	You'll be fine, Sam. The children will love you.	__

DICTATION

7 2.35 Listen. Then listen again and write down what you hear.

SELF-ASSESSMENT Think about this unit. What did you learn? What do you need help with? **WORKBOOK p. 50**

BBC

CULTURE

What is the happiest profession?

The happiest profession

You might be thinking, 'What job can I do when I leave school? Which one will bring me the most job satisfaction? Which one could be the most useful to society?' And what about *where* you'll work? Will you be sitting at a desk all day, running around meeting people or travelling around the world? Will you be doing an unusual job, like tea tester for example? But you might not have asked yourself a simple but very basic question: 'Which job is going to make me *happiest*?'

Well, data from a recent survey revealed some surprising results. It shows that a top salary, the possibility of promotion and a high status in society are not the only important criteria. Flexible hours, a good relationship with colleagues and seeing fast results in your work are also key factors to being happy at work. Professions such as bankers, lawyers and accountants do badly in the survey because they often work long hours, which can get very stressful.

In contrast, the top jobs in the survey are hairdressers, gardeners, plumbers and florists! Why? Because all four have a high job satisfaction rating. Workers see very fast results and their customers are usually happy with the outcome. These workers also feel that their training has paid off because they use these skills on a daily basis, something which many people in office jobs don't experience. People who have set up their own business are also happier because they have more choice about what work to do and when.

To celebrate these 'happy jobs', the BBC recently ran a different kind of talent contest. Instead of focusing on singers and dancers, the producers wanted to showcase the skills needed in everyday jobs, rather than in glamorous ones. Young people between sixteen and twenty-five were tested on their skills at farming, gardening, plumbing and hairdressing. The challenges may be more modest but they are no less important to society.

GLOSSARY
criteria (n) standards that you use to judge or decide about sth
key factor (n) important point
rating (n) a number that shows how good, popular, important, etc. sth is
set up (a business) (phr v) start (a business)
showcase (v) show the best qualities or parts of sth

EXPLORE

1 In pairs, discuss the questions.

1 What are the most stressful jobs?
2 What are the least stressful jobs?
3 Which jobs are the happiest?

2 Read the article and choose the correct option.

1 The article is aimed at *workers* / *people about to start work*.
2 The results of the survey are *expected* / *unexpected*.
3 High status jobs *don't do* / *do* well in the happiness survey.
4 Hairdressers are happy because they *see fast results* / *meet lots of people*.
5 The BBC contest features jobs that are often *ignored* / *unskilled*.

3 Choose the best summary for the article.

1 Surprisingly, job satisfaction is not about status or money. It's about using the skills that you have learnt. We should celebrate professions like hairdressing for this reason.
2 Money is not the most important consideration when choosing a future career. You may be much happier doing a more modest job. This is because you will always be on the move.

4 In pairs, discuss the questions.

1 Has your opinion about the jobs in the photos changed after reading the article?
2 Which jobs do you think make people the happiest/unhappiest where you live? Why?

EXPLORE MORE

5 4.5 Watch Part 1 of a video about a new talent show. In pairs, discuss the questions.

1 Which of the adjectives below do you think best describe the contestants who enter this type of contest?

arrogant confident funny hard-working lazy nervous proud shy talented

2 Would you like to enter a contest like this?

6 4.6 Watch Part 2 of the video. Complete the sentences with the words below.

competition creative extremely hair love passion stand working

1 Lisa really wants to win this ________. She says she's going to go in there and do what she does best, which is ________!
2 Serafina is ________ passionate about hairdressing. It's her life. Doing hairdressing is how she can be ________.
3 This is what Becky's been ________ towards. Hopefully, she'll be able to ________ out and show off a bit.'
4 For Jake, hairdressing is like a massive ________. It's like his first big ________.

7 4.7 Watch Part 3 of the video. Mark the sentences T (true) or F (false). Correct the false sentences.

1 ☐ Becky's style is more alternative than Serafina's.
2 ☐ The final competition is only about the hairstyle.
3 ☐ The judges are very proud of both contestants.
4 ☐ It was easy to decide the winner.
5 ☐ Becky is surprised that she won.

8 In pairs, discuss the questions.

1 What's your opinion of this kind of talent contest?
2 Are there programmes like this in your country? If so, what kind of hobbies or professions are they about?

YOU EXPLORE

9 CULTURE PROJECT In groups, prepare a questionnaire about happiness at work.

1 Write your questionnaire. Use the ideas below to help you:

challenges choices colleagues job satisfaction responsibility routine work environment working hours

2 Interview a number of different working people for the questionnaire.
3 Share your results with the class.

5

Light years away

VOCABULARY
Space | Dimensions and distance | Large numbers | Space science

GRAMMAR
Zero, First and Second Conditionals | Third Conditional

Grammar: Night sky

Speaking: Don't crash!

BBC Culture: George Moyes – skydiver

Workbook p. 65

BBC VOX POPS

CLIL 3 > p. 140

5.1 VOCABULARY Space

I can talk about space and use large numbers.

1 CLASS VOTE Have you ever:

- learned the names of stars?
- used a telescope?
- watched a programme about space?

2 Check your understanding of the words in the Vocabulary A box. Which words can you find in the pictures?

Vocabulary A Space

astronaut astronomer comet Earth galaxy moon orbit planet planetarium satellite solar system space station spacecraft star telescope

3 2.36 Listen to a presentation at a planetarium and answer the questions.

1 What kind of information can satellites send?
2 What is a galaxy?
3 What is the name of the galaxy we live in?
4 Is the light that stars send always the same colour?
5 What colour is the Earth from space?
6 Can we see the International Space Station from the Earth?

4 Complete the quiz questions with words from the Vocabulary A box.

What do you know about space? Try our quiz and find out!

1 The Earth travels around the sun in a(n) *orbit*, which is
a a perfect circle.
b an ellipse (similar to an oval).
c a star shape.

2 The sun is a giant star. Which is the third ______ from the sun?
a Mars b Venus c Earth

3 A(n) ______ is an icy rock travelling through space. We can see its 'tail' of gas when
a it's near the sun.
b it's travelling fast.
c it's getting smaller.

4 The ______ travels round the Earth. Its light
a comes from hot gas inside it.
b is reflected from the sun.
c is very bright.

5 If you want to see galaxies, you need a(n) ______. They work best
a in dark countryside skies.
b in a bright city.
c on a cloudy night.

5 2.37 In pairs, do the quiz in Exercise 4. Listen and check.

6 2.38 **WORD FRIENDS** Study the Word Friends and Watch out! boxes. Complete the sentences below with words from the Word Friends box. Listen and check.

Word Friends

The box is forty centimetres **long/wide/high**.
The **length/width/height** of the box is forty centimetres.
London is ten kilometres **away**. (= We're ten kilometres **from** London.)
The **speed limit** is eighty kilometres/fifty miles **per/an hour**.
It **takes two hours** to get to London.

Watch OUT!

In the USA they use different length units:
1 mile = about 1.6 kilometres
1 foot = about 30 centimetres
1 inch = 2.54 centimetres
In the UK they use miles too, but they don't use feet or inches anymore.

1 A speed of twenty miles *per* hour is the same as thirty-two kilometres ______ hour.
2 My notebook is twenty centimetres ______ and fifteen centimetres ______.
3 I think that wall is about six metres ______.
4 My home town is about ten kilometres ______ Mexico City.
5 What is the ______ of that route?
6 The school is not far from here. It's only 400 metres ______.

7 2.39 Study the Vocabulary B box. Listen to the numbers.

Vocabulary B Large numbers

100 = a hundred 1,000 = a thousand
1,000,000 = a million 1,000,000,000 = a billion

- We do not normally use plurals with large numbers: 4,700 = four **thousand** seven **hundred**
- In British English, we put *and* between *hundred* and a different number: 1,403 = one thousand four hundred **and** three
- We use a hyphen when we write numbers 21–99: twenty-one, ninety-nine
- In writing, we separate each thousand with a comma: 3,000,000
- We can make very big numbers simpler by using *point*: 1,700,000 (one million seven hundred thousand) = 1.7 million (one point seven million)

8 2.40 Write the numbers as words. Listen and check.

1 935 ______
2 7,268 ______
3 2,400,000 ______
4 8.1 billion ______
5 54,322,641 ______
6 6,000,000,000 ______

9 Work in pairs. Take it in turns to write a number on a piece of paper. Your partner has to read it aloud.

10 2.41 Read the article. Choose the correct option. Listen and check.

Did you know?

Mars is millions of kilometres [1]*away* / *far* but actually, the distance between Mars and the Earth changes all the time – from over 50 to 401 [2]*million* / *millions* kilometres. For that reason, it's difficult to calculate the [3]*long* / *length* of time it takes to get there.

The fastest [4]*satellite* / *spacecraft* can travel at 58,000 kilometres [5]*per* / *the* hour, so theoretically, we should get to Mars in thirty-nine days. However, this is not possible because the distance is never short for a long time. Also, you can't travel in a straight line. So it [6]*takes* / *gets* much longer! In 1969 Mariner 6 took 155 days to get to Mars, but Viking 2 took twice that time – 333 days!

11 Answer the questions.

1 What is the distance between Mars and Earth? Why does it change?
2 Why does getting to Mars take such a long time?
3 When would the journey probably take the shortest time possible?

12 In pairs, choose any three space objects or phenomena from this lesson or from other information sources. Write a short description, including their size, distance, speed or another large number. **And YOU**

Light travels at a speed of 299,792 kilometres per second.

5.2 GRAMMAR Zero, First and Second Conditionals

I can talk about things that are always true, possible situations and imaginary situations.

VIDEO NIGHT SKY

Nina: You've got some weird things, Skye.
Skye: I know. That's a bit of a meteorite. My dad found it. And that's my telescope. Astronomers use them if they want to look at planets. Oh, I think Jay's here.
Jay: Hi! You guys ready to go outside?
Nina: Why? It's cold out there. I don't want to stand around in the dark!
Skye: You'll be fine if you borrow my scarf and gloves. Come on.
Nina: Why have you brought the tripod, Jay? Are you going to take a photo of my new hairstyle in the dark?
Jay: Ha ha! No, we want a photo of the comet for our space project.
Nina: Are you sure we'll be able to see it?
Jay: Good question! The comet is millions of miles away. If we didn't have a good camera and the tripod, it would be really tricky.
Skye: Don't worry, guys. I'm on it!
Nina: Oh my days! I can see for miles. Hey, a moving light!
Jay: Wow! Quick! Take a photo, Skye. And silence now. It'll take twenty seconds.
Nina: Er, guys, I think those are fireworks.
Skye: You're kidding!
Nina: If I were you, I'd give up now.

OUT of class
I'm on it! *Oh my days!*
You're kidding!

1 CLASS VOTE Do you think astronomy is interesting? Why? / Why not?

2 5.1 2.42 Watch or listen. What does Nina see?

3 Study the Grammar box. Find more examples of conditionals in the dialogue.

Grammar Zero, First and Second Conditionals

Zero Conditional: for things that are always true
if + Present Simple, Present Simple
Astronomers watch the sky if the sky is clear.

First Conditional: for possible situations in the future
if/unless + Present Simple, *will* + infinitive/imperative
If you don't go outside, you won't see the comet.
I will buy a telescope unless it costs too much.
If you want to see a comet, check online.

Second Conditional: for imaginary situations
if + Past Simple, *would* + infinitive (without *to*)
If I won the lottery, I'd buy a ticket to Mars.
I wouldn't wait any longer if I were you.

GRAMMAR TIME > PAGE 122

4 2.43 Match the two halves of each sentence. Listen and check. Are they Zero or First Conditionals?

1 Ice melts [c] *Zero Conditional*
2 If you don't put your coat on, [ ] ______
3 We won't go home early [ ] ______
4 If you look at the sun, [ ] ______

a unless it starts raining.
b you need special glasses.
c if you heat it.
d you'll feel cold.

5 Complete the Second Conditional sentences using the correct form of the verbs in brackets.

1 If Sara *had* (have) enough time, she *would show* (show) me how to use the telescope.
2 If we ______ (not have) a Science test tomorrow, we ______ (not feel) stressed.
3 What ______ you ______ (do) if you ______ (win) a trip into space?
4 If I ______ (be) you, I ______ (use) the binoculars to look for the comet.
5 If we ______ (have) a good camera, we ______ (take) a photo of that comet.

6 In pairs, complete the sentences to make them true for you. **And YOU**

1 I'll do my homework this evening unless …
2 I get really cross if …
3 If the weather is good tomorrow, …
4 I would feel very excited if …

5.3 READING and VOCABULARY A big adventure

I can understand specific detail in an article and talk about space travel.

1 CLASS VOTE Do you think it's a good idea to send people into space? Why? / Why not?

2 Look at the title of the article and the photo. What do you think the girl's dream is?

The future is far away!

Alyssa Carson is a teenager and she already has big ambitions for her future. If her dreams come true, she'll fly into space. But she doesn't want to orbit the Earth on the space station or go to the moon. Alyssa wants to travel to Mars, the red planet.

So, is this just a dream? No. Alyssa made the decision when she was three years old because the idea was exciting and 'no one's been there!' After that she read lots of books on Mars and attended her first space camp when she was seven. Since then she's learned a lot about travel to other planets. It's an expensive trip, which requires many years of training. This is a problem for Alyssa's family, but they try to support her. As her father explains, 'If you see the passion she has, you have to be there for her.' Alyssa believes we are 'the Mars generation' and that the mission to Mars will help us get to know the planet better.

More than 100,000 people have already applied for a journey to Mars. If they pass the tests, like Alyssa, they will start a training programme. It's also important to speak several languages if you want to be an astronaut. Alyssa speaks Spanish, French, Chinese and some Turkish, so this should be enough! She also has a certificate in scuba diving and is already working on her pilot's licence. Both these things, as well as a certificate in skydiving, are important for an astronaut's training.

Only a few people can go on the first Mars mission. The flight to Mars won't be easy. They will spend hundreds of days together in a very tight space! So, if you were an astronaut on Mars, what would life be like? You would live in an extremely small space called a 'pod' and you would wear a space suit all the time. If you made a phone call home, it would take half an hour for the sound to reach Earth! Also, if you got ill, there wouldn't be any hospitals. Life wouldn't be as easy, that's for sure! But it would be really exciting.

3 Read the first paragraph of the article. Check your ideas from Exercise 2.

4 2.44 Read the whole article. Choose the correct answers.

1 Alyssa decided to go to Mars because she
  - a read about it in a book.
  - b liked the idea of doing something different.
  - c went to space camp.
  - d enjoyed travelling and exploring.

2 What is Alyssa's parents' opinion of her ambition?
  - a They think it's too expensive and try to discourage her.
  - b They want to help her fulfill her dream because they are also 'Mars generation'.
  - c They don't mind because they have a lot of money to spend.
  - d They find it difficult because of the expense, but they try to help her.

3 Which of these things is *not* important for an astronaut's training?
  - a learning to fly a plane
  - b learning to dive
  - c attending a space camp
  - d speaking foreign languages

4 If you lived on Mars, what would life be like?
  - a It would be possible to phone your friends and family.
  - b There would be plenty of people to talk to.
  - c You would wear your own clothes at the station.
  - d Homes would be similar to large houses on Earth.

5 Look at the highlighted words in the article. Check your understanding. Use a dictionary if necessary.

6 In pairs, discuss the questions about the article.

1 Is the author mainly giving advice, giving information or describing a place?
2 What idea do you have of Alyssa's character?
3 How would you summarise the text in one sentence?

7 [VOX POPS ▶ 5.2] Would you like to go to Mars? Why? / Why not?

AND YOU

Yes, I would. It would be really exciting.
No, I'd miss my family and friends.

5.4 GRAMMAR Third conditional

I can talk about unreal situations in the past.

1 CLASS VOTE Should we spend millions of pounds on space experiments? Why? / Why not?

2 Read the interview quickly. How long did the flight take?

This week in ***Space*** magazine, astronomer **Guy Greenwood** talks about a historic mission to catch a comet.

Space: The Rosetta mission cost 1.7 billion dollars. That's a lot of money! What was your aim?

Guy: Our aim was to discover more about comets. The Rosetta spacecraft flew 6.4 billion kilometres to comet 67P, which is about four kilometres wide. The flight took ten years!

Space: What would have happened if your calculations had been wrong?

Guy: Well, lots of scientists worked on this project, so we were confident that we'd got it right. We would have been very disappointed if the mission had failed. If the mission hadn't been successful, we wouldn't have had these incredible close-up photos or this analysis of the comet's surface.

Space: They are amazing photos. So, tell us more about the lander, the little spacecraft which landed on the comet.

Guy: Yes. The lander sent us the first pictures of the icy surface of a comet. There were lots of scientific experiments on the lander. If the lander's solar panels had been in sunlight, it would have been OK. But it landed in a large shadow which was quite dark. So it didn't have much power and it went to sleep. Luckily, even though it worked for two hours only, it managed to get enough information about the comet's surface.

3 Read the interview again. Answer the questions.

1 Were the scientists' calculations right?
2 Was the mission successful?
3 What was a result of the mission?
4 Were the lander's solar panels in sunlight?

4 Study the Grammar box. Find more examples of the Third Conditional in the interview.

Grammar Third Conditional

for unreal situations in the past
if + Past Perfect, *would have* + past participle
The experiment would have ended if the lander had broken. (It didn't break.)

GRAMMAR TIME > PAGE 122

5 Match 1–3 with a–c to make sentences.

1 If the lander had had more solar power,
2 The Rosetta mission would have been quicker
3 If the European Space Agency hadn't spent millions of euros,

a if the comet had been nearer to Earth during the mission.
b the scientists would have gathered more data.
c the Rosetta Mission wouldn't have happened.

6 2.45 Complete the Third Conditional sentences in the article using the correct form of the verbs in brackets. Listen and check.

Moon landings: *fact or fiction?*

Did you know some people believe that astronauts have never landed on the moon? They believe NASA faked the landing. Here are some of their reasons.

They say that the flag [1]*wouldn't have waved* (not wave) if the astronauts [2]________ (film) it on the moon because there is no air on the moon. They also think some stars [3]________ (be) visible if the astronauts [4]________ (take) the photos on the moon. Another mystery is that although we can see the astronauts' footprints on the surface, we can't see any traces of the landing module. If the module [5]________ (land) on the surface of the moon, it [6]________ (leave) some traces!

7 2.46 Listen to the second part of the article. What are the arguments against the ideas in Exercise 6? What's your view?

8 [VOX POPS 5.3] Complete the sentences to make them true for you.

And YOU

1 If I hadn't come to this school, …
2 If I hadn't met my best friend, …
3 If I had learned how to …
4 If I had been born in a different country, …

5.5 LISTENING and VOCABULARY Fearless Felix

I can understand the main points of a report and talk about space science.

1 CLASS VOTE **Would you jump out of a plane or a hot air balloon? Why? / Why not?**

2 2.47 **Study the Vocabulary box. Choose the correct option. Listen and check.**

Vocabulary Space science

atmosphere balloon capsule engine force gravity helium oxygen parachute sound barrier

1 Humans need *oxygen* / *helium* to breathe.
2 The Concorde was a jet plane which broke the *engine* / *sound barrier*.
3 The force which attracts objects towards the Earth is *parachute* / *gravity*.
4 Helium is a very light gas which is used in *balloons* / *parachutes*.
5 A jet *engine* / *atmosphere* is very powerful.
6 Greenhouse gases damage the Earth's *sound barrier* / *atmosphere*.

3 **Find words from the Vocabulary box in the pictures.**

4 **Look at the pictures and read the information. What do you think happened? Explain your ideas.**

5 2.48 **Listen to the first part of a report about Felix Baumgartner. Were your ideas correct? Use the prompts to summarise what happened.**

1 First, Felix put on …
2 Then he got into …
3 The balloon took him …
4 When he reached the right height, …
5 Finally, he opened …

6 2.49 **Listen to the second part of the report. Complete the notes with a word or phrase.**

Name:	Felix Baumgartner
Date of jump:	1 **14 October** 2012
Location:	2 ________, USA
Nationality:	3 ________
Age:	42
Height of jump:	about 4 ________ kilometres
Speed:	5 ________ kilometres per hour
Time in free fall:	6 ________ minutes and ________ seconds
Cost:	7 ________ of US dollars

7 **What is your opinion of Baumgartner's achievement?**

8 **In pairs, decide what you would do and how you would feel in each situation.** And YOU

What would you do if:

1 you had to climb ten metres up a climbing wall to win a big prize?
If I had to climb ten metres up a climbing wall, …
2 you won a bungee jump as a prize in a school lottery?
3 your friend invited you to fly in a hot air balloon?

5.6 SPEAKING Warnings and prohibition

I can give a warning and tell somebody not to do something.

VIDEO **DON'T CRASH!**

Jay: Skye, I've got a great idea for our Science project. We didn't get a photo of the comet, but we can make a great film with this!
Skye: What is that?
Jay: It's my birthday present. It's a drone with a small camera on it – here. You can get them for a good price now.
Skye: That's so neat! How fast does it fly?
Jay: I don't know. Let's try it. Right, the camera's on. We're off! Mind out!
Skye: Awesome! Be careful – don't fly too high. You mustn't get in the way of planes.
Jay: I don't think it's that high. I'm sure we're getting some good pictures.
Skye: Can I have a go?
Jay: Sure. Here's the control.

Later:

Jay: Watch out! You can't do that! If you're not careful, you'll … crash!
Skye: Well, if you hadn't pressed the wrong button, it wouldn't have crashed!
Jay: It's OK. There's no damage. Phew! Let's check the recording.
Skye: That's amazing! This will be perfect for our project.

That's so neat! *We're off!*
Can I have a go?
OUT of class

1 CLASS VOTE Do you think people should be allowed to use drones? Why? / Why not?

Drones are not a good idea because they can be a danger to planes.

2 Look at the photo. What are Skye and Jay doing? What problems might they have?

3 5.4 2.50 Watch or listen and answer the questions.

1 What are they using the drone for?
2 Was Jay's drone expensive?
3 What does Skye think of the drone?
4 Was the crash Skye's fault?

4 Study the Speaking box. Find examples of warnings and prohibition in the dialogue.

Speaking Warnings and prohibition

Warnings
Mind out!
Mind the steps/ladder/wet floor.
Look out!
Watch out!/Be careful!
Watch out for the people/bicycles/dogs!
If you're not careful, you'll ...

Prohibition
You can't/mustn't do that!
You aren't allowed to ... it when ...
Don't fly too high/go too fast.
Keep off the flower beds/grass/carpet.
Make sure you don't ...

5 In pairs, take it in turns to explain what each sign means. Tell the class.

Skateboards and bikes are not allowed in the park.

Smoking prohibited

No camping permitted.
No fires or barbecues.

It is forbidden to take photos in this exhibition.

6 What would you say in each situation? Use phrases from the Speaking box. **And YOU**

- You see a cyclist riding towards your friend quite fast.
- Your little brother is playing online games all evening.
- There is ice on the path where you and your friends are walking.
- Your dad is driving the wrong way up a one-way street.

5.7 WRITING An essay

I can write an essay discussing advantages and disadvantages.

1 CLASS VOTE If you won a trip into space, would you rather go to the moon, to Mars or visit the International Space Station?

2 In pairs, make a list of the advantages and disadvantages of space travel. Compare your ideas with the class.

3 Read Nina's essay. Order the sections as they appear in the essay.

- [ ] conclusion
- [1] introduction
- [ ] advantages
- [ ] disadvantages

In your opinion, is space travel useful?

Since the first space flight in 1961, many people have dreamed of travelling into space. But is space travel really useful?

On the one hand, I believe space travel might be useful for humans in the future. For example, the main advantage is that we can look for another planet to live on, like Mars. This would be useful if we had climate problems here on Earth. Another reason for space travel is that we can test new technology.

On the other hand, I think space travel is too expensive as things like hospitals and education are more important. Another disadvantage is that it's very dangerous because of the speed and the distance. Also, if you had to travel to Mars, you might not come back!

To sum up, if I had to choose, I would forget about space travel and try to look after planet Earth better.

4 Work in pairs. List the advantages and disadvantages Nina gives for space travel. Are they the same as your ideas in Exercise 2?

5 Do you agree with Nina's opinions? Explain your reasons to the class.

6 Study the Writing box. Find examples of these phrases in Nina's essay.

Writing An essay

Introduction
Nowadays many/more and more people ...
Many people believe/have wanted ...
But is ... really useful/good ...?
Is ... worth ...?

Arguments for and against
On the one hand, ... On the other hand, ...
Firstly, .../Secondly, .../Moreover, ...
One/Another/The main advantage/disadvantage is (that) ...
One/Another reason for ... is ...
Finally, ...

Giving and justifying opinions
I believe ...
In my opinion, ...
It seems ...
For example, ...
This is because ...

Ending
To sum up, ...
In conclusion, ...

Writing Time

7 Write an essay discussing this question: *Would you ever travel to space as a tourist?* In your essay you should:

- write a short introduction and conclusion.
- list your reasons for and against, and your final decision.
- give reasons for your opinions.
- use linking words (e.g. *also*, *in addition*, *however*, *but*, *because*).

TIP
Make sure your essay is clearly related to the title. Organise your arguments for and against in two main paragraphs.

WORDLIST Space | Dimensions and distance | Large numbers | Space science

ambition /æmˈbɪʃən/
astronaut /ˈæstrənɔːt/
astronomer /əˈstrɒnəmə/
atmosphere /ˈætməsfɪə/
attend /əˈtend/
balloon /bəˈluːn/
billion /ˈbɪljən/
binoculars /bɪˈnɒkjələz/
calculate /ˈkælkjəleɪt/
calculation /ˌkælkjuˈleɪʃən/
capsule /ˈkæpsjuːl/
certificate /səˈtɪfɪkət/
comet /ˈkɒmət/
crash /kræʃ/
damage /ˈdæmɪdʒ/
data /ˈdeɪtə/
descent /dɪˈsent/
distance /ˈdɪstəns/
drone /drəʊn/
Earth /ɜːθ/
ellipse /ɪˈlɪps/
engine /ˈendʒɪn/
experiment /ɪkˈsperəmənt/
force /fɔːs/
free fall /friː fɔːl/
footprint /ˈfʊtˌprɪnt/
galaxy /ˈgæləksi/
gravity /ˈgrævɪti/
helium /ˈhiːliəm/
hundred /ˈhʌndrəd/
land /ˈlænd/
lander /ˈlændə/
landing /ˈlændɪŋ/
light year /laɪt jɪə/
Mars /mɑːz/
meteorite /ˈmiːtiəraɪt/
million /ˈmɪljən/
mission /ˈmɪʃən/
moon /muːn/
orbit /ˈɔːbɪt/
oxygen /ˈɒksɪdʒən/
parachute /ˈpærəʃuːt/
pilot's licence /paɪləts laɪsns/
planet /ˈplænət/
planetarium /ˌplænəˈteəriəm/
press /pres/
reach /riːtʃ/
record-breaking /ˈrekɔːd ˌbreɪkɪŋ/
reflect /rɪˈflekt/
require /rɪˈkwaɪə/
satellite /ˈsætəlaɪt/
scientific /ˌsaɪənˈtɪfɪk/
solar system /ˈsəʊlə ˌsɪstəm/
sound barrier /saʊnd ˈbæriə/
space camp /speɪs kæmp/
space station /speɪs ˈsteɪʃən/
space suit /speɪs suːt/
spacecraft /ˈspeɪskrɑːft/
speed /spiːd/
star /stɑː/
support /səˈpɔːt/
surface /ˈsɜːfəs/
telescope /ˈteləskəʊp/
thousand /ˈθaʊzənd/
training programme /ˈtreɪnɪŋ ˌprəʊgræm/
unit /ˈjuːnɪt/
Venus /ˈviːnəs/
visible /ˈvɪzəbl/
wave /weɪv/
writer /ˈraɪtə/

WORD FRIENDS

The box is forty centimetres long/wide/high.
The length/width/height of the box is forty centimetres.
London is ten kilometres away. (= We're ten kilometres from London.)
The speed limit is eighty kilometres/fifty miles per/an hour.
It takes two hours to get to London.

VOCABULARY IN ACTION

1 Use the wordlist to find:

1. four man-made objects you can find in space *lander, …*
2. two gases *oxygen, …*
3. six verbs *crash, …*
4. two devices you can use to see a long way *binoculars, …*
5. two people *astronaut, …*

2 In pairs, write definitions for two words from the wordlist. Give your definitions to another pair. Can they guess the words?

3 Work in pairs. Choose two words from the wordlist each. Your partner must write a sentence including both words.

A: balloon, thousand
B: I wouldn't like to travel a thousand kilometres in a balloon!

4 2.51 PRONUNCIATION Listen to the sentences. Notice the pronunciation of weak forms in the underlined words.

1. I'd find out more if I were you.
2. If I hadn't phoned you, I wouldn't have known about it.
3. It's travelling at a speed of 1,000 miles an hour.
4. If I won the lottery, I'd buy a ticket to the moon.
5. What would have happened if they had missed?
6. I'd love to travel to Mars.

5 2.51 Listen again and repeat the sentences.

Revision

VOCABULARY

1 **Write the correct word for each definition.**

1 an item of clothing that astronauts wear
s*pace* s*uit*
2 a place where you can learn about planets
p ___________
3 the measurement of how fast something travels s _____
4 a small, light flying machine with a camera
d _____
5 how long an object is from one end to the other l ______
6 a moving space object with a long bright 'tail'
c _____

2 **2.52 Complete the quiz with the nouns below. There is one extra noun. Listen and check.**

Earth light year ~~million~~ solar system thousand Venus

Did you know that:

1 the sun is about the same size as one *million* Earths?
2 there are thousands of planets in the universe, but only eight in our __________ ?
3 two of those eight planets, __________ and Mercury, don't have any moons?
4 ancient astronomers believed that the __________ was at the centre of the universe?
5 the edge of space is called the Karman Line? It's one hundred __________ metres above the Earth (that's 100 kilometers!)

GRAMMAR

3 **Complete the Zero and First Conditional questions using the correct form of the verbs in brackets.**

1 What *will* you *do* (do) tomorrow if the weather is good?
2 What do you eat if you __________ (be) really hungry?
3 If your friend __________ (text) you in a lesson, do you reply?
4 __________ you __________ (help) me if the teacher gives us lots of homework today?
5 If your home phone rings, __________ you __________ (answer) it?

4 **2.53 Complete the Second Conditional sentences in the article with the correct form of the verbs in brackets. Listen and check.**

Life in space

Life as an astronaut is very strange. First of all, it's very quiet. Radio waves can travel in space, but sound waves can't. So astronauts wouldn't hear the other astronauts if they [1]*didn't wear* (not wear) radio headphones! Then, of course, there's no gravity. What [2]__________ (happen) if an astronaut cried in space? Or if he [3]__________ (drop) his sandwich? Well, the tears and the sandwich [4]__________ (stay) in the air! And at bedtime, they [5]__________ (not fall) asleep unless they fixed themselves to the 'bed'. However, one good thing happens as a result of zero gravity: your back stretches about five or six centimeters. So if you [6]__________ (want) to grow taller, you should travel into space!

5 **Complete the Third Conditional sentences with the correct form of the verbs in brackets.**

1 We *wouldn't have seen* (not see) the stars if the sky *hadn't been* (not be) clear.
2 She __________ (not become) an astronaut if she __________ (not be) to space camp.
3 If somebody __________ (tell) me about the space documentary, I __________ (watch) it.
4 If he __________ (not read) that book about space, he __________ (not study) Physics.

SPEAKING

6 **Match the sentences with the situations. What else could you say?**

1 ☐ You see a young child running to pick up a ball from the road.
2 ☐ Your teacher is carrying a lot of books and can't see that the floor is wet.
3 ☐ Your sister is going to fly a drone in a busy children's play park.

a Be careful! You might slip!
b You mustn't use it here. You'll have to go somewhere else.
c Mind out! There's a car coming.

DICTATION

7 **2.54 Listen. Then listen again and write down what you hear.**

SELF-ASSESSMENT Think about this unit. What did you learn? What do you need help with? **WORKBOOK** p. 62

BBC

CULTURE

Can you run a marathon in space?

Sports in space!

Tim Peake is no ordinary astronaut. Apart from his duties on the International Space Station (ISS), he also likes to do sport. Amazingly, he took part in the London Marathon – from space! He did it to raise money for charity. How? Easy – with a harness to keep him tied to the running belt.

The ISS is a zero-gravity lab where a crew of six people live and work. They travel in the space station, which orbits the Earth every ninety minutes, at a speed of 28,800 km per hour. So, Tim Peake not only ran the usual 42 km but also travelled more than 100,000 km during his marathon run! But what other sports are possible in space?

American astronauts often play weightless baseball or basketball, and sometimes even golf. You can even throw a boomerang and it returns to you in orbit just like on earth! But of course, for most sports, the rules change dramatically in the absence of gravity. The astronauts have to adapt to their surroundings.

For the rest of us on 'terra firma', the closest we get to an astronaut's experience is probably skydiving. But jumping out of a plane is not for everyone. It seems too risky. So, what other safer sports can we do that challenge gravity?

Zorbing comes from New Zealand. You roll down a hill in a giant ball, or 'orb', made from transparent plastic – but you need a lot of space! If you're in the city, you could try parkour, which is like an urban obstacle course. If you come across an obstacle, you have to get round it by jumping off walls or onto other buildings. Parkour fans also go to skate parks alongside skateboarders, BMX riders and other urban sports lovers.

But a skate park in space? Now that is hard to imagine!

GLOSSARY

harness (n) a piece of equipment that holds sb or sth in place
crew (n) a group of people working together on a ship, aircraft, etc.
weightless (adj) having no weight, especially because you are in space
surroundings (n) the place where you are and the things that are in it
obstacle course (n) a race in which you have to get over a series of objects

EXPLORE

1 Look at the photo and the title of the article. In pairs, discuss the questions.

1 Who do you think the man is?
2 What is he doing?

2 Read the article and answer the questions.

1 Why did Tim Peake run the London Marathon in space?
2 What are the American astronauts' favourite sports?
3 What is necessary in order to do sport in space?
4 Why isn't skydiving very popular with many people?
5 What do you need for zorbing?
6 Where do fans of parkour like to go in the city?

3 In pairs, discuss which of the sports mentioned in the article you would like to do and why.

EXPLORE MORE

4 5.5 Watch Part 1 of the video about unusual people doing extreme sports. Mark the sentences T (true) or F (false).

1 ☐ George has done skydiving before.
2 ☐ His family are frightened about him doing it.
3 ☐ George is also very nervous about the jump.
4 ☐ The trainer thinks George is a little crazy.
5 ☐ If he could, George would like to try skydiving again.

5 5.5 Watch the video again without the sound. Choose the correct option.

1 George *sits* / *doesn't sit* on the floor during the training.
2 He *is* / *isn't* connected to the skydiving trainer during the skydive.
3 George is wearing *black* / *white* gloves.
4 The parachute is blue and *pink* / *orange*.
5 George *was* / *wasn't* wearing a tie during the jump.

6 5.6 Watch Part 2 of the video and complete the text with the words below. There are two extra words.

beaches brother competes extreme fun skate parks perform tricks wheelchairs

Aaron Fotheringham is an [1]______ wheelchair athlete from Las Vegas. He usually practises his sport in [2]______. His [3]______ loved skating and he encouraged Aaron to do the sport for the first time. Now Aaron [4]______ internationally – he travels to many different countries to [5]______ his skills. He helps other people in [6]______ to do the same. He is very experienced but he still gets nervous before big [7]______ and stunts.

7 5.6 Watch the video again and answer the questions.

1 What colour is Aaron's wheelchair?
2 What image can you see on his T-shirt?
3 What is the name of the special event?
4 Where do you see Aaron doing his wheelchair tricks?

8 What's your opinion of George's and Aaron's feats? Whose achievement is more amazing? Why? What crazy activities can the elderly and disabled do in your country? Discuss in pairs.

YOU EXPLORE

9 CULTURE PROJECT In groups, prepare a digital presentation about an elderly or disabled person in your country who has done something extraordinary.

1 Use the internet to research the person.
2 Write a short script to describe your ideas. Write about their personality and what they achieved. Choose images or videos that you would like to use.
3 Share your presentation with the class. What information in the other presentations surprised you? What do you think of the people's achievements?

6

Take a deep breath

VOCABULARY
Health problems | At the doctor's | Adjectives and nouns for illness | Extreme sports

GRAMMAR
Reported statements and questions | Reported commands and requests

Grammar: First aid

Speaking: I hate hiccups!

BBC Culture: An allergy epidemic

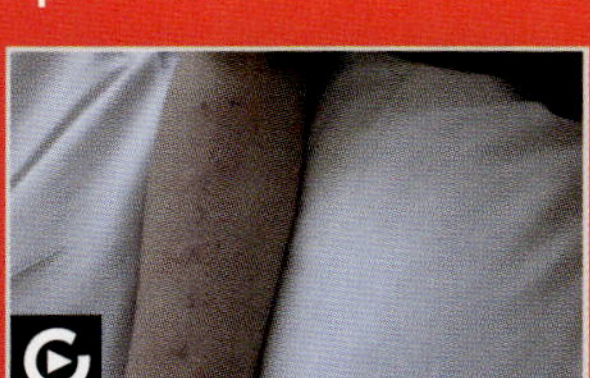

Workbook p. 77

BBC VOX POPS

EXAM TIME 2 > p. 130
CLIL 4 > p. 141

6.1 VOCABULARY Sickness and health

I can talk about health problems.

1 CLASS VOTE **How are you today? Choose from the phrases below. Compare how you feel with the class.**

I've never felt better. ☺☺ I'm fine. ☺ I don't feel too good. 😐
I'm coming down with something. ☹ I feel awful. ☹☹

2 **Study the Vocabulary box. In pairs, use the words and phrases to describe the people in the picture.**

I think the girl has got asthma. *Perhaps the boy has got a virus.*

Vocabulary	Health problems
allergy asthma bug food poisoning hay fever infection injury insomnia migraine travel sickness virus	

3 I KNOW! **What other words and phrases related to health problems can you use to describe the people in the picture?**

The woman has got a headache. *The boy is sneezing.*

4 **Look at the posters from the doctor's waiting room. Choose the correct explanation for each poster.**

1 a Wait here if you think you have a food allergy.
  b You don't have to wait for a food allergy test.
  c Everybody should get a food allergy test now.
2 a If you want to go to the asthma clinic, arrange a time with the nurse.
  b You can check the hours of the asthma clinic with the nurse.
  c The nurse will be at the asthma clinic.
3 a Sealegs wristbands are for sale at the chemist's.
  b You can get free Sealegs wristbands at the chemist's.
  c You can buy Sealegs wristbands from the doctor.

5 3.01 **WORD FRIENDS** **Complete the Word Friends box with the words below. Listen and check.**

a check-up ~~a rash~~ a temperature some tablets your blood pressure your voice

Word Friends

Feeling ill

- [ ] **come down with** the flu/something
- [ ] **have** [1]*a rash*/a runny nose/[2]________/ a nose bleed/a cough/an infection
- [ ] **lose** your appetite/[3]________

Seeing the doctor

- [ ] **get** a prescription
- [ ] **have** [4]________
- [ ] **listen to** your chest
- [ ] **take** your temperature/[5]________

Getting better

- [ ] **get** lots of rest
- [ ] **stay** in bed
- [ ] **take** medicine/[6]________

6 3.02 **Listen to a conversation between a doctor and a patient. Tick the phrases you hear in the Word Friends box.**

7 3.02 **Listen again. Answer the questions.**

1. What is the boy's problem?
2. What does the doctor do?
3. What is the doctor's advice?
4. Is the boy happy with the doctor's advice? Why? / Why not?

8 **Study the Speaking box. Who says what? Write *D* for doctor or *P* for patient.**

Speaking — At the doctor's

- [*D*] Now, take a deep breath.
- [ ] Where does it hurt?
- [ ] It's painful when I swallow.
- [ ] Is it serious?
- [ ] It's nothing to worry about.
- [ ] What seems to be the matter?
- [ ] Here's something for the pain.
- [ ] Is there anything I can take for it?

9 **In pairs, take it in turns to be the doctor or the patient. Choose a health problem from the Vocabulary box and have a short conversation.**

Doctor: Now, what seems to be the matter?
Patient: I think I've got food poisoning.

10 3.03 **WORD BUILDING** **Study the table. Complete the words in the factfile below. Listen and check.**

Adjectives from nouns	Adjectives from verbs
-ic	***-ed***
allergy – allergic	depress – depressed
asthma – asthmatic	infect – infected
dyslexia – dyslexic	injure – injured
-ful	stress – stressed
pain – painful	
Nouns from verbs	**Nouns from adjectives**
-ion	***-ness***
depress – depression	blind – blindness
infect – infection	deaf – deafness
operate – operation	dizzy – dizziness
prescribe – prescription	ill – illness
	sick – sickness

Did You know?

Your whole body can feel [1]p*ain* except for the brain. That's why doctors can do an [2]o________ on somebody's brain while they're awake!

Humans are sometimes [3]a________ to their pets, but cats and dogs can also have [4]a________ to humans!

Chewing gum helps you to calm down when you're [5]s________, but it isn't a new idea. The ancient Greeks chewed gum from the mastic tree thousands of years ago.

Have you cut your finger? Sugar can stop an [6]i________ from developing, but if it gets worse, always see your doctor.

It's not unusual to suffer from [7]sea-________ during a cruise, but some people also feel [8]d________ when they arrive home – even sailors – and it can last for months or years!

Ten percent of the population are [9]d________ and can find reading difficult. However, people with [10]d________ are often brilliant at doing puzzles.

11 **In pairs, ask and answer the questions.** And YOU

1. Do you or does anyone in your family have an allergy?
2. What do you do when you feel stressed?
3. When did you last have a virus? How did you feel and what did you do?

6.2 GRAMMAR Reported speech

I can report what somebody else has said.

1 CLASS VOTE **If a person can't see different colours, why is it difficult to do the things below?**

cook   choose clothes   drive a car   read a Geography book

2 **Look at the photo in the text. What sort of test do you think this is?**

When twelve-year-old George said that he was getting headaches at school, his dad made an appointment for an eye test. The optician showed him some coloured images and asked him what numbers he could see, but George found the task difficult. The optician then asked him what his plans were for the future. George said that he hoped to be a pilot. 'That might be difficult,' said the doctor, 'because you're colour-blind'. She told George that he probably wouldn't be able to fly planes in the future. He was very disappointed.

Later at home, his mum told him that colour-blindness ran in the family and said his grandad had the same problem, but that he had learned to live well with it. She said that he couldn't tell the difference between some colours. George asked if that was why his grandad didn't drive a car. 'No,' said his mum. 'You can drive when you're colour blind. He just never enjoyed driving.'

3 **Read the text quickly. Why did George go to the doctor?**

4 **Study the Grammar box. Find more examples of reported speech in the text.**

Grammar | **Reported statements and questions**

Present Simple → Past Simple
'I have a headache.' He said (that) he had a headache.
Present Continuous → Past Continuous
'I'm getting better.' She said (that) she was getting better.
Past Simple → Past Perfect
'I wanted to be a doctor.' He said (that) he had wanted to be a doctor.
will → would
'My mum will do it'. He said (that) his mum would do it.
can → could
'I can't see anything'. She said (that) she couldn't see anything.
Questions
'**Do** you **work** in a hospital?' She asked me if I worked in a hospital.
'**What time is it?**' He asked what time it was.
Other changes
We often change pronouns, time phrases and place adverbials.
now → then   here → there   this month → that month
yesterday → the previous day/the day before
tomorrow → the following day
'**My** brother was **here yesterday**.' The girl said her brother had been there the day before.

GRAMMAR TIME > PAGE 123

5 **Complete the sentences.**

1 'The doctor was very kind.'
I told him that the doctor *had been* very kind.
2 'The medicine tastes horrible, but it will help.'
He said that the medicine ______ horrible, but that it ______.
3 'I tried to sleep but I wasn't tired.'
She said that she ______ to sleep, but that she ______ tired.
4 'Anne's visiting her aunt in hospital, so she can't come.'
I told her that Anne ______ her aunt in hospital, so she ______.

6 **Rewrite the questions in reported speech.**

1 'What time does the doctor finish?' I asked.
I asked what time the doctor finished.
2 'When are they leaving?' Rachel asked.
3 'Does it hurt?' the nurse asked.
4 'When did you take the medicine?' he asked me.
5 'Did Emma see the doctor?' I asked.
6 'Can I make an appointment?' Liam asked.
7 'What time did you call Dr Bower?' I asked her.
8 'Are you feeling better?' Lindsay asked me.

7 **Work in pairs. Think of the last time somebody told you some important news. What did they say? How did you feel?** And YOU

My friend told me she was going to live in a different town. I was really sad.

6.3 READING and VOCABULARY What to do if you've got a cold

I can understand specific detail in different types of text.

1 CLASS VOTE How often do you get a cold? Do you try to avoid a person who's got a cold? Why? / Why not?

2 Look at the poster. Where do you think you might see this information?

Achoo! Have you got a cold? Read on for some great tips!

Always feed a cold. Perhaps you don't feel like eating, but your body needs vitamins, so eat small amounts regularly.

Try hot chicken soup. Your body needs food and water. Hot soup clears your nose and the water in it hydrates you.

Fresh air won't make your cold worse and might make you feel better. But if you go outside, remember to wear warm clothes.

Don't get too hot. Some people think it's good to sweat if you've got a cold, but you will feel worse.

Get lots of vitamin C. You don't have to drink loads of orange juice. Some green vegetables have more vitamin C in them. So try some broccoli.

3 3.04 Read the poster. Mark the sentences T (true) or F (false).

1 ☐ You should try to stop eating when you've got a cold.
2 ☐ Soup can help a cold, but you must drink water with it.
3 ☐ Going outside can help when you've got a cold.
4 ☐ Sweating won't make you feel better.
5 ☐ Orange juice is the best source of vitamin C.

4 3.05 Read the blog post quickly. Have you heard of any of these remedies before?

I've always blogged about keeping healthy, but guess what! Today I'm sweating, my throat hurts, my nose is running and my head feels like it's going to explode. Yes, I've caught a cold and I've got a party on Saturday! I hope it's just a twenty-four-hour virus. I don't want to take any more tablets, so I think it's time to find some cool ideas to help me get better fast.

Eating well is super important. Fruit and vegetables are a must, but I've read that onions can fight a virus if you eat them raw – just like eating an apple! Yuk! I might try it, but I don't think anyone will want to talk to me at the party! Another remedy is chocolate. Apparently, dark chocolate can stop a cough, so I'm definitely going to try that. Hot chocolate with chilli works best because the spice fights the cold. Yum!

Some ideas are simply crazy. Another blogger told me that wet socks could help. First you put on cold, wet, cotton socks on warm feet (e.g. after a bath), then a pair of dry woollen socks and then you go straight to bed. He said that the cold socks helped the circulation in the feet and that cleared the head. I have no idea where the idea comes from, but he said he'd tried it and it had worked. So, that's it for today. I've got a virus but I'm going to put on two pairs of socks, grab some chocolate and go to bed. Wishing you all a happy and healthy weekend!

5 Read the blog post again. Answer the questions. Do not use more than three words.

1 What does the blogger normally write about?
2 How long does the blogger hope the virus will last?
3 What effect do raw onions have on a virus?
4 What is dark chocolate good for?
5 Who has tried the sock remedy?

6 Look at the highlighted words in the two texts. Check your understanding. Use a dictionary if necessary.

7 [VOX POPS 6.1] In pairs, take it in turns to answer the questions. Use information from the two texts and your own experience.

And YOU

1 What do you think are the best remedies for a cold?
I always drink hot lemon and honey.
2 How do you feel when you've got a cold? Do you try to carry on with your life or do you usually stay in bed and rest?

6.4 GRAMMAR Reported commands and requests

I can use reported speech to talk about commands and requests.

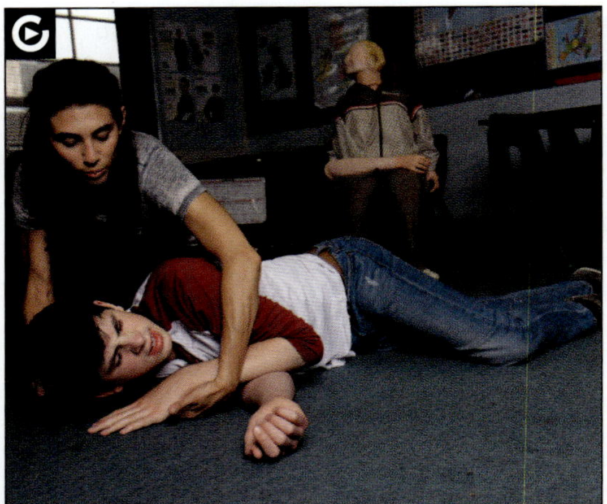

VIDEO **FIRST AID**

Nina: You go first, Dan. Lie down, please. What are you doing?

Dan: You asked me to lie down!

Nina: Yes, but not with your legs up on that chair! Come on, Dan. Please be serious! I really want to learn this. I'd love to be a first aider at festivals one day.

Dan: OK, I was just messing about.

Nina: Now, the instructor told us to start by bending this arm – like this. And then I pull your other hand and put it on your cheek. I asked you to be serious!

Dan: Sorry!

Nina: Then he told us to bend the knee and then I need to pull the leg over.

Dan: Gently!

Nina: Oh yes! Sorry, Dan. Now I need to move your head a bit so you can breathe OK. Anything else?

Dan: Yes. Call an ambulance!

Nina: Very funny!

Please be serious!
I was just messing about.
Very funny!

OUT of class

1 CLASS VOTE **Have you ever done a first aid course? Do you think schools should teach first aid?**

2 **Look at the photo. What are Dan and Nina doing? Why is it important to put someone who is hurt in the recovery position?**

3 **6.2 3.06 Watch or listen. Why does Nina lift Dan's head?**

4 **What do the verbs below mean? Which ones can you find in the dialogue?**

bend lie down lift pull push

5 **Study the Grammar box. Find more examples of reported commands and requests in the dialogue.**

Grammar | **Reported commands and requests**

Commands

'Move the left leg first.' I **told** you **to move** the left leg first.
'Don't rush.' She **told** us **not to** rush.

Requests

'Can you help me, please?' He **asked** them **to help** him.
'Please don't touch the medical equipment.'
She **asked** us **not to touch** the medical equipment.

GRAMMAR TIME > PAGE 123

6 **Rewrite the commands and requests in reported speech.**

1 'Put a bandage on my arm.'
She told me *to put a bandage on her arm*.

2 'Please don't use mobile phones in the hospital.'
The nurse asked us ______.

3 'Don't do any sports for the next six weeks.'
The doctor told him ______.

4 'Please help me with my Biology homework.'
Sarah asked her mum ______.

7 **3.07 Complete the text with the correct form of the verbs in brackets. Listen and check.**

Young first AIDERS
Matt's story

Matt Hanford is a first aid specialist at festivals and events – and he's just sixteen years old. It all began when Matt's teacher [1] *asked* (ask) his class *to take* (take) part in a first aid course. Matt really enjoyed it and his local first aid organisation [2] ______ (ask) him ______ (become) a first aider. The first event Matt helped at was a rock music festival. He was a bit nervous at first, but his colleagues [3] ______ (tell) him ______ (not worry) and he loved the experience. Last week his first aid team leader [4] ______ (ask) him ______ (help) at a rugby match. When we [5] ______ (ask) Matt ______ (explain) why he likes being a first aider, he told us it's because he loves helping people – and going to lots of great events!

8 **Think of a time when you hurt yourself or felt unwell. What did people ask you or tell you to do?**

And YOU

Once I fell off my bike and cut my knee.
My mum told me to wash it and put a plaster on it.

6.5 LISTENING and VOCABULARY Extreme sports

I can listen for specific detail and talk about extreme sports.

1 CLASS VOTE **Which sports can you see in the photos? Which do you think look the most exciting? Why?**

2 3.08 **Study the Vocabulary box. Write the words in the correct category. Use a dictionary if necessary. Listen and check.**

Vocabulary Extreme sports

abseiling BMXing bodyboarding bungee jumping free running hang-gliding (ice) climbing kite-surfing parachuting paragliding sandboarding sky-diving snowboarding white-water rafting

- **on land:** ______, ______, ______, ______, ______, ______
- **in the air:** ______, ______, ______, ______, ______
- **on/in the water:** ______, ______, ______

3 3.09 **Complete the sentences with words from the Vocabulary box. Listen and check.**

1. I love *BMXing* and I just got a new bike for my birthday.
2. On our holiday in Tunisia, we went ______ in the desert.
3. We're going ______ on the Salmon River – I hope I don't fall in!
4. My dad went ______ once, but he was too scared to jump out of the plane!
5. We do ______ around our town. It's a mix of athletics and acrobatics.
6. I tried ______ for the first time today. We wore ropes and went down a ten-metre rock.

4 3.10 **Listen to a boy talking about extreme sports. Put the parts of the body in the order you hear about them.**

heart [ ] blood [ ] lungs [ ] brain [ ] muscles [*1*]

5 3.10 **Listen again. Answer the questions.**

1. Why does the boy think extreme sports are good?
2. Who should be careful about doing extreme sports?

6 3.11 **Listen to a girl leaving a message about her birthday party. Which of the sports in the Vocabulary box is she going to do at her party?**

7 3.11 **Listen again. Complete the notes.**

Harriet's extreme party!

- *Where:* [1] ______ *(opposite* [2] ______ *and next to the leisure centre)*
- *When: Saturday @* [3] ______ *a.m.*
- *Tell Harriet's mum about any* [4] ______
- *Must wear:* [5] ______ *and trousers*
- *Phone Katy's mum about lift (mobile no:* [6] ______*)*

8 [VOX POPS 6.3] **Have you ever tried an extreme sport? Discuss in pairs.**

And YOU

- If so, which one? How did you feel?
- If not, which extreme sport would you like to try? Why?

I've never tried an extreme sport, but I'd like to try hang-gliding because I think it's the nearest thing to flying! It would be amazing to see everything from high up.

6.6 SPEAKING Asking for and giving advice

I can ask for and give advice.

VIDEO **I HATE HICCUPS!**

Nina: You've got to help me. I can't get rid of these hiccups. It's driving me mad! Any ideas what to do?
Skye: Have you tried holding your breath?
Nina: Yes. It didn't work!
Tommo: I know it sounds weird, but if I were you, I'd try drinking some water upside down. Drink from the opposite side of the glass.
Nina: OK. I'll give it a go. Oh no, the water has gone everywhere!
Skye: I know! I saw this on TV. Try blocking your ears and nose and drinking the water. It's supposed to work every time!
Nina: OK, I'll block my ears, but …
Skye: I'll hold your nose.
Jay: And I'll take the glass of water. Take a sip.
Nina: What are you doing, Dan?
Dan: You looked so funny, Nina. I had to take a photo!
Nina: Please don't! What do you suggest, Jay?
Jay: I wish I could help, but I've got to go. Boo!
Nina: Aargh! What did you do that for? Wait a minute. My hiccups have gone! Thanks, Jay!

> *It's driving me mad!*
> *I know it sounds weird, but …*
> *I'll give it a go.*
>
> **OUT of class**

1 CLASS VOTE **Do you know a cure for hiccups? What is it and does it work?**

I've heard that eating a slice of lemon can stop hiccups, but I haven't tried it because I don't like lemons!

2 Look at the photo. What do you think is happening?

3 6.4 3.12 **Watch or listen. Do the friends stop Nina's hiccups? How?**

4 Study the Speaking box. Find more examples in the dialogue.

Speaking Asking for and giving advice

Asking for advice
What do you suggest?
If you were me, what would you do?
What's your advice?
Any ideas what to do?

Giving advice
If I were you, I'd drink some honey and lemon.
You'd better see a doctor.
You should/ought to go home.
It might be a good idea to …
Have you thought about making an appointment to see the doctor?
Have you tried putting some cream on it?
Try holding your nose.
I'd recommend/advise/suggest taking an aspirin.

Being unable to give advice
I don't know what to advise/suggest, I'm afraid.
I wish I could help/suggest something, but I …
I'm afraid I can't really help you.

5 3.13 **Complete the dialogues with words from the Speaking box. Listen and check.**

1 A: I've got a rash on my stomach. What's your *advice*?
B: It might be a good ______ to see a doctor. It could be something serious.

2 A: I've had a runny nose for a few days. What do you ______?
B: I don't know ______ to advise, I'm afraid. I think you'll just have to wait for it to go.

3 A: I feel a bit dizzy. ______ ideas what to do?
B: If I ______ you, I'd have something to eat and sit down for a while.

6 3.14 **Listen to four dialogues. Respond with advice in each situation. Listen, check and compare your advice with what you heard.**

7 In pairs, choose one of the problems below each. Take it in turns to ask for and give advice.

- a bad headache
- a sore throat
- itchy eyes and sneezing

And YOU

6.7 ENGLISH IN USE Quantifiers

I can use quantifiers to talk about activities and sports.

Girl: What happened to your arm?
Boy: I was at the snowboarding competition yesterday. I won both a silver and a gold medal!

Girl: Impressive! What about Al and Carl? Did either of them win a medal?
Boy: No, neither Al nor Carl won anything.

Girl: So, was it a dangerous jump? Were you going too fast? Did you fall over?
Boy: Umm … actually, it was none of those things. I fell out of bed!

1 **Look at the cartoon. How did the boy hurt his arm? Do you think he wanted to tell the girl how he hurt it?**

2 **Study the Language box. Find more examples of quantifiers in the cartoon.**

Language Quantifiers

Two people/things
Both sports are good for you.
Did you try either of the two sports?
I didn't try either of the two sports.
I tried neither of the two sports.

More than two people/things
All the sports listed are easy.
Did you try any of the sports listed?
I didn't try any of the sports listed.
I tried none of the sports listed.

both ... and
Both Mark and Liam love BMXing.
Mark and Liam both love BMXing.
Mark loves both BMXing and bodyboarding.

either ... or
You can go either climbing or skateboarding.
You either love extreme sports or you don't.

neither ... nor
Nicola's neither adventurous nor sporty.
Neither Joe nor Ann like running.

3 **Complete the dialogues with quantifiers.**

1 A: Where are Simon and Rebecca?
B: They're *both* ill. ______ of them can come.
2 A: Are there any films on TV tonight?
Yes, we can ______ watch an action film ______ a thriller.
3 A: So have you asked all your friends about going snowboarding?
B: Yes, but ______ of them wants to join me.
4 A: Can Tom and Harry go to the beach with us?
B: No. ______ Tom ______ Harry can go.

4 3.15 **Choose the correct answers. Listen and check.**

[1] *Neither* Lily nor I have ever done any extreme sports before. Snowboarding is going to be a new experience for [2] ______ of us. Lily and I have been friends for years and we both have asthma. In the past, neither Lily [3] ______ I imagined we could ever try snowboarding. When I found out I had asthma, I was worried I'd [4] ______ have to stop sport altogether or only do very gentle, boring sports! [5] ______ of my friends or family have asthma, so I didn't know what to expect. I soon realised that with medicine I could control my asthma. So next week it's Lily's birthday, and we're going to go snowboarding – I can't wait!

	a	b	c	d
1	a Either	b Both	c (Neither)	d None
2	a both	b neither	c all	d either
3	a and	b nor	c or	d none
4	a neither	b none	c both	d either
5	a None	b Neither	c All	d Both

5 **Complete the sentences to make them true for you.**

None of my friends have ever …
Neither myself nor my best friend like …
I enjoy playing both … and …
This weekend I'm going to either … or …

And YOU

WORDLIST Health problems | Adjectives and nouns for illness | Extreme sports

abseiling /ˈæbseɪəlɪŋ/
acrobatics /ˌækrəˈbætɪks/
allergic /əˈlɜːdʒɪk/
allergy /ˈælədʒi/
ambulance /ˈæmbjʊləns/
amount /əˈmaʊnt/
appointment /əˈpɔɪntmənt/
asthma /ˈæsmə/
asthmatic /æsˈmætɪk/
athletics /æθˈletɪks/
bandage /ˈbændɪdʒ/
bend /bend/
blind /blaɪnd/
blindness /ˈblaɪndnəs/
block /blɒk/
blood /blʌd/
BMXing /ˌbiː em ˈeksɪŋ/
bodyboarding /ˈbɒdi ˌbɔːdɪŋ/
brain /breɪn/
breath /breθ/
breathe /briːð/
bug /bʌg/
bungee jumping /ˈbʌndʒi ˌdʒʌmpɪŋ/
carsick /kɑːsɪk/
cheek /tʃiːk/
chemist's /ˈkemɪsts/
circulation /ˌsɜːkjəˈleɪʃən/
climbing /ˈklaɪmɪŋ/
clinic /ˈklɪnɪk/
cold /kəʊld/
colour-blind /ˈkʌlə blaɪnd/
colour-blindness /kʌlə blaɪndnəs/
come down with /kʌm daʊn wɪð/
cream /kriːm/
deaf /def/
deafness /ˈdefnəs/
depress /dɪˈpres/
depressed /dɪˈprest/
depression /dɪˈpreʃən/
dizziness /ˈdɪzinəs/
dizzy /ˈdɪzi/
dyslexia /dɪsˈleksiə/
dyslexic /dɪsˈleksɪk/
explode /ɪkˈspləʊd/
extreme sports /ɪkˈstriːm spɔːts/
eye test /aɪ test/
feed /fiːd/
first aid /fɜːst eɪd/
first aider /ˌfɜːst ˈeɪdə/
food poisoning /fuːd ˈpɔɪzənɪŋ/
free running /friː ˈrʌnɪŋ/
hang-gliding /ˈhæŋ ˌglaɪdɪŋ/
hay fever /heɪ ˈfiːvə/
headache /hedeɪk/
heart /hɑːt/
hold your breath /həʊld jə breθ/
hiccups /hɪkʌps/
hurt /hɜːt/
hydrate /ˈhaɪdreɪt/
ice climbing /ˈaɪs ˌklaɪmɪŋ/
ill /ɪl/
illness /ˈɪlnəs/
infect /ɪnˈfekt/
infected /ɪnˈfektɪd/
infection /ɪnˈfekʃən/
injure /ˈɪndʒə/
injured /ˈɪndʒəd/
injury /ˈɪndʒəri/
insomnia /ɪnˈsɒmniə/
itchy /ˈɪtʃi/
kite-surfing /kaɪt sɜːfɪŋ/
knee /niː/
lie down /laɪ daʊn/
lift /lɪft/
lungs /lʌŋz/
migraine /ˈmiːgreɪn/
muscle /mʌsl/
operate /ˈɒpəreɪt/
operation /ˌɒpəˈreɪʃən/
optician /ɒpˈtɪʃn/
pain /peɪn/
painful /ˈpeɪnfəl/
parachuting /ˈpærəˌʃuːtɪŋ/
paragliding /ˈpærəˌglaɪdɪŋ/
plaster /ˈplɑːstə/
prescribe /prɪˈskraɪb/
prescription /prɪˈskrɪpʃən/
pull /pʊl/
push /pʊʃ/
raw /rɔː/
recovery position /rɪˈkʌvəri pəˌzɪʃən/
remedy /ˈremədi/
run in the family /rʌn ɪn ðə ˈfæmli/
sandboarding /ˈsændbɔːdɪŋ/
seasickness /ˈsiːsɪknəs/
sick /sɪk/
sickness /ˈsɪknəs/
serious /ˈsɪəriəs/
sky-diving /skaɪ ˈdaɪvɪŋ/
sneeze /sniːz/
snowboarding /ˈsnəʊbɔːdɪŋ/
sore throat /sɔː θrəʊt/
source /sɔːs/
stress /stres/
stressed /strest/
suffer from /ˈsʌfə frəm/
swallow /ˈswɒləʊ/
sweat /swet/
tablet /ˈtæblət/
temperature /ˈtemprɪtʃə/
tired /taɪəd/
tiredness /ˈtaɪ̯ədnəs/
travel sickness /ˈtrævəl ˈsɪknəs/
virus /ˈvaɪərəs/
white-water rafting /waɪt ˈwɔːtə ˈrɑːftɪŋ/
wrist band /rɪst bænd/

WORD FRIENDS

Feeling ill
come down with the flu
have a rash
have a runny nose
have a temperature
have a nose bleed
have a cough
have an infection
lose your appetite
lose your voice

Seeing the doctor
get a prescription
have a check-up
listen to your chest
take your temperature
take your blood pressure

Getting better
get lots of rest
stay in bed
take medicine
take some tablets

VOCABULARY IN ACTION

1 Use the wordlist to find:

1. five adjectives that describe how you feel *stressed, ...*
2. four adjectives that describe a medical condition *asthmatic, ...*
3. three verbs of movement *push, ...*
4. three extreme sports you do in/on water *kite-surfing, ...*
5. two extreme sports you do in cold weather *snowboarding, ...*

2 Choose the correct option.

1. What do you do if you *take* / *have* a nose bleed?
2. What can you do if you *lose* / *get* your appetite?
3. When did you last *have* / *take* a check-up?
4. Has the doctor ever *had* / *taken* your temperature? If so, when?

3 In pairs, ask and answer the questions in Exercise 2.

A: What do you do if you have a nose bleed?
B: I put a wet towel on my nose.

4 3.16 PRONUNCIATION Listen and repeat the groups of words. Sometimes the stress moves, depending on the part of speech. Sometimes it stays the same.

Stress moves: operate, operation
Stress doesn't move: injure, injury, injured

5 3.17 Mark the stress in the words below. Write them in the correct category in Exercise 4. Listen and check.

allergy, allergic asthma, asthmatic
depress, depression dyslexia, dyslexic
infect, infection, infected prescribe, prescription

Revision

VOCABULARY

1 Write the correct health problem for each situation.

1 It's like a terrible headache and I need to stay in the dark. m*igraine*

2 I ate some fresh fish, but I was sick as soon as I got home. f___ p_________

3 I go to bed tired, but I lie awake for hours. i_______

4 Sometimes I find it difficult to breathe. a_____

5 I cut my finger and didn't clean it properly. It's very red and painful. i________

6 I fell and hurt my back doing sport, but it's getting better. i_____

2 Have you ever suffered from any of the problems in Exercise 1? Discuss in pairs.

3 Complete the text with the words below.

~~dizzy~~ dizziness ill painful prescribe tiredness travel sickness

Motion sickness

It's that horrible feeling that starts in your stomach. You feel [1]*dizzy*, you feel sick and for some people it ends with a [2]__________ headache. Although it's often called [3]__________, it's really motion sickness. Some people get it on exciting rides at the fair or even watching 3D movies where they complain of [4]__________ and nausea. In very serious cases, the doctor might [5]__________ tablets, but there are other remedies such as ginger or wristbands that don't cause [6]__________. Other remedies include sitting on brown paper! Maybe it's worth trying as nobody wants to be [7]__________ on holiday.

GRAMMAR

4 Read the dialogue. Complete the text below with one or two words in each gap.

Alice: I feel awful. I can't get rid of my headache.
Mark: I had a bad one last week and my teacher sent me home. Have you talked to your teacher?
Alice: Yes, she just gave me a glass of water! Do you have an aspirin?
Mark: No, I don't. Sorry. Go and see the school nurse.

Alice told Max she [1]*felt* awful. She said she [2]__________ get rid of her headache. Mark said that he had had a bad one the week [3]__________ and that his teacher [4]__________ sent him home. He asked Alice [5]__________ she had talked to her teacher. She said the teacher had just [6]__________ her water. Then Alice asked Mark if he [7]__________ an aspirin. Mark said he [8]__________ and told Alice [9]__________ go and see the school nurse.

5 Complete the sentences with the words below.

all ~~both~~ either none nor

1 *Both* Emma and Diane love their BMX bikes.
2 They all went hang-gliding, but __________ of them enjoyed it.
3 Neither Carl __________ Jane enjoyed paragliding.
4 Never again. I tried three sports and __________ of them made me sick!
5 She looks hot. __________ it's the weather or she's got a temperature.

SPEAKING

6 Work in pairs. Student A, your partner is ill. Find out what's wrong and give him/her some advice. Student B, imagine you have a health problem. Tell your partner about it. Follow the instructions below.

A: Say hello. Ask your friend how he/she is.
B: Say you aren't well. Explain what the problem is.
A: Give your friend advice.
B: Say you've tried that, but it doesn't work.
A: Suggest something else.
B: Again, tell your friend that doesn't work and way.
A: Say you can't help, but hope your friend feels better soon.
B: Thank your friend.

DICTATION

7 3.18 Listen. Then listen again and write down what you hear.

SELF-ASSESSMENT Think about this unit. What did you learn? What do you need help with?

WORKBOOK p. 74

BBC

CULTURE

Are you allergic to where you live?

Living with allergies

Sixteen-year-old Diana Brampton suffers from a very unusual allergy. She has a condition called cold urticaria – she is allergic to the cold. It didn't help that she was brought up in Ontario, Canada, one of the coldest areas on earth.

When the temperature goes below 5°C, she develops an allergic reaction. Her feet can swell up and turn a purple colour and she can get a rash all over on her body. But it's not just the weather – she can't swim in cool water or even have a drink with ice cubes. Because her allergy is so unusual, it took a long time to get a proper diagnosis.

For years, she couldn't understand what was wrong with her. Luckily, her family were able to move to Florida to help her. There are only about ten days a year when the temperature drops below 5°C there, so Diana can live more comfortably.

The UK doesn't have a particular problem with extreme cold weather, but it is a very green country and twenty-five percent of the population suffer from hay fever in spring time. 1.1 million children in the UK currently receive treatment for asthma. But why are some people more prone to them than others? One teenager gave us his opinion.

'My father was allergic to pollen and I guess that's why I am. My doctor told me that you are fifty percent more likely to be allergic if you have a parent with an allergy. I have terrible symptoms – a rash, a runny nose and sneezing. It happens just when the weather gets better after winter. Also, where I live doesn't help much. Birmingham is a big industrial city and the pollution makes the symptoms worse. In the spring, I have to stay indoors. At least I'm not the only one in my class with this problem!'

GLOSSARY
swell up (phr v) become larger than normal
get a diagnosis (phr) find out what disease you have
receive treatment (phr) use drugs, etc. to get better
be prone to sth (phr) be likely to suffer from sth bad

EXPLORE

1 In pairs, discuss the questions.

1 What are some things people are allergic to?
2 What are the symptoms of allergies?

2 Read the article and choose the correct option.

1 Living in Canada made Diana's condition much *worse* / *better*.
2 Her symptoms include *breathing problems* / *problems with her skin*.
3 It took a *long* / *short* time to get Diana's condition diagnosed.
4 In Florida, Diana doesn't suffer *at all* / *as often* from her allergy.
5 Many people get hay fever in the UK because of *the landscape* / *people's diet*.
6 Matt says that *other* / *no other* people have the same the allergy as him.

3 Read the article again. In pairs, discuss the questions.

1 Were you surprised by Diana's allergy?
2 Why are some people more likely to have an allergy than others?

EXPLORE MORE

4 6.5 **Watch Part 1 of a documentary about allergies and answer the questions.**

1 What allergies does Morgan have?
2 Why are there numbers on Emma's arm?

5 6.5 **Watch the video again. Mark the sentences T (true) or F (false).**

1 ☐ Twenty-five percent of people in the UK suffer from allergy attacks.
2 ☐ More than 200,000 people go to hospital each year with allergy attacks.
3 ☐ The body reacts in different ways depending on what it is allergic to.
4 ☐ The doctor writes numbers up to twelve on Emma's arm.
5 ☐ Emma scratches her arm after the treatment.
6 ☐ Allergic reactions are never very serious.

6 6.6 **Watch Part 2 of the video and choose the correct option.**

There is no one factor behind the [1]*allergy* / *virus* epidemic. However, changes in [2]*our diet* / *the environment* could have a significant effect. If scientists can discover what these changes are, there is some hope for children. Surprisingly, spending time [3]*inside* / *outside* is recommended as you come into contact with [4]*good* / *bad* bacteria. We can learn from dogs because their instinct is to [5]*search for* / *kill* these micro-organisms. If you live in the city and don't have a dog, head for [6]*some green space* / *the mountains*.

7 What is the advice at the end of the programme?

1 Avoid contact with people in cities.
2 Reconnect with nature, learn from animals.
3 Find out as much as possible about allergies.

8 Do you think allergies are increasing where you live? If so, which ones? Discuss in pairs or small groups.

YOU EXPLORE

9 CULTURE PROJECT **In small groups, prepare a survey about allergies where you live.**

1 Brainstorm different common allergies: nuts, dust, pollen, seafood, etc.
2 Write some survey questions. Use the ideas below and your own ideas.
   - Are you allergic to … ?
   - Do you know anybody who is allergic … ?
   - What happens when you have an allergic reaction?
3 Share your results with the class.

7

A clear message

VOCABULARY
Non-verbal communication | Word building: verbs and nouns for communication | Advertising

GRAMMAR
The Passive: Present Simple, Past Simple, Present Perfect, *can* and *must* | The Passive with *will*

Grammar: Communication breakdown

Speaking: Brown bananas

BBC Culture: Learning English abroad

Workbook p. 89

BBC VOX POPS

face2face: Did you know that 80–90 percent of communication is non-verbal? Top seven ways we communicate without words!

1 *Posture*: The position of your body can say a lot of things to other people – for example that you're bored, or tired.

2 ________: Looking into someone's eyes can show you are engaged in the conversation. Looking away shows just the opposite!

3 ________: Muscle movements in our face can instantly show a range of feelings, from happiness to sadness.

4 ________: This is a clear way to communicate 'Yes' or 'No' – agreement or disagreement.

5 ________: How we move our hands and arms not only shows our emotions, but also our personality.

6 ________: Putting your arm around someone can communicate feelings of love and friendship. But be careful: not everyone feels comfortable sharing their personal space!

7 ________: How loudly or quietly we speak can communicate how we're feeling.

7.1 VOCABULARY Non-verbal communication

I can talk about different forms of communication.

1 CLASS VOTE How do you prefer to communicate with your friends? Why?

by email   by phone   by text   face-to-face   using instant messaging

2 I KNOW! How many other forms of communication can you think of in three minutes?

3 3.19 Study the Vocabulary box. Complete the headings in the poster. Listen and check.

Vocabulary Non-verbal communication

body contact   eye contact   facial expressions   gestures
head movements   posture   voice

4 Which of the ways of communicating in Vocabulary A do you think is the most important when you meet someone for the first time? Which is the least important?

5 3.20 WORD FRIENDS Match each phrase in the Word Friends box with one of the forms of communication in the poster. Listen and check.

Word Friends

bow/shrug your shoulders   give sb a hug   look sb in the eye
make eye contact   nod/shake your head   raise/lower your voice
raise your eyebrows   point a finger

6 3.21 **Listen to a psychologist talking about non-verbal communication. Mark the sentences T (true) or F (false). Correct the false sentences.**

1 ☐ Children learn a lot of non-verbal communication from their parents.
2 ☐ Children learn to read sad facial expressions first.
3 ☐ Facial expressions usually mean the same thing in different cultures.
4 ☐ Nodding your head always means 'yes'.
5 ☐ People of the same nationality sometimes use different forms of non-verbal communication.

7 **Complete the questions with words from the Word Friends box. In pairs, ask and answer the questions.**

1 Do you think you're good at reading people's facial *expressions*?
2 Do you ______ your friends a hug when you meet up with them?
3 In what situations do you ______ your eyebrows?
4 Do you ever raise or ______ your voice when you talk to your friends? If yes, when?
5 Is it important to ______ eye contact when you're speaking to someone?

8 3.22 WORD BUILDING **Complete the table. Use a dictionary if necessary. Listen and check.**

Verb	Noun
communicate	*communication*
interrupt	______
explain	______
describe	______
define	______
suggest	______
pronounce	______
repeat	______
discuss	______
inform	______

9 3.23 **Complete the sentences with the correct form of words from Exercise 8. Listen and check.**

1 Every time I try to say something, my brother i*nterrupts* me; he never lets me finish a sentence!
2 It took me a long time to remember the correct **p**______ of *Edinburgh*.
3 I went to bed really late last night because I had a long **d**______ with my parents about school.
4 Anna tried to **e**______ to Matt why she was late, but he didn't listen.
5 I often have to **r**______ myself when I talk to my grandma because she can't hear very well.

10 3.24 **Complete the blog with the words below. Listen and check.**

~~communication~~ describe explanation facial expressions hand gestures

My blog

Do we still prefer face time to screen time?

It's no secret that most teens love online [1]*communication*. However, research reports that nearly fifty percent of teens still prefer talking to a friend face-to-face rather than using technology. So what's the [2]______ for this?

One reason is that although texting and messaging is great, it's not always easy to [3]______ our feelings clearly. Without [4]______, such as a smile or frown, it's easy to misunderstand what the other person is saying. It's also more fun talking to friends in person. For example, you definitely add more laughs to a story when you use [5]______ and your voice!

11 **In pairs, discuss the questions. Compare your answers with the class.**

1 Why do many teens still prefer face-to-face communication?
2 Do you think adults or elderly people prefer face-to-face communication? Why?
3 Can you think of situations in which online communication is better?

12 [VOX POPS 7.1] **In what situations do you find communicating difficult?**

When I'm in a group of people, I often feel shy and I find it hard to think of things to say.

And YOU

7.2 GRAMMAR The Passive

I can use verbs in the Passive.

VIDEO COMMUNICATION BREAKDOWN

Jay: You're in a rush!
Skye: We're going to a workshop. The last one was organised by the Drama teacher.
Jay: What workshop?
Nina: We were sent an email last week. Look at the poster: 'Improve your communication skills and have fun. All equipment is provided.'
Skye: Come on. It'll be a laugh.
Teacher: Hi, guys. OK, today's game has been designed to help you communicate better with each other. In this game obstacles are placed around the room. The obstacles are chairs, a table, cushions and some water. One person is blindfolded and has to get to the other side of the room.
Jay: Cushions … cool. Can I be blindfolded?
Teacher: Sure. Now, when the instructions are given, listen carefully. OK. Dan, Nina and Skye, decide where you want the obstacles. … I think we're ready. Remember: *clear* instructions must be given.
Dan: Jay! I said turn right.
Jay: Clear instructions weren't given.
Nina: They were! You weren't listening!
Teacher: Guys, this should be fun!

You're in a rush!
It'll be a laugh.

OUT of class

1 CLASS VOTE **Look at the photo. Do you think this type of actitivity helps your communication skills? Why? / Why not?**

2 7.2 3.25 **Watch or listen and answer the questions.**

1 How did Nina, Dan and Skye hear about the workshop?
2 What obstacles does the teacher mention?

3 **Study the Grammar box. Find more examples of the Passive in the dialogue.**

Grammar The Passive

Present Simple and Past Simple
Special equipment **is used**.
The message **wasn't sent**.

Present Perfect
The poster **has been printed**.
The obstacles **haven't been moved**.

can* and *must
The game **can't be played** in groups.
More information **must be given**.

by
The workshop was organised **by** the students.

GRAMMAR TIME > PAGE 124

4 3.26 **Write questions and short answers for these sentences from the Grammar box. Listen and check.**

1 Is special equipment *used*? (✓) *Yes, it is.*
2 Was the message ______? (✗) ______
3 Has the poster ______? (✓) ______
4 Have the obstacles ______? (✗) ______
5 Can the game ______? (✗) ______

5 **Write the past participle form of the verbs below.**

find keep lose make say see show speak teach write

6 **Rewrite the sentences in the Passive.**

1 A schoolboy has found a message in a bottle.
A message in a bottle *has been found by* a schoolboy.
2 Most people don't write letters now.
Letters ______ most people now.
3 We can make some food for the workshop.
Some food ______ for the workshop.
4 They didn't keep their letters for the grandchildren.
Their letters ______ for the grandchildren.
5 This teaches students to work in a team.
Students ______ to work in a team.
6 The students must speak English in this class.
English ______ the students in this class.

7.3 READING and VOCABULARY Communicating with family members

I can understand a text about communication between family members.

1 CLASS VOTE Do you communicate with different people in different ways? Think about your parents, brother or sister, grandparents, neighbours.

2 3.27 Read the texts quickly. Which forms of communication do Sam and Amelia mention?

Sam

I don't talk much at home. It's not that I don't enjoy talking, it's just that sometimes I don't want to. This often happens when I get home from school and my mum **fires questions** at me. 'How was the Maths test? Was your homework given back to you? How did you do?' If I don't answer, she raises her voice and repeats them. It **drives me mad** – especially when I'm chatting online with my friends. Sometimes we're interrupted by my mum telling me to tidy my room or walk the dog. **Don't get me wrong** – my mum is great, but I find that really annoying! She likes texting me to find out where I am. I remember once, I came home, said hi to my dad and went straight to my bedroom. A few minutes later, my mum came in from the garden and texted me. 'Sam, where are you? Your dinner's ready!' 'Mum, I'm in my room!' I replied. That made us both laugh!

Amelia

I've always been **chatty** like my grandma and we talk about everything. I love her stories of when she was young and a bit of a **rebel**. We often talk about what it was like without a mobile phone or a computer. She didn't like talking to her friends on the phone at home because everyone could hear her. When she had a boyfriend, she had to go to a phone box near the house. It was used by lots of people, so she often had to wait in the cold. Gran was a good dancer and wanted to study Dance at college. Her parents wouldn't even have a discussion about it. 'That's how it was,' she says. The best thing about Gran is she can read my facial expressions. If something's worrying me, she knows and we talk about it. She never thinks I'm being silly. Gran texts me sometimes, but she's **hilarious**. She writes, 'Hello, America'. That's because in **predictive text** my name appears as 'America'!

3 Read the texts again. Mark the sentences T (true) or F (false).

1 ☐ Sam always likes talking to his mum when he gets home.
2 ☐ Sam's mum often has to ask the same questions more than once.
3 ☐ Sam doesn't generally get on well with his mum.
4 ☐ Sam's dad sent him a text about dinner.
5 ☐ Amelia and her grandma both talk a lot.
6 ☐ Amelia's grandma preferred using a public phone when she was young.
7 ☐ Amelia's grandma's parents wanted her to study Dance.
8 ☐ Her grandma often gets Amelia's name wrong in her texts.

4 Which person in the texts:

1 is good at reading body language? ______
2 is annoyed by interruptions? ______
3 sometimes talks in a loud voice? ______
4 sometimes gets texts from a person who's worried? ______
5 is sometimes very funny? ______
6 likes hearing about life in the past? ______

5 Look at the highlighted words in the texts. Check your understanding. Use a dictionary if necessary.

6 In pairs, discuss the questions.

1 What type of person do you think Sam is? What about Amelia?
2 What differences are there in the way Sam communicates with his mum and Amelia communicates with her grandma?

7 In groups, imagine you are writing a leaflet called *A parent's guide to talking to teenagers*. What suggestions would you include?

Parents shouldn't ask questions about homework at meal times.

And YOU

7.4 GRAMMAR The Passive with *will*

I can change active sentences into passive sentences.

1 CLASS VOTE **Does your school offer sign language classes? If not, do you think it would be good idea to add them? Why? / Why not?**

2 **Read the news story. Who has hearing difficulties?**

I can't wait until we can chat just like other mates.

When Luke Hamilton discovered that his new neighbour, Dominic, had hearing difficulties, he decided to look for a sign language course. He soon found one. From September, sign language classes will be taught at Luke's school. They'll be offered to students and parents, and Luke's very excited about it. 'The course will be taught by a qualified teacher after school. Homework won't be given, although students can do online exercises,' he says. The head teacher is sure the classes are a good idea. 'Sign language courses aren't offered in many schools in this area, so we thought it would be popular. If this goes well, more courses will be planned for the future,' he explained. During the course, students will learn basic signs for everyday use. Luke doesn't know how quickly he'll learn, but he's sure of one thing: 'My sign language will be used with Dominic,' he says. 'I can't wait until we can chat just like other mates.'

3 **Read the news story again. Answer the questions.**

1. Why did Luke decide to learn sign language?
2. How does Luke feel about starting the course?
3. Why does the head teacher think the course will be popular?

4 **Study the Grammar box. Find more examples of the Passive with *will* in the news story.**

Grammar | **The Passive with *will***

A science fair will be organised at the school.
These classes won't be taught during school hours.

Sometimes you can form two passive sentences from one active sentence:

Active: The school will offer free classes to parents.
Passive: Free classes will be offered to parents.
Parents will be offered free classes.

GRAMMAR TIME > PAGE 124

5 **Complete the sentences using the Passive with *will*.**

1. Next year, the course *will be offered* (offer) to all students.
2. A lot of new classes ______ (organise) for next year.
3. The suggestion ______ (not discuss) until tomorrow.
4. The information ______ (write) on the board for you.
5. Books ______ (not use) in class today because we're playing a game.

6 3.28 **Read the text. Complete the sentences below using the Passive with *will*. Listen and check.**

From next week, students from Hong Kong University will teach Chinese at Harwood School. Teachers believe more schools will offer Chinese lessons to students in the future. The university students will teach writing and speaking skills. They won't test the pupils, but they will organise a weekly quiz. At the end of the course they will prepare a Chinese meal to celebrate.

1. From next week, Chinese *will be taught at Harwood School by students from Hong Kong University*.
2. Teachers believe students ______ by more schools in the future.
3. Writing and speaking skills ______ .
4. The pupils ______ , but a weekly quiz ______ .
5. At the end of the course, a Chinese meal ______ to celebrate.

7 **In pairs, make passive sentences that are true for you.** And YOU

1. a school trip / organise / for my class soon
   A school trip will be organised for my class soon.
2. extra homework / give / today
3. the answers to this exercise / discuss / in class
4. a big party / plan / for the end of school

7.5 LISTENING and VOCABULARY Advertising

I can understand key information in short conversations and describe a TV commercial.

1 CLASS VOTE **Adverts must communicate their message clearly. What do you think makes a good TV commercial?**

a famous person colour humour
music other?

2 3.29 **Study the Vocabulary box. Complete the sentences. Listen and check.**

Vocabulary Advertising

~~billboard~~ brand commercials flyers logo
poster slogan target audience

1 There's a huge *billboard* at the side of the road. It's advertising the new cinema.
2 The ______ for this sports company is 'Everyone's a winner'.
3 The ______ for Lacoste clothing is a green crocodile.
4 A man is handing out ______ for the music festival next weekend.
5 There are too many ______ on TV. It's really annoying when you're watching a film.
6 The ______ for this advert is children – that's why they put it on after school.
7 Can I put this ______ up on your notice board, please?
8 I always buy the same ______ of shampoo.

3 3.30 **Listen to five extracts from TV commercials. Match the commercials (1–5) with the products (a–h). There are three extra products.**

a ☐ chocolate
b ☐ trainers
c ☐ perfume
d ☐ toothpaste
e ☐ washing-up liquid
f ☐ nail varnish
g ☐ a hamburger
h ☐ a mountain bike

4 3.30 **Listen again. Answer the questions.**

1 Who is the target audience for each commercial?
2 Which commercial mentions a new product of a well-known brand?
3 Which commercial do you think is the most successful?
4 Which one did you like best? Why?

5 3.31 **Listen to four short dialogues. Choose the correct answers.**

1 What is the logo of the jeans that Anna wants to buy?

A

B

C

2 What is offered for free with a flyer from the pizza restaurant?

A

B

C

3 Where will Sam's poster be put?

A

B

C

4 What time does Joe want to go football training?

A
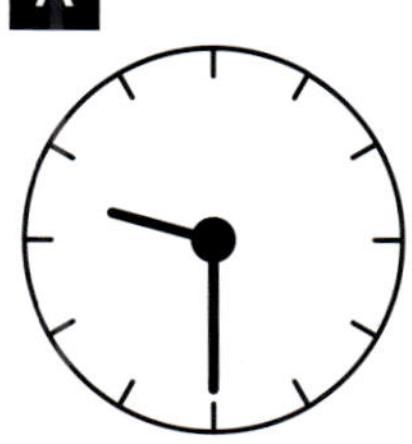
B
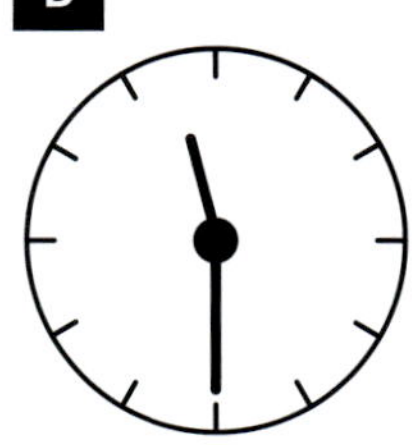
C

6 [VOX POPS ▶ 7.3] **In pairs, tell each other about your favourite TV commercial. Describe the advert and say why you like it.**

And YOU

7.6 SPEAKING Indicating objects and clarifying

I can indicate different objects, ask for and give clarification.

VIDEO BROWN BANANAS

Nina: Just a minute, Dan. I need a drink. Any idea where my bag is?
Dan: Do you mean this one, under your jacket?
Nina: That's it. I've got a great drink. It's that new one that's been on TV. Oh no! I've left it at home.
Dan: Don't worry. Let's make a drink instead. Come on.
Nina: Cool. What do you want me to do?
Dan: First, wash the fruit and cut them into small pieces.
Nina: OK. When you said wash the fruit, did you mean the bananas and pineapple?
Dan: Sorry, I meant to say wash those strawberries next to the sink.
Nina: Yuk! Look at these bananas. This one's black.
Dan: OK, but that one there is fine. Just cut that up.
Nina: You've got a pineapple. That's a bit tricky. Have you got a tin instead?
Dan: What do you mean, 'a tin'?
Nina: A tin of pineapple. It's much easier.
Dan: Brilliant! OK, let's put it all in the blender with some milk.
Nina: And now let's turn it on.
Dan: No, no, no!

OUT of class

Any idea where … is?
That's a bit tricky.

1 CLASS VOTE **Do you sometimes buy a drink or snack because you've seen it on TV? Think of an example.**

2 7.4 3.32 **Watch or listen. What fruits are mentioned?**

3 **Study the Speaking box. Find more examples of indicating and clarifying in the dialogue.**

Speaking Indicating objects and clarifying

Indicating objects
That's it/them!
This one/These ones here.
That one/Those ones over there.
Look at this/that/these/those …
It's that new/old one that …
These/Those are the ones which …

Asking for clarification
Do/Did you mean …?
What/Which one do you mean?
When you said … what did you mean?
When you said …, did you mean …
Could you say that again?

Giving clarification
Sorry, I meant to say …
What I was trying to say was …
When I said …, I meant …

4 3.33 **Jay and Skye are looking at phones. Complete the dialogue with words and phrases from the Speaking box. Listen and check.**

Jay: [1] *Look at that* phone! I might get it with my birthday money.
Skye: Which [2] ______?
Jay: That one [3] ______. It's got an awesome camera.
Skye: I thought your old phone was fine.
Jay: It was until it stopped working.
Skye: [4] ______, 'it stopped working'?
Jay: Sorry, [5] ______ until I dropped it in the swimming pool. Then it stopped working!

5 **Work in pairs. Choose one of the items below that you would like to buy and have a short conversation. Then swap roles.** **And YOU**

headphones jeans a rucksack a smarthpone a sports shirt

A: I want those cool headphones.
B: Which ones?
A: Those ones.
B: What's wrong with the ones you've got?
A: They aren't very good.
B: What do you mean …?

7.7 WRITING A review

I can write a review and offer opinions and points of view.

1 CLASS VOTE **Which of the language learning aids below can you see in the photos? Which of these do you consider most effective and which most enjoyable?**

books/films in original language
coursebook dictionary flashcards
language learning website mobile phone app

2 Read Jo's review and answer the questions.

1 What website is she reviewing and what is her opinion of it?
2 Who is the review written for?

Is Wordfit the right website for you?

So many websites have been created for language learners that it can be hard to know which is the best to use. Wordfit is one of the most popular websites, but is it as good as they say?

I was impressed by the design of the website. It looks really attractive and is easy to use. There is a wide variety of online activities and lots of fun things to do, like quizzes and games. I particularly like the fact that you can chat with other language learners on the site. The only disappointing thing about the website is that very little listening practice is provided and there's no opportunity to practise pronunciation.

All in all, I think Wordfit is a useful website and I would definitely recommend it to other learners. However, if you only want to practise listening and speaking skills, it's probably not the website for you.

3 Order the information as it appears in the review.

a ☐ Jo gives her overall opinion and recommendation.
b ☐ Jo says what she is reviewing and why she chose to review it.
c ☐ Jo explains what she thinks the advantages and disadvantages of the website are.

4 Underline the adjectives in Jo's review.

5 Write the adjectives below in the correct column. Add the adjectives you underlined in Exercise 5.

~~amazing~~ awful boring brilliant
confusing fantastic poor weak

Positive	Negative
amazing	

6 Study the Writing box. Find examples of these phrases in Jo's review.

Writing A review

What you are reviewing and why
Lots of people have asked me about …
… is one of the most popular …
… but is it as good as they say?

Advantages and disadvantages
I was impressed by …
It looks attractive/confusing.
I particularly like …
The only disappointing thing about … is …
Unfortunately, …

Personal opinion and recommendation
All in all, I think …
I would/wouldn't recommend it to …
This is one of the best … I have ever used/read/watched.

Writing Time

7 Write a review of a method of language learning that you have used (e.g. an app, a book, a website, a language course). In your review, you should:

- say what you are reviewing and give a brief description.
- explain what you think the advantages and disadvantages are.
- give your personal opinion and say whether you would recommend it to others.

TIP
Organise your review into clear paragraphs and remember to use a range of adjectives.

WORDLIST Non-verbal communication | Advertising

advert /ˈædvɜːt/
amazing /əˈmeɪzɪŋ/
app /æp/
attractive /əˈtræktɪv/
awful /ˈɔːfəl/
be engaged in (sth) /bi ɪnˈɡeɪdʒd ɪn/
billboard /ˈbɪlbɔːd/
blindfold /ˈblaɪn(d)ˌfəʊld/
body contact /ˌbɒdi ˈkɒntækt/
boring /ˈbɔːrɪŋ/
brand /brænd/
brilliant /ˈbrɪljənt/
chatty /ˈtʃæti/
commercial /kəˈmɜːʃəl/
communicate /kəˈmjuːnɪkeɪt/
communication /kəˌmjuːnɪˈkeɪʃən/
communication skill /kəˌmjuːnɪˈkeɪʃən skɪl/
confusing /kənˈfjuːzɪŋ/
define /dɪˈfaɪn/
definition /ˌdefɪˈnɪʃən/
describe /dɪˈskraɪb/
description /dɪˈskrɪpʃən/
disappointing /ˌdɪsəˈpɔɪntɪŋ/
discuss /dɪˈskʌs/
discussion /dɪˈskʌʃən/
don't get me wrong /dəʊnt get mi rɒŋ/
drive (sb) mad /draɪv mæd/
emotion /ɪˈməʊʃ(ə)n/
equipment /ɪˈkwɪpmənt/
explain /ɪkˈspleɪn/
explanation /ˌekspləˈneɪʃən/
eye contact /aɪ ˈkɒntækt/
face-to-face /ˌfeɪs tə ˈfeɪs/
facial expression /ˌfeɪʃəl ɪkˈspreʃən/
fantastic /fænˈtæstɪk/
fire questions (at sb) /ˌfaɪər ˈkwestʃnz/
flashcards /ˈflæʃˌkɑːdz/
flyer /ˈflaɪə/
frown /fraʊn/
gesture /ˈdʒestʃə/
head movement /hed ˈmuːvmənt/
hilarious /hɪˈleəriəs/
impressed /ɪmˈprest/
impressive /ɪmˈpresɪv/
in a rush /ɪn ə rʌʃ/
instant messaging /ˈɪnstənt ˈmesɪdʒɪŋ/
interrupt /ˌɪntəˈrʌpt/
interruption /ˌɪntəˈrʌpʃən/
logo /ˈləʊgəʊ/
message /ˈmesɪdʒ/
misunderstand /ˌmɪsʌndəˈstænd/
muscle /ˈmʌsəl/
nail varnish /neɪl ˈvɑːnɪʃ/
non-verbal /nɒn ˈvɜːbəl/
obstacle /ˈɒbstəkəl/
perfume /ˈpɜːfjuːm/
personal space /ˈpɜːsənəl speɪs/
poor /pɔː/
poster /ˈpəʊstə/
posture /ˈpɒstʃə/
predictive text /prɪˈdɪktɪv tekst/
pronounce /prəˈnaʊns/
pronunciation /prəˌnʌnsiˈeɪʃən/
rebel /ˈrebəl/
recommend /ˌrekəˈmend/
repeat /rɪˈpiːt/
repetition /ˌrepəˈtɪʃən/
research /rɪˈsɜːtʃ, ˈriːsɜːtʃ/
sign language /saɪn ˈlæŋgwɪdʒ/
slogan /ˈsləʊgən/
suggest /səˈdʒest/
suggestion /səˈdʒestʃən/
target audience /ˈtɑːgət ˈɔːdiəns/
text /tekst/
toothpaste /ˈtuːθpeɪst/
tricky /ˈtrɪki/
voice /vɔɪs/
washing-up liquid /ˈwɒʃɪŋ ʌp ˈlɪkwəd/
weak /wiːk/
workshop / ˈwɜː(r)kˌʃɒp /

WORD FRIENDS

make eye contact
nod/shake your head
raise/lower your voice
raise your eyebrows
read facial expressions
use hand gestures

VOCABULARY IN ACTION

1 Use the wordlist to find:

1 five compound nouns related to communication *body contact, ...*
2 five negative adjectives used to describe a website *confusing, ...*
3 three ways of advertising a product *flyer, ...*
4 two kinds of cosmetics *perfume, ...*
5 four adjectives to describe positive feelings/ experiences *amazing, ...*

2 Complete the sentences with the adjectives below.

awful chatty disappointing ~~hilarious~~ impressive tricky

1 That film was *hilarious*! We couldn't stop laughing!
2 Although her marks were good, they were still ________ as she expected to get 100 percent.
3 I'm not sure I can answer this question. It's really ________; the other ones were much easier.
4 My friend's really ________ and loves talking to people.
5 The weather's not just bad – it's absolutely ________! There's no way we can play football!
6 I think the most ________ building in London is the Gherkin. It's amazing.

3 3.34 PRONUNCIATION Underline the sound the words below all have in common. Listen and check.

commercial explanation shake

4 3.35 The most common way of spelling the /ʃ/ sound is *sh*, but in the middle of a word it is sometimes spelled *ci* or *ti*. In pairs, find more examples of the sound in the wordlist. Listen and check.

words with 'sh'	words with 'ci'	words with 'ti'
flashcards	commercial	communication

Revision

VOCABULARY

1 Write the correct word for each definition.

1 a type of product sold by a particular company **b**_r a n d_
2 talking about something to exchange opinions **d** _ _ _ _ _ _ _ _ _
3 movement of the hands or arms to express an idea **g** _ _ _ _ _ _
4 a symbol used by a company to advertise its product **l** _ _ _
5 the way in which someone holds their body **p** _ _ _ _ _ _
6 a short phrase used to advertise a product or company **s** _ _ _ _ _

2 3.36 Complete the quiz questions with the noun form of the verbs in brackets. Listen and check.

Are you good with words? Take our quiz and find out!

1 Give your partner a __________ (describe) of a place in your town. Can he/she guess what it is?
2 What is a good phrase to use when making a __________ (suggest) in English?
3 What is the correct __________ (pronounce) of the famous river that runs through London?
4 What is the __________ (define) of the adjective *chatty*?
5 Can you name three types of non-verbal __________ (communicate)?
6 What is the most common __________ (explain) students give when they're late for class?

3 In pairs, do the quiz in Exercise 2.

GRAMMAR

4 Complete the text with the correct passive form of the verbs in brackets.

At school yesterday we [1]_were taught_ (teach) how to improve our communication skills. The lesson [2]__________ (not hold) in the classroom, but out on the school field. We [3]__________ (organise) into teams and the plan was to make a bridge. I love this type of activity because it [4]__________ (do) in groups. You always have lots of problems, but they [5]__________ (can/solve) when everybody works together. [6]__________ my team's bridge __________ (build) perfectly? No, and it definitely [7]__________ (can/not/use), but we had fun!

5 Write sentences. Use the Passive with *will*.

1 the ideas / discuss / in tomorrow's lesson
The ideas will be discussed in tomorrow's lesson.
2 the information / not send / to you / by email
3 team members / select / next week / ?
4 the festival / advertise / in the local paper
5 we / put / into new groups / at school / ?
6 the winner / not announce / until the end of the day

SPEAKING

6 Complete the dialogue with the words and phrases below.

I thought you said   that one   this one   ~~those~~   which one do you mean

Julia: Look at [1]_those_ dogs in the magazine advert. I'd love [2]__________.
Tom: [3]__________? The little brown one?
Julia: No. [4]__________ – the black and white one.
Tom: [5]__________ your mum was allergic to pets.
Julia: She is, but I can always dream!

7 In pairs, talk about which of the clubs below you would like to join and why.

basketball club   dance club
gardening club   painting club
photography club

A: Look at all these clubs. I'd love to join that one.
B: Which one do you mean?
A: This one here – photography club.
B: I thought you said you didn't like taking photos.
A: When I said that, I meant I don't like people taking photos of me! I love taking photos.

DICTATION

8 3.37 Listen. Then listen again and write down what you hear.

Why do languages change?

BBC CULTURE

How languages evolve

All languages are in flux. In other words, they are constantly changing. This is especially true of English, which is a real global language. There are now nearly three times more non-native speakers of English than native speakers. 950 million people speak it as a foreign language, while only 340 million speak it as a mother tongue. So why is English changing and is this a good thing?

One reason is globalisation. These days business meetings can be held with people from all over the world – like Brazil, Nigeria and Japan. The only language spoken will be English. This has led to the creation of a new language variety, called International English. It's a kind of simplified English which can be understood by everyone. Some linguists don't like this because for them it is a corruption of the language. But it could be the future of communication in today's globalised world.

In some countries, English has a different role. In Singapore, Hong Kong and the Philippines, English is spoken as a second language. Around 600 million people speak English in this way, meaning that they are bilingual. In the Philippines, Tagalog – the country's main language – and English merge to create a variety called Taglish. It can be difficult to understand if you're not a local.

Languages also evolve because new words and phrases are coined all the time. Nouns such as *emoticon*, *spam* or *blog* and verbs like *google*, *Photoshop* or *Skype* have all been introduced thanks to digital technology. There is much discussion about whether these words should be in the dictionary or not – and some new words never make it!

The use of slang also changes a language. For example, colloquial terms such as *innit?* (*isn't it?*) and *like*, are used so much in contemporary English that they are now a kind of punctuation. But if people use these terms to communicate, why shouldn't they count as 'real words'?

GLOSSARY
mother tongue (n) the main language you learn as a child
linguist (n) sb who scientifically studies languages and how they work
corruption (n) a change from its original form
merge (v) combine; join together
coin (v) invent (a new word or expression)

EXPLORE

1 In pairs, discuss the questions.

1 Does your language have different varieties or dialects?
2 Do you use English words in your language? Which ones?

2 Read the text and answer the questions.

1 Why is English considered to be a 'global language'?
2 What is International English?
3 How many people speak English as a second language?
4 How has digital technology changed language?
5 Why are some words not considered to be 'real' words?

3 Read the article again. In pairs, discuss the questions.

1 What information in the text surprised you?
2 Do you think your language is changing as much as English? If so, in what way?
3 Do you agree that terms like *to google* are real words? Why? / Why not?

EXPLORE MORE

4 7.5 **Watch Part 1 of a video about the English language. Choose the correct option.**

1 People study English in the Philippines because *the teaching is better* / *it is cheaper*.
2 *One hundred* / *Ten* million people live in the Philippines.
3 Taglish is *difficult* / *easy* for foreigners to understand.
4 The number of foreign students in the Philippines is *stabilising* / *increasing*.
5 Elizaveta also considered studying in *Australia and New Zealand* / *Russia*.

5 7.6 **Watch Part 2 of the video. Choose the words you hear.**

1 *chav* / *chap*
2 *ain't* / *innit*
3 *LOL* / *IMO*

6 Match words 1–6 to their definitions a–f.

1 LOL
2 IMO
3 ain't
4 innit
5 chav
6 chap

a isn't it
b in my opinion
c an offensive word to describe a young person who is agressive and often wears sportswear
d am not / aren't / isn't
e a man, especially one you like
f laugh out loud

7 7.6 **Watch the video again and answer the questions.**

1 Why are some words written in black?
2 Why are some words written in red?
3 How many words are there in the *Oxford English Dictionary*?
4 When does a word become a word?

8 What did you learn about English in these videos? Would you go and study English in the Philippines? Why? / Why not? Discuss in pairs or small groups.

YOU EXPLORE

9 CULTURE PROJECT **In groups, prepare a digital presentation about different words in your language.**

1 Discuss these questions:
   - What new words are currently used?
   - What kind of people use them?
   - Which words come from other languages?
   - How many English words are used?
   - What do you think of these words?
2 Write a short script based on your discussion.
3 Share your presentation with the class.

8

Creative energy!

VOCABULARY
Art | Literature and books | Art and literature | The press

GRAMMAR
Ability | Obligation and prohibition

Grammar: Crazy painting

Speaking: Basil's song

BBC Culture: Graffiti in Bristol

Workbook p. 101

BBC VOX POPS

8.1 VOCABULARY Art and literature

I can describe works of art and talk about books.

1 CLASS VOTE Do you think you learn enough about art and literature at school? Why? / Why not?

2 3.38 Write the words below in the correct category in the Vocabulary A box. Listen and check.

contemporary art   landscape   oil painting   sculpture   sketch

Vocabulary A Art

Types of art
abstract art   graffiti   graphic art   pop art   ______   ______

Types of paintings
illustration   portrait   still life   watercolour   ______   ______   ______

3 Match the works of art (A–F) with their titles (1–6).

1 ☐ *Starry Night*, Vincent Van Gogh
2 ☐ *Girl with a Pearl Earring*, Johannes Vermeer
3 ☐ *Black Square*, Kazimir Malevich
4 ☐ *Café Guerbois*, Édouard Manet
5 ☐ *Splash*, Tomas Misura
6 ☐ *Still Life with Basket*, Paul Cézanne

4 3.39 Listen to two descriptions. Which of the works of art above are the speakers describing?

5 Study the Speaking box. In pairs, take it in turns to ask and answer about the other paintings.

> **Speaking** | **Talking about art**
>
> What type of art is it?
> It's modern/abstract/impressionist.
>
> What type of painting is it?
> It's an oil painting/a still life.
>
> Can you describe the painting/drawing?
> It's a portrait of a young woman.
> There are some mountains in the background/in the middle.
> There are some lines/shapes/images.
> I like the colours/atmosphere.
> I can't make out what it is. Maybe it's a ...
> It's unusual/simple/complicated/colourful.
> It reminds me of ...

6 3.40 Study the Vocabulary B box. Choose the correct option. Listen and check.

> **Vocabulary B** | **Literature and books**
>
> author autobiography biography chapter character cover fiction non-fiction novel novelist play playwright poem poet poetry plot scene

1. Interesting *authors* / *characters* are more important in a book than a good plot.
2. I usually read one or two *chapters* / *poems* of a book before I go to sleep.
3. I prefer reading *fiction* / *non-fiction* such as science books and biographies.
4. I find long *novels* / *novelists* boring.
5. I believe there aren't enough *playwrights* / *plays* about teenagers.

7 Are the sentences in Exercise 6 true for you?

8 I KNOW! Work in pairs. How many different types of books can you name?

crime novels, romantic fiction, …

9 Look at the book titles. What type of book do you think each one is?

1. *Goldfinger*, Ian Fleming
2. *The Three Musketeers*, Alexandre Dumas
3. *The Shadow of the Wind*, Carlos Ruiz Zafón
4. *David Beckham*, David Beckham
5. *City of the Beasts*, Isabel Allende
6. *The Hound of the Baskervilles*, Arthur Conan Doyle
7. *The Maze Runner*, James Dashner

Goldfinger, by Ian Fleming, is a spy story.

10 Study the Speaking box. In pairs, talk about a book you enjoyed or didn't enjoy.

I loved Lord of the Rings. It's fiction and it's set in a place called Middle Earth. It's about …

> **Speaking** | **Talking about books**
>
> It's called ...
> It was written by ...
> It's about .../It tells the story of ...
> It's set in ...
> It's a true story/fiction/non-fiction.
> In the first/last chapter ...
> It starts/ends with ...
> It's fantastic/amazing/weak/boring.

11 WORD FRIENDS 3.41 Complete the blog entry with the correct form of verbs from the Word Friends box. Listen and check.

> **Word Friends**
>
> **appear** in the news
> **do** a painting
> **get** good/bad reviews
> **give** a (poetry) reading/a speech
> **hold** an exhibition
> **promote** your work/ideas
> **win** an award
> **write** a bestseller/a play/a novel

Jesslovesart.blog

Do you [1] *write* plays or [2] ______ paintings that you want to show others? Then why not try an art festival? It's the perfect place to [3] ______ your work.

I've just been to a brilliant festival with lots of artists and writers. I met a novelist who had [4] ______ his first award when he was twelve. He [5] ______ a funny speech about how he wrote stories during Science lessons at school! He said the best thing about his job is [6] ______ good reviews.

My favourite activity was a Japanese haiku poetry workshop. A haiku poem has three lines. The first and the last line have five syllables and the middle line has seven. We wrote a poem and then we [7] ______ our own poetry reading. At the end we had a party and some journalists came. The next day we all [8] ______ in the news!

12 [VOX POPS 8.1] In pairs, talk about a famous novelist or artist from anywhere in the world.

And YOU

8.2 GRAMMAR Modal verbs for ability: *can, could, be able to, manage to*

I can talk about ability in the present, past and future.

1 CLASS VOTE **What comics did you read when you were younger? Did your friends read the same ones? Do you like reading comics or graphic novels?**

2 **In pairs, discuss the questions.**

1 Do you enjoy reading novels?
2 What do you prefer: watch a film based on a book or read the book? Why?

3 **Read the text. According to the writer, why are graphic novels a good idea?**

I can read books and enjoy pictures!

I can't remember how many different comics I read when I was little, but I know I loved them. I managed to collect a big pile of them. Then I started collecting superhero comics like *Spiderman* because they were exciting. I loved manga comics and tried to copy the drawings, but I couldn't do them very well. When I started to read novels, I couldn't always follow the story and missed the pictures. Then I discovered graphic novels! They're great if you aren't able to read very quickly because the pictures help you to stay interested. I've read fiction and non-fiction ones. There's even a graphic book about the life of Gandhi called *My Life is my Message*. When we started reading Shakespeare's play *Hamlet* at school, I couldn't follow the plot. My dad managed to find a graphic novel of it in the library, so I'll be able to understand the story and the characters. This doesn't mean I won't be able to read longer novels in the future. It just means that I'll be able to enjoy types of books that I wouldn't normally read.

4 **Study the Grammar box. Find more examples in the text.**

Grammar | **Ability**

Present
She can/can't paint.
They're able to/aren't able to speak French.

Past
They could/couldn't understand the story.
Jack was/wasn't able to come.
He managed to/didn't manage to read the book in a day.

Future
I'll be/won't be able to finish this today.

Questions
Can/Could he paint? No, he can't/couldn't.
Is/Was she able to speak French? Yes, she is/was.
Will you be able to read more books? No, I won't.
Did he manage to read the book in day? Yes, he did.

Be able to is more formal than *can.*
Could is used to describe general ability in the past.
Managed to describes specific achievements in the past.

GRAMMAR TIME > PAGE 125

5 3.42 **Complete the dialogues with the correct form of *can, could, be able to* or *manage to*. Listen and check.**

Mum: What's the matter, love?
Oscar: I [1]*couldn't* sleep last night and now I [2]________ concentrate.
Mum: Why don't you read a nice book before you go to sleep? It [3]________ help you to relax.

The next day:

Oscar: Hi, mum. I [4]________ get a great book from the library.
Mum: Oh, that's good. Tonight you'll [5]________ read it in bed and you'll soon fall asleep.
Oscar: It's a horror story!
Mum: That's no good, Oscar! You [6]________ to sleep after that!

6 **Complete the questions with the correct form of the words in brackets. Give answers that are true for you.**

1 *Did you manage to* (you/manage to) fall asleep quickly last night?
No, I didn't. I couldn't sleep for ages.
2 ________ (you/can) swim when you were four?
3 ________ (your best friend/can) tell funny jokes?
4 ________ (you/able to) do homework and listen to music at the same time?
5 ________ (you/be able to) finish this exercise before the end of the lesson?

8.3 READING and VOCABULARY Art for teens

I can identify detail in a text about an artist and talk about different types of exhibitions.

1 CLASS VOTE Do you enjoy visiting art exhibitions? Why? / Why not?

2 Look at the photos in the article. Which type of art do you prefer? Why?

3 3.43 Read the article. How many types of art or paintings does it mention?

4 Read the article again. Choose the correct answers.

1 What does Charlotte try to do in this text?
   - a give a review of an art gallery
   - b apologise for being noisy in art galleries
   - c explain how to enjoy art galleries more
   - d describe different types of art

2 What was the school trip to the art gallery like?
   - a It was successful although the students behaved badly.
   - b It was stressful for the teacher and not much fun for the students.
   - c It was better than the students thought it would be.
   - d It was interesting because they had studied the artist at school.

3 What does Charlotte think about art galleries now?
   - a They should have more events for young people.
   - b You don't need to visit them to enjoy them.
   - c There are more exhibitions for teens now than before.
   - d You can enjoy them if you find events especially for teens.

4 Charlotte finds Kristián Mensa's work interesting because
   - a he uses extraordinary, unique objects in his pictures.
   - b he puts a lot of effort into each work of art.
   - c he's got original ideas and is very creative.
   - d he uses different techniques at the same time.

5 Look at the highlighted words in the text. Check your understanding. Use a dictionary if necessary.

Art has something for everyone, but you have to look for it!

By Charlotte, 17

At school, Art is fun because we **experiment** with different **techniques**. We do portraits, make sculptures and generally get creative! However, a school trip to an art gallery is often **disappointing** if you're a teen. For example, last year my Art teacher organised a trip to an exhibition of abstract art by Mark Rothko. The gallery was full of older people, who obviously didn't want to be with noisy school kids. We all got bored and we couldn't stop **giggling**. Our teacher was getting stressed and kept telling us to be quiet.

The next day we talked to our teacher about the **lack** of activities for visitors our age at art galleries. She agreed that a visit should be both educational and fun. That's when I decided to go online and look for art galleries that have special events for teens. I managed to find a huge **range** of activities and proposed some of them to the teacher. Next month we're going to see an exhibition of pop art and meet an artist who specialises in it. So, if you say art galleries are boring, I can show you where to look for **inspiring** ideas!

It's also a good idea to use the internet to learn about artists. Recently I managed to find a contemporary artist from Czechia, called Kristián Mensa. I've already seen artists who **combine** different techniques, but this is totally different. He does unique illustrations with ordinary **household objects** such as mobile phones, headphones and even biscuits. His art is very simple, but it makes you see things differently. For example, he notices that a flower is similar to a mop – and puts this idea into life by drawing a little man and giving him a real flower mop. It's hilarious! I hope I'll be able to go to an exhibition of his work in the future.

6 In pairs, read the adverts for different art exhibitions. Which one would you like to go to? Why? And YOU

- Giant tree sculptures in the park
- Wild animals in watercolour
- Contemporary art from China
- Impressionist gardens by Monet

I'd like to see 'Wild animals in watercolour'. I love the facial expressions of animals, so it will be interesting to see how the colours work.

8.4 GRAMMAR Modal verbs for obligation and prohibition: *must* and *have to*

I can talk about obligation and prohibition in the past, present and future.

VIDEO CRAZY PAINTING

Skye: OK. First, we have to spread this plastic on the ground. And then we add the paint.
Nina: This is a great idea for painting T-shirts.
Skye: I know. We should ask school if we can do it on the last day.
Nina: No, we won't be allowed to do it. It's too messy.
Skye: Dan, hi. Listen, you'll have to hurry up. We're nearly ready.
Nina: What's up?
Skye: Dan's left the T-shirts at home. He had to go back for them, but he won't be long.
Nina: It's OK. Mum won't be home until later. She says we're allowed to do this, but we have to clean up before she gets back.
Dan: Sorry I'm late. You didn't have to wait for me.
Skye: You've got the T-shirts, Dan!
Nina: OK. Let's put on the T-shirts, then get some water on the plastic and we're ready.
Skye: Are there any rules?
Nina: No, just run and slide, but we mustn't push each other. Off we go!
Skye: Oh no! Your mum's home. We have to clean up.
Nina's mum: Hi! That looks fun. Can I try it?
Skye: Sure, you'll have to change first though!

OUT of class

What's up? *Sorry I'm late.* *Off we go!*

1 CLASS VOTE **Look at the photo. Would you like to try this? Why? / Why not?**

2 8.2 3.44 **Watch or listen. Why can't they start the activity?**

3 **Study the Grammar box. Find more examples in the dialogue.**

Grammar **Obligation and prohibition**

Obligation

You must/have to leave.	Do/Did/Will you have to leave?
They had to leave.	Yes, I do/did/will.
I will have to leave.	

Lack of obligation

You don't have to come.
She didn't have to come.
He won't have to come.

Prohibition

You mustn't/aren't allowed to go.
I wasn't allowed to go.
He won't be allowed to go.
Are/Were you allowed to stay late?
Will you be allowed to stay late?

Must and *mustn't* don't have past or future forms. We use different verbs instead.
In question forms we usually use *have to*.

GRAMMAR TIME > PAGE 125

4 **Write questions and short answers about the dialogue.**

1 they / be allowed / paint T-shirts / in Nina's garden / ?
Are they allowed to paint T-shirts in Nina's garden?
Yes, they are.
2 they / be allowed / paint T-shirts / on the last day of school / ?
3 why / Nina and Skye / have to / wait for Dan / ?
4 what / they / have to / do / before Nina's mum arrives / ?
5 Nina's mum / have to / change her clothes / ?

5 **Complete the second sentence so that it means the same as the first one. Use the word in brackets.**

1 You mustn't paint on the walls. (allowed)
You *aren't allowed to* paint on the walls.
2 It was necessary to tidy the room. (have to)
They ______ tidy the room.
3 It will be necessary to stay after class. (have to)
They ______ stay after class.
4 Writing in your book is not allowed. (must)
You ______ in your book.
5 It won't be necessary for Jack to come. (have to)
Jack ______ come.

8.5 LISTENING and VOCABULARY In a newspaper office

I can understand a conversation between friends and talk about the press.

1 CLASS VOTE **Who in your family listens to or reads the news?**

2 3.45 **Match the groups of words in the Vocabulary box with the headings below. Listen and check.**

in the news people types of press

Vocabulary **The press**

________ : broadsheet magazine online news site tabloid
________ : designer editor journalist paparazzi reporter
________ : adverts celebrity gossip commercials headlines horoscope local/national news weather forecast

3 **Complete the sentences with words from the Vocabulary box.**

1 My sister works as an ____________ in a fashion magazine.
2 I don't buy newspapers. I read the news on an online ____________ .
3 This magazine is all about ____________ : who is dating who, where an actor went on holiday or what they were wearing at a party.
4 The ____________ says it's going to rain at the weekend.
5 A ____________ is a type of newspaper that has a lot of photos and not much serious news.

4 **In pairs, answer the questions. Compare your answers with the rest of the class.**

1 What do the paparazzi do?
2 What's the difference between a reporter and an editor?
3 Why is a good headline important?
4 What's the difference between a tabloid and a broadsheet?

5 **Look at the picture. Why do you think there's a pony in a newspaper office?**

6 3.46 **Listen to Freddie and Ava talking about Freddie's day in a newspaper office. Did Freddie win a prize for his short story or his photos?**

7 3.46 **Listen again. Mark the sentences T (true) or F (false).**

1 ☐ Freddie went to the office with another winner.
2 ☐ When Freddie arrived, he met the editor.
3 ☐ The office was busy when Freddie was there.
4 ☐ The football player signed a shirt for Freddie.
5 ☐ The owner of the pony got angry in the reception.

8 3.46 **Listen again. Match 1–6 with a–f to make sentences.**

1 The editor
2 The reporters
3 Ava
4 Freddie
5 The football player
6 The pony

a wasn't pleased about the photo.
b wrote a funny headline.
c wasn't happy about the visit to the office.
d introduced Freddie to the reporters.
e thought the bird story was funny.
f were looking for news stories.

9 **In pairs, tell each other what you remember about Freddie's day at the newspaper office.**

First, he met …

10 **In pairs, take it in turns to ask and answer the questions.** And YOU

1 Do you prefer national or local news?
2 Is there too much celebrity gossip in newspapers?
3 Do you ever read your horoscope?
4 What kinds of magazines do you like reading?

8.6 SPEAKING Comparing ideas and expressing opinions

I can compare and contrast ideas and express opinions.

VIDEO BASIL'S SONG

Tommo: I could be wrong, but I bet she's got her headphones on.

Nina: Let's throw a stone at her window.

Skye: Hi, guys. Sorry, I didn't hear you. I really need your help. I'm trying to write a song for the school show, but it's exactly the same as my last one.

Nina: Is it a sad song again?

Skye: Sort of. One friend moves away and the other friend is lonely.

Nina: It seems to me that you need some fresh ideas, Skye. What do you think, Tommo?

Tommo: I think Nina's right. Why not write about Basil?

Skye: Basil! Are you mad? People don't write about their pet snakes!

Tommo: Personally, I think Basil is more interesting than two sad friends.

Nina: In my opinion, Tommo's right, Skye. It's got to be fun. OK, we'll write one line each about Basil and see how it goes.

Later:

Nina: And now let's do a rap. My fun won't end with you as my friend.

Tommo: I'm not gonna lie. I'll never say bye!

Skye: I've had a few pets, but you're the best.

Nina: He might be a snake, but Basil's my mate!

Skye: Nina, you're brilliant! If you ask me, we've got a hit song! Now let's write some more lines.

I bet … *Sort of.*
… and see how it goes.

OUT of class

1 CLASS VOTE What do you think is more important in a song: the lyrics or the music?

2 Work with a partner. What are songs often about?

3 8.3 3.47 Watch or listen. Why doesn't Skye open the door to Nina and Tommo?

4 Study the Speaking box. Find more examples in the dialogue.

Speaking Comparing ideas and expressing opinions

Comparing ideas

- ☐ On the one hand, … but on the other hand, …
- ☐ Personally, I think … is better/more interesting than …
- ☐ … is the best idea because …
- ☐ It's exactly/almost the same as …
- ☐ … is totally different from …

Expressing opinions

- ☐ In my opinion, … is brilliant/amazing /awful.
- ☐ As I see it, …
- ☐ I think you're right.
- ☐ As far as I can see, …/As far as I'm concerned, …
- ☐ It seems to me that …
- ☐ If you ask me, …
- ☐ I'm not sure …
- ☐ I could be wrong, but …

5 3.48 Complete the dialogue with words from the Speaking box. Listen and check.

A: In my [1] *opinion*, the best song ever written is *Starman* by David Bowie.

B: What makes it special for you?

A: Well, as I [2] ________ it, it's a message about hope.

B: [3] ________, I think *Space Oddity* is better.

A: You might be right. I'm not [4] ________, but I think he wrote it after watching the film *2001: A Space Odyssey*.

B: If you [5] ________ me, all of his songs are brilliant.

6 3.49 Listen to two short dialogues. What is each dialogue about?

1 ________ 2 ________

7 3.49 Listen again. Tick the phrases from the Speaking box that you hear.

8 [VOX POPS 8.4] In pairs, talk about:

- the most boring book you've ever read.
- your favourite song.
- a disappointing film.

And YOU

8.7 ENGLISH IN USE Phrases with prepositions

I can understand and use phrases with prepositions.

Hamish: Is everything on display, Olivia?
Olivia: Nearly, Hamish. We're waiting for the final painting. It's on loan from another gallery.

Olivia: It's been sent to another gallery by mistake!
Hamish: But the exhibition opens in ten minutes! We're in trouble, Olivia.

Olivia: Well done, Hamish. Thanks to you, the exhibition started on time.
Visitor: At last, *real* art!

1 Look at the cartoon. What's the problem at the art exhibition?

2 Study the Language box. Find more examples of phrases with prepositions in the cartoon.

Language	Phrases with prepositions
at all/first/last/least by coincidence/hand/mistake in a hurry/a mess/advance/danger/fashion/ ink/pencil/trouble on display/fire/foot/loan/purpose/sale/time	

3 Choose the correct option.

1. At *first* / *last*, Ellie was a nervous Art student but now she paints with confidence.
2. I'll draw a picture of you in *pencil* / *fashion* first. Then I'll add colour.
3. We can't leave this room in a *mess* / *trouble*. Let's clean up.
4. I'm sorry. I didn't break it on *display* / *purpose*. It was an accident.
5. Someone left the door open by *hand* / *mistake* and a thief stole the painting.
6. We'd like at *least* / *all* 100 people to come to the poetry reading.

4 3.50 Complete the blog post with prepositions. Listen and check.

Can you judge a book by its cover?

Choosing the right book is difficult, but [1] *at* last there's an exciting new way to do it. I've discovered a company called Blind Date With a Book. The books are wrapped [2] ______ hand in brown paper and a few words are written on the cover. Nothing else! They're [3] ______ sale in shops and online. When I get my mystery parcel, I'm always [4] ______ a hurry to open it. The last book was *Pride and Prejudice*, by Jane Austen. [5] ______ coincidence, I had just seen the film! In the past, I've bought boring books [6] ______ mistake just because I liked the cover. Now I find out [7] ______ advance what the book is about and so far, I haven't been disappointed!

5 In groups, play a game of *Blind Date With a Book.* **And YOU**

- Choose a book you've read and write four clues about it. Don't write the title or the author's name.
- Read your clues to the rest of the group.
- Vote for the best book. Say why you would like to read it.
- Can you guess the titles of all the books?

WORDLIST Art | Literature and books | The press | Phrases with prepositions

abstract art /ˈæbstrækt ɑːt/
advert /ˈædvɜːt/
art gallery /ɑːt ˈɡæləri/
artist /ˈɑːtɪst/
at all /ət ɔːl/
at first /ət fɜːst/
at last /ət lɑːst/
at least /ət liːst/
author /ˈɔːθə/
autobiography /ˌɔːtəbaɪˈɒɡrəfi/
be set in /bi set ɪn/
bestseller /ˌbest ˈsel ə/
biography /baɪˈɒɡrəfi/
broadsheet /ˈbrɔːdʃiːt/
by coincidence /baɪ kəʊˈɪnsədəns/
by hand /baɪ hænd/
by mistake /baɪ məˈsteɪk/
celebrity gossip /səˈlebrəti ˈɡɒsəp/
chapter /ˈtʃæptə/
character /ˈkærəktə/
colourful /ˈkʌləfəl/
combine /kəmˈbaɪn/
comic /ˈkɒmɪk/
commercial /kəˈmɜːʃəl/
complicated /ˈkɒmplɪkeɪtəd/
contemporary art /kənˈtempərəri ɑːt/
cover /ˈkʌvə/
designer /dɪˈzaɪnə/
disappointing /ˌdɪsəˈpɔɪntɪŋ/
draw /drɔː/
editor /ˈedətə, ˈedɪtə/
exhibition /ˌeksəˈbɪʃən/
experiment /ɪkˈsperɪmənt/
extraordinary /ɪkˈstrɔːdnri/
fiction /ˈfɪkʃn/
giggle /ˈɡɪɡl/
graffiti /ɡræˈfiːti/
graphic art /ˈɡræfɪk ɑːt/
graphic novel /ˈɡræfɪk ˈnɒvəl/
headline /ˈhedˌlaɪn/
horoscope /ˈhɒrəskəʊp/
household object /ˈhaʊshəʊld ˈɒb dʒekt/
illustration /ˌɪləˈstreɪʃən/
image /ˈɪmɪdʒ/
impressionist /ɪmˈpreʃnɪst/
in a hurry /ɪn eɪ ˈhʌri/
in a mess /ɪn eɪ mes/
in advance /ɪn ədˈvɑːns/
in danger /ɪn ˈdeɪndʒə/
in fashion /ɪn ˈfæʃən/
in ink /ɪn ɪŋk/
in pencil /ɪn ˈpensəl/
in trouble /ɪn ˈtrʌbəl/
in the background /ɪn ðə ˈbækˌɡraʊnd/
in the news /ɪn ðə njuːz/
inspiring /ɪnˈspaɪərɪŋ/
journalist /ˈdʒɜːnəlɪst/
judge /dʒʌdʒ/
lack /læk/
landscape /ˈlændskeɪp/
line /laɪn/
local news /ˈləʊkl njuːz/
lyrics /ˈlɪr ɪks/
magazine /ˌmæɡəˈziːn/
messy /ˈmesi/
national news /ˈnæʃnəl njuːz/
newspaper office /ˈnjuːsˌpeɪpə ˈɒfəs/
non-fiction /nɒn ˈfɪkʃn/
novel /ˈnɒvəl/
novelist /ˈnɒvələst, ˈnɒvəlɪst/
oil painting /ɔɪl ˈpeɪntɪŋ/
on display /ɒn dɪˈspleɪ/
on fire /ɒn faɪə/
on foot /ɒn fʊt/
on loan /ɒn ləʊn/
on purpose /ɒn ˈpɜːpəs/
on sale /ɒn seɪl/
on time /ɒn taɪm/
online news site /ˈɒnlaɪn njuːz saɪt/
paparazzi /ˌpæpəˈrætsi/
play (n.) /pleɪ/
playwright /ˈpleɪraɪt/
plot /plɒt/
poem /ˈpəʊəm/
poet /ˈpəʊət/
poetry /ˈpəʊətri/
pop art /pɒp ɑːt/
portrait /ˈpɔːtrət/
the press /ðə pres/
range /reɪndʒ/
reception /rɪˈsepʃən/
recite /rɪˈsaɪt/
reporter /rɪˈpɔːtə/
review /rɪˈvjuː/
scene /siːn/
sculpture /ˈskʌlptʃə/
shape /ʃeɪp/
simple /ˈsɪmpəl/
sketch /sketʃ/
still life /stɪl laɪf/
syllable /ˈsɪləbəl/
tabloid /ˈtæblɔɪd/
technique /tekˈniːk/
unique /juːˈniːk/
unusual /ʌnˈjuːʒuəl/
watercolour /ˈwɔːtəˌkʌlə/
weather forecast /ˈweðə ˈfɔːkɑːst/
weak /wiːk/
wrapped /ræpt/

WORD FRIENDS

appear in the news
do a painting
get/good bad reviews
give a poetry reading/ a speech
hold an exhibition
promote your work/ideas
win an award
write a bestseller/a play/ a novel

VOCABULARY IN ACTION

1 Use the wordlist to find:

1 five people who write for a living *author, …*
2 four things you find in a magazine or newspaper *adverts, …*
3 four types of art *abstract, …*
4 three things you find in a book or play *chapter, …*
5 three things that can happen if you write a good book *win an award, …*

2 Complete the sentences with the correct form of verbs from Word Friends.

1 If you want to *promote* your work, contact a magazine.
2 When a new bookshop opens, a famous author usually ________ a speech.
3 I'd like to ________ a painting of my house before we move.
4 The art gallery ________ an exhibition of paintings by Picasso. We must go.
5 Her teacher knew that she would ________ a bestseller one day.
6 He's a famous novelist, but he doesn't like to ________ in the news.

3 3.51 PRONUNCIATION **Listen and repeat the words.**

Oooo	oOoo	ooOo
complicated	unusual	exhibition

4 3.52 **Write the words below in the correct column in Exercise 3. Listen and check.**

biography celebrity disappointing experiment illustration paparazzi watercolour

5 3.52 **Listen again and repeat.**

Revision

VOCABULARY

1 **Write the correct word for each definition.**

1 photographers who follow famous people and take photos **p** *aparazzi*
2 a painting of objects, often flowers or fruit **s** _ _ _ _ **l** _ _ _
3 the person who decides what goes in a book or newspaper **e** _ _ _ _ _
4 a newspaper that is small, with lots of pictures and no serious news **t** _ _ _ _ _ _
5 one part of a book **c** _ _ _ _ _ _
6 a work of art made from wood, stone, etc **s** _ _ _ _ _ _ _ _

2 **Complete the text with the words below. There are two extra words.**

appear illustrations plays poems ~~poet~~ poetry reviews

Picasso

Did you know that Pablo Picasso spent a short time as a [1]*poet*? At the age of fifty-three, he stopped painting and drawing, and started writing. He moved to France and soon managed to [2]______ in the French press although he didn't always get good [3]______. He wrote two [4]______ for the stage and produced [5]______ for more than fifty books. However, he soon returned to his life as a painter.

3 **Complete the sentences with prepositions.**

1 Although the bus was late, we got to the exhibition *on* time.
2 Her paintings are ______ sale at a gallery in town.
3 ______ coincidence, I met the editor of a newspaper and he offered me a job.
4 There's paint everywhere – we can't leave this room ______ a mess like this.
5 I've finished this chapter, ______ last! It took ages!
6 Have you seen the headlines? The art gallery is ______ fire!

GRAMMAR

4 3.53 **Complete the text with the words below. Listen and check.**

able are ~~can~~ can't couldn't managed will

Robots [1]*can* beat humans at chess, but [2]______ they able to be creative? In a recent poetry competition, a poem written by a computer [3]______ to win second prize. While some people [4]______ believe the result, others weren't surprised. Experiments have shown that robots are [5]______ to produce beautiful portraits and landscapes, although they [6]______ work alone – a human needs to draw the shape first. Some scientists believe that in the future, robots [7]______ be able to paint and write as well as humans.

5 **Complete the sentences with the correct form of the verbs in brackets.**

1 I *have to* (have to) go out now. You ______ (have to) tell me the rest of the story tomorrow.
2 The students ______ (not be allowed to) leave until they had finished their poems.
3 We ______ (not have to) pay for the books because somebody gave them to us.
4 The book's a surprise. You ______ say anything. (must not)

SPEAKING

6 **Complete the dialogue with the words below.**

~~ask~~ me opinion sure wrong

A: Do you like the play we're reading at school?
B: Well, if you [1]*ask* me, it's more interesting than a long novel.
A: I'm not [2]______. It seems to [3]______ that it would be better to watch it at the theatre.
B: I know what you mean. I could be [4]______, but I think the teacher is organising a trip.
A: That's brilliant. In my [5]______, we should watch plays first and then study them.

7 **In pairs, talk about the artwork in your town or school. Use Exercise 6 to guide you.**

DICTATION

8 3.54 **Listen. Then listen again and write down what you hear.**

SELF-ASSESSMENT Think about this unit. What did you learn? What do you need help with? **WORKBOOK** p. 98

BBC

CULTURE

Graffiti: street art or vandalism?

Bristol: UK capital of street art

If you want to see art, it's normal to go to an art exhibition in a gallery. There you'll find paintings, landscapes and sketches. But wouldn't it be more fun to see these works in the street? Well, there's a city in the UK whose biggest tourist attraction is street art: Bristol!

There are historical reasons for this fame. The city was badly bombed in World War II, leaving large areas that were empty and required new buildings. Many of these new constructions were put up in a hurry and the buildings quickly became abandoned. The concrete walls were perfect canvases for street art. Today you can find art everywhere – on bridges, in alleys and on the main streets in the city centre. The whole place seems like a giant outdoor gallery!

If you're able to stay for a while, book onto one of Bristol's popular street art walking tours. Experts will tell you about the artists who have decorated the city's streets. The most famous of them is Banksy, with his stencilled graffiti designs. He is celebrated all over the world for his funny and, at times, controversial murals but nobody knows his real identity. Most of his early work was removed by the local council but there is one famous work that survives. It shows a man hanging from a painted window on the side of a large wall.

Of course, some people call Banksy's creations street art and others call it graffiti. What's the difference? Well, the debate is open. Some people say that graffiti is destructive and political, while street art is constructive and creative. But others say that the only difference is that graffiti includes letters – people's 'tags' or special signatures. Whatever you think, a lot of these works are now worth large sums of money at auctions. Is that a good thing or are people just paying for acts of vandalism?

GLOSSARY

abandoned (adj) if a builiding is abandoned, no one lives in it
canvas (n) a surface on which an artist paints
stencilled (adj) painted using a piece of metal, plastic, etc. into which shapes have been cut
controversial (adj) causing disagreement or discussion
mural (n) wall painting

EXPLORE

1 In pairs, discuss the questions.

1 What can you see in the photo? What do you think is the message?
2 Is it graffiti or street art? Why? What do you think is the difference?
3 Do you think street art can be worth money? Why? / Why not?
4 Is there a lot of graffiti/street art where you live? Is it often removed?

2 Read the article and choose the correct option.

1 The writer believes that it's *normal* / *unusual* to see art in the street.
2 Street art became popular in Bristol because there were many *abandoned buildings* / *street artists* there.
3 *Not many* / *A lot of* people know about the city's art tours.
4 Banksy's art *is* / *isn't* well-known.
5 There is *not much* / *a lot* of Banksy's art on the streets of Bristol today.
6 People *agree* / *disagree* about the difference between graffiti and street art.

EXPLORE MORE

3 In pairs, discuss the questions.

1 Is there any interesting graffiti or street art where you live?
2 What would you prefer to look at – street art or graffiti? Why?

4 8.5 Watch Part 1 of the video. Mark the sentences T (true) or F (false).

1 ☐ The council believes that all street art is worth saving.
2 ☐ Bansky has inspired other artists to use the street as a canvas.
3 ☐ The first man interviewed likes the graffiti that he is shown.
4 ☐ The woman likes the first work but not the second.
5 ☐ The journalist suggests that saving street art might make it more popular.

5 8.5 Check your memory. Choose the correct option for the things you saw in the video. Then watch the video again and check your answers.

1 a boy on a *bicycle* / *motorbike*
2 a *boy* / *girl* with a skipping rope
3 a *skull* / *face* with big teeth and pink lips
4 two giant *ears* / *eyes*
5 *Big Ben* / *The Statue of Liberty*
6 photo of a street art *tree* / *flower*

6 8.6 Watch Part 2 and choose the correct option.

1 According to the reporter, Banksy and Beverly Hills are a *normal* / *strange* combination.
2 The buyer likes the street art because it was *painted in America* / *the artist is British*.
3 All the money from the sale of Banksy's art went to *a charity* / *the auction house*.
4 The two main Banksy pieces sold for *less* / *more* than expected.

7 Who do you think should own street art? If you had the money, would you buy this kind of art? Why? / Why not? Discuss in pairs or small groups.

YOU EXPLORE

8 CULTURE PROJECT In groups, have a discussion about graffiti and street art in your town.

1 Share photographs of graffiti and street art near where you live.
2 Discuss these questions:
- What kind of street art can you find? Where is it?
- Which examples do you consider artistic and which acts of vandalism?
- Which would you remove and which would you keep? Why?

3 Do you think any of the pieces could be worth money? Why? / Why not? Do you all agree?

9

Let's get together

VOCABULARY
Celebrations | Phrases for special occasions | National celebrations | Sounds

GRAMMAR
Defining and non-defining relative clauses | Indirect questions

Grammar: Travelling in style!

Speaking: Time to celebrate

BBC Culture: The Insomnia festival

Workbook p. 113

BBC VOX POPS

EXAM TIME 3 > p. 134
CLIL 5 > p. 142

A 

B 

C 

D 

9.1 VOCABULARY Celebrations

I can talk about special occasions.

1 4.01 **Study the Vocabulary A box. What is being celebrated in each photo? Listen and check.**

Vocabulary A Celebrations

dinner party cultural festival family get-together house-warming party leaving party Mother's Day name day New Year's Eve party religious ceremony school prom wedding reception

2 4.02 WORD FRIENDS **Listen and tick the phrases from the Word Friends box that you hear.**

Word Friends

- ☐ **blow out** candles
- ☐ **bring** good/bad luck
- ☐ **celebrate** a birthday
- ☐ **follow** the tradition of
- ☐ **hire** a limo
- ☐ **let off** fireworks
- ☐ **make** a toast
- ☐ **put up** decorations
- ☐ **throw** a (street) party
- ☐ **turn** eighteen/a year older
- ☐ **(un)wrap** presents

3 4.03 **Complete the dialogues with the correct form of verbs from the Word Friends box. Listen and check.**

1 A: In the UK, seeing a black cat is supposed to *bring* good luck.
B: Really? In my country it's bad luck!
2 A: Aren't you going to ______ your presents?
B: No, not before my friends arrive.
3 A: Can I ______ the candles on my cake now?
B: Just wait a minute. I want to take a photo first!
4 A: What are you doing, Tom?
B: I'm ______ decorations for my little sister's party.
5 A: Do you remember when our football team won the championship?
B: Of course! And the neighbours ______ a street party. Brilliant!

4 I KNOW! **How many more celebrations can you think of in three minutes?**

fancy-dress party, Christmas, …

5 4.04 **Study the Speaking box. Choose the most suitable phrase for each situation. Listen and check.**

Speaking | **Phrases for special occasions**

Congratulations!
Cheers!
Happy Birthday/Anniversary/Mother's Day!
Happy Christmas/New Year!
Have fun!

1 I'm going to a party tonight.
2 I've just won a gold medal for swimming!
3 Has everyone got a drink? Here's a toast to the best mum!
4 It was thirty years ago today that your grandad and I got married.
5 Look! It's nearly midnight! Five, four, three, two, one …

6 CLASS VOTE **How do you usually celebrate your birthday?**

- with friends?
- in a restaurant?
- at a party?
- with parents?

7 **Complete the quiz with verbs from the Word Friends box.**

Birthday traditions around the world

True or false?

1 In Vietnam, you don't *celebrate* your birthday on the day you were born. You turn a year older on 'Tet' (New Year's Day), no matter when you were born during the year.
2 In Brazil, when it's a child's birthday, the parents often ________ decorations which are brightly-coloured paper flowers.
3 In the UK, children usually ________ fireworks on their birthday.
4 In parts of Canada, the birthday boy or girl's nose is greased with butter. This is supposed to ________ good luck.
5 In Hungary and Argentina, the birthday boy or girl's ears are pulled as they ________ their presents.
6 In Ireland, when a boy or girl turns sixteen, the parents ________ a street party.
7 Many Jamaicans ________ the tradition of 'flouring', or covering the birthday boy or girl in baking flour.
8 In Venezuela, some people follow the custom of pushing the person's face into the birthday cake when they ________ their candles!

8 4.05 **In pairs, discuss which of the traditions in the quiz you think are true and which are false. Listen and check.**

9 4.06 **Study the Vocabulary B box. Read the text and choose the correct option. Listen and check.**

Vocabulary B | **National celebrations**

custom display flag national symbol parade public holiday spectators traditional costume

Maisy's blog: I ♥ Ireland

Yesterday was 17 March and it was St Patrick's Day. It's a public [1]*holiday* / *display* in Ireland and that means that everyone was out celebrating. It was amazing! There was a huge [2]*custom* / *parade* in the centre of Dublin, Ireland's capital city. There were lots of people, all dressed in [3]*national symbol* / *traditional costume* or fancy dress.

Crowds of people came to watch and most of the [4]*spectators* / *displays* were dressed up in green. This [5]*flag* / *custom* comes from the shamrock, which is a kind of green leaf and the [6]*national symbol* / *traditional costume* of Ireland. As you'll see in my blog photos, I joined in the fun, wore a really funny tall green hat and bought an Irish [7]*custom* / *flag*. The festival also included a street party, an awesome fireworks [8]*parade* / *display* and loads of street performances. It was definitely the best day of my trip to Ireland so far.

10 **Read the blog post again. Answer the questions.**

1 When and where is the celebration held?
2 What happens?
3 What can you see?
4 How are the people dressed?

11 [VOX POPS ▶ 9.1] **In pairs, ask and answer about a celebration you have enjoyed. Use the questions in Exercise 10 to help you.**

And YOU

9.2 GRAMMAR Defining and non-defining relative clauses

I can be specific about people, things and places.

VIDEO TRAVELLING IN STYLE!

Skye: Just a minute. I've forgotten something.
Jay: Skye, you're always the one who's late!
Skye: Sorry, everyone! I'm ready now!
Nina: OK. Before we leave, let's make a toast.
Dan: Is that champagne?
Nina: No, it's the bottle of sparkling grape juice that my mum gave me. Anyway, here's to great friends and a great night!
All: Cheers!
Tommo: So, shall we go now?
Skye: But where's the car?
Dan: There is no car.
Nina/Skye: What?
Skye: You were the one who was supposed to organise the transport.
Dan: Don't worry, I have. Give us two minutes.
Nina: Space hoppers! You must be joking!
Skye: We can't go on those. Look at the dresses we're wearing!
Jay: They're great fun! My uncle, who owns a toy shop, got them for us.
Tommo: Come on. It'll be a laugh!
Skye: Oh all right. Actually, it's quite fun.
Dan: Well, they say your school prom is a night that you never forget!

OUT of class

Let's make a toast. Here's to … Cheers!

1 CLASS VOTE **How would you like to travel to your school prom? Why?**

limo rickshaw skateboard space hopper

2 **Look at the photo. How do you think the friends have prepared for their evening?**

3 9.2 4.07 **Watch or listen and answer the questions.**

1 Why do Skye and Nina get annoyed with Dan?
2 How do they feel about the transport in the end?

4 **Study the Grammar box. Find more examples of relative clauses in the dialogue.**

Grammar Relative clauses

Defining relative clauses
That's the car which/that we hired for the prom.
Students who/that go to the prom usually have fun.
That's the place where we're meeting Jack.
Sara's the girl whose mum teaches at my school.

Non-defining relative clauses
Our school prom, which was last month, was great.
Tom Evans, who is a musician, played the piano.
The hall, where the dance was held, was huge!
Our Maths teacher, whose daughter also graduates this year, will lead the ceremony.

GRAMMAR TIME > PAGE 126

5 **Complete the sentences with *who*, *which*, *whose* or *where*. Decide if the relative clauses are defining (D) or non-defining (ND).**

1 [D] Look at the tuxedo *which* I bought in the sales last week.
2 [ ] This is the Olive Tree restaurant, ________ we celebrated my parents' wedding anniversary.
3 [ ] Is that Ann Miller, ________ was at your birthday party?
4 [ ] Is this the cake ________ you made?
5 [ ] This is the street ________ the parade will start.
6 [ ] That's Jessica Brown, ________ brother is getting married next month.

6 4.08 **Listen to a teenager talking about school proms in Britain and answer the questions.**

1 How old are British students when they go to their first prom?
2 When do some students go to a second prom?
3 What do students usually wear to a prom?

And YOU

7 **In pairs, plan an end-of-year celebration for your school.**

We should hold the celebration in a place where …

9.3 READING and VOCABULARY Fun attractions

I can understand the main points of an article and talk about tourist attractions.

1 CLASS VOTE **What's the best place for a visitor to your town or city to go to? Why?**

2 4.09 **Read the texts. What four attractions are described? Which one would you like to visit?**

Fun attractions in Tokyo!

A Experience Japanese culture

Spend an unforgettable day at the Shiokawa Recreation Centre learning about Japanese culture by taking part in a tea ceremony and dressing up in a kimono. A kimono is the traditional costume of Japan, which is still often worn for festivals and celebrations.

Opening times: Saturdays, 10.30–3.30; **Price:** adults 5,500 yen, children (twelve and under) 3,500 yen.

B Cats … everywhere!

Why not take a break from shopping and visit the Kyoshi café, which is one of Tokyo's many pet cafés? Pet cafés are a place where people can stroke and sit with animals.

Opening times: 10.00 a.m.–10.00 p.m.; **Charge for one hour:** 1,000 yen (weekdays) 1,200 yen (weekends); Children must be twelve years old or over to enter.

C A visit to the future

If you love futuristic things, you'll love the Naomichi Museum, a small private museum of science and technology. The main attraction is Jin, a walking robot that also plays football. So, play a game with Jin or observe the solar system. And shop for books on science, experiment kits and souvenirs in the museum shop.

Open daily, from 10.00 to 5.00; **adults:** 620 yen, **children:** 210 yen; free admission for young people aged eighteen and under on Saturdays

D Bean-throwing festival

Enjoy the Japanese ceremony of bean-throwing, which is part of the Setsubun celebration. Setsubun celebrates the start of spring and the custom of throwing soya beans is believed to bring good luck. Sushi lovers will be happy to taste makisushi and it's also a custom to eat roasted soya beans. You can also admire beautiful costumes and masks. The Zojoji Temple will hold a bean-throwing ceremony between 12.00 and 1.00 p.m. on Wednesday 3 February. Entry is free.

3 4.10 **Three young people are looking for things to do in Tokyo. Match the people with attractions A–D.**

Sophie ☐

Sophie's been in Tokyo for a week. She's visited lots of historical sites with her parents and has already learned a lot about Japanese culture. On her last day, which is Saturday, she would like to do something different, which is free of charge. She loves animals and technology.

Max ☐

Max and his brother Sam are visiting his uncle in Tokyo. He's pleased that they'll be able to meet the rest of the family: his uncle's having a family get-together on Wednesday at 1.30. Max and Sam want to do something before the rest of the family arrive. They're both keen on Japanese culture. They also love robots and enjoy shopping, but have already spent all their money!

Emma ☐

Emma arrives in Tokyo on the evening of 3 February and is staying until Sunday 7 February. She prefers learning about old things rather than modern science and technology. She loves Japanese culture and is especially interested in art and fashion. She enjoys Japanese food, but she has to be careful as she's allergic to some kinds of food, as well as animal hair.

4 Look at the highlighted words in the texts. Check your understanding. Use a dictionary if necessary.

5 4.11 **In pairs, ask and answer the questions. Listen and check.**

1 What kind of tea is served at a tea ceremony?
2 What do you think the Japanese word *kimono* means?
3 Why do you think pet cafés or cat cafés are popular in Tokyo?
4 How many roasted soya beans do you think people eat at Setsubun?

6 [VOX POPS ▶ 9.3] **Think of the last attraction you visited. What did you do there? Would you recommend it to others?**

And YOU

9.4 GRAMMAR Indirect questions

I can ask questions politely.

1 CLASS VOTE Do you prefer to have friends over to your house or to go and visit your friends in their own homes? Why?

2 4.12 Do the quiz and compare your results with the class. Listen and check.

Are you an ideal guest or host? Take the test and find out!

1 **You have invited guests to your house, but it's very late and you are tired. What do you say?**

- **a** I wouldn't say anything. If you have invited some guests, you have to stay up until they want to leave.
- **b** 'I was wondering when you're going home. I feel sleepy.'
- **c** 'How long are you going to stay? I feel a bit sleepy. Maybe we can meet tomorrow.'
- **d** 'Do you mind if I go to bed? You can stay here as long as you want. Just close the door when you leave!'

2 **Your girlfriend's/boyfriend's parents have invited you to dinner. They are well-known actors and you'd like to know how much they earn. What do you say?**

- **a** 'How much do you earn?'
- **b** 'I'd like to know how much you earn.'
- **c** I would never ask such a question. You shouldn't ask people about money.
- **d** 'Wow, you're so famous! Are you very rich?'

3 **You need the bathroom at a party. You have to ask your friend's parents. What do you say?**

- **a** 'Where's the bathroom?'
- **b** 'Could you tell me where the bathroom is?'
- **c** 'Do you have any idea where the bathroom is?'
- **d** I wouldn't ask. I'd look for the bathroom myself.

3 Do you agree with the 'correct' answers given in the quiz? Discuss in pairs.

4 Study the Grammar box. Find more examples of indirect questions in the quiz.

Grammar Direct and indirect questions

***Wh-* questions**

Direct: Where's the party?
Indirect: Could you tell me where the party is?
Direct: When will you be back?
Indirect: I'd like to know when you will be back.

Wh-* questions with *does* or *did

Direct: What time does the party start?
Indirect Do you have any idea what time the party starts?
Direct: Where did you go after the party?
Indirect: I was wondering where you went after the party.

***Yes/No* questions**

Direct: Is Tom having a birthday party?
Indirect: Do you know if Tom is having a birthday party?
Direct: Can I use your phone?
Indirect: Do you mind if I use your phone?

GRAMMAR TIME > PAGE 126

5 Order the words to make indirect questions.

1. you / tell me / how much / cost / the tickets / could / ?
   Could you tell me how much the tickets cost?
2. when / the next bus / know / arrives / you / do / ?
3. if / have / you / I'd / to know / a boyfriend / like
4. any idea / who / you / she / have / do / is / ?
5. is / how / was / I / wondering / expensive / it

6 Change the indirect questions in Exercise 5 into direct questions.

7 Write indirect questions. Use phrases from the Grammar box.

1. How old are you?
   Could you tell me how old you are?
2. Where are you from?
3. Do you like this music?
4. Have you been to the UK?
5. When did you go there?
6. Did you have a good time?

8 In pairs, ask and answer about each situation. Use indirect questions. And YOU

- You've forgotten someone's name.
- You're not sure what's on the menu.
- You need to know the way to the bus station.

9.5 LISTENING and VOCABULARY Do you enjoy firework displays?

I can identify specific detail in a radio interview and talk about sounds.

1 CLASS VOTE **Do you enjoy firework displays? Why? / Why not?**

2 4.13 **Study the Vocabulary box and listen to the sounds.**

Vocabulary	Sounds
bang buzz cheer clap crackle fizz These words are both verbs and nouns.	

3 4.14 **Match the definitions with the words in the Vocabulary box. Listen and check.**

1. A happy crowd makes this noise when they shout. *cheer*
2. You hear this noise when you open a can of soft drink. ______
3. The flames of a fire make this noise. ______
4. A happy crowd makes this noise with their hands. ______
5. The sound of a door slamming shut. ______
6. Bees and flies make this noise. ______

4 4.15 **Listen to a radio programme about fireworks. When is the interview taking place?**

a Thanksgiving Day
b New Year's Eve
c Independence Day

5 4.15 **Listen again. Choose the correct answers.**

1. According to the presenter, China
   a has the most firework displays in the world.
   b makes the most fireworks in the world.
   c makes the largest fireworks in the world.
2. According to An Li, the first fireworks came from
   a China. b India. c Syria.
3. When the fireworks were made by putting powder inside a bamboo, they were
   a hotter. b brighter. c louder.
4. Assistants at firework displays in England wore hats of leaves because
   a it made people laugh.
   b it protected their heads.
   c it was an English tradition.
5. Italians changed fireworks by
   a making them colourful.
   b making them bigger.
   c making displays safer.
6. The first firework display in the United States was in
   a 1608 b 1776 c 1777

6 **In pairs, discuss your answers in Exercise 5. Give reasons for your choices and explain why you think the other two options are not correct. Listen again if necessary.**

7 **Think of the last time you saw a firework display. In pairs, take it in turns to describe the event.** And YOU

SPEAKING Talking about future plans

I can use verb phrases with *to*-infinitives and *-ing* forms to talk about future plans.

VIDEO TIME TO CELEBRATE

Skye: It's so hot on the dance floor. I'm dying for a drink!
Nina: Me too! What I really want is some nice cold water. I hope Jay and Tommo hurry up with our drinks.
Dan: Have you two got any plans for the summer?
Skye: Well, Mum and Dad are going to Iceland. I'd love to see some volcanoes. What have you got planned, Nina?
Nina: I'm going back to Colombia for a holiday. I can't wait to see the sun again!
Dan: I wish I could come with you!
Nina: In your dreams!
Tommo: We're back! Drinks for everyone!
Skye: Thanks, guys.
Jay: No worries. Here's to a great summer. I hope we all have fun.
All: Yes. Cheers, everyone!
Nina: Right. Who feels like a dance? I love this music.
Jay: Hang on a minute. What's that noise?
Tommo: It's the firework display. It's just starting.
Nina: I hope it's not cold outside!
Skye: Come on, Nina. It's fine! Anyway, we could all do with some fresh air.
Dan: The fireworks are amazing. Look!

I'm dying for …
In your dreams!
No worries.

OUT of class

1 CLASS VOTE **How do you feel about coming to the end of the school year? Why?**

disappointed excited happy sad worried

2 **Look at the photo. How do you think the friends are feeling?**

3 9.4 4.16 **Watch or listen and answer the questions.**

1 What are Tommo and Jay doing while the others are waiting for them? Why?
2 Who would like to travel with a friend?
3 Why do they go outside?
4 Why is Nina worried about going outside?

4 **Study the Speaking box. Find more examples in the dialogue.**

Speaking Talking about future plans

Asking about future plans
What are your plans for the summer/the future?
What have you got planned?
Have you got any plans for the weekend?
What would you like to do?
What do you fancy doing?

verb + *to*-infinitive
I'd love/like to go to India.
I need to visit my grandparents.
I'm planning to learn to surf this summer.
I can't wait to have a rest!
I'm dying to try my new skateboard.

verb + noun/*-ing*
I fancy a concert/going to a concert.

Other structures
I wish I could go to the beach.
I hope we have a good time.
I'm looking forward to the trip/going on a trip.
I feel like a swim/going for a swim.

5 4.17 **Choose the correct option. Listen and check.**

1 I'd like *to get* / *getting* a ticket for the prom.
2 They fancy *to watch* / *watching* the fireworks.
3 I can't wait *to go* / *going* on holiday.
4 What have you got *planned* / *planning* for tomorrow?
5 I wish we *have* / *could have* a party.
6 Are you looking forward to *go* / *going* away for the weekend?

6 **In pairs, talk about what you would like to do in the school holidays. Use phrases from the Speaking box. Then tell the class about your partner.**

Lisa is planning to go to Greece.

And YOU

9.7 WRITING An informal invitation

I can write an email inviting a friend to a celebration.

1 CLASS VOTE **Which of the information below would you give a friend or relative who was coming to stay with you during the holidays? What other information might you include?**

a description of your house   advice on what to bring
places to go   plans for things to do

2 Read Dan's email to Mike. Whose birthday is it?

Hi Mike,
How are your summer holidays going? What have you been up to? We're throwing my brother Ed a surprise twenty-first birthday party. Would you like to come? He came back from the USA yesterday and he's staying for a couple of weeks. The party's on Saturday 19 August at our house. Mum and dad said you could stay at our house for the weekend. Do you think you'll be free?

On the Sunday after the party we're planning to go to the Atlantis Water Park. It's absolutely amazing there! So, you could do with some swimming trunks. We could hang out with my cousins. Do you remember them? They'll be at the party too.

By the way, you don't need to wear anything smart to the party – you can wear whatever you want. I hope you can come. Let me know as soon as possible!

Speak soon,
Dan

3 Read the email again and mark the sentences T (true) or F (false).

1 ☐ Ed doesn't know about the party.
2 ☐ Ed's in the USA at the moment.
3 ☐ Mike has met Dan's cousins before.
4 ☐ Mike needs to bring smart clothes for the party.

4 Why do you think people often like to celebrate their twenty-first birthday? Are there any other special birthdays that are important in your country?

5 Study the Writing box. Complete gaps 1–5 with phrases from Dan's email.

Writing An informal invitation

Starting your email
How are things?
How are your summer holidays going?
1 ______

Offering an invitation
Do you fancy coming to ...?
Do you want to meet up ...?
2 ______

Explaining your plans
I'd like to show/take you ...
I hope we can ...
3 ______

Before you finish
I hope you can come.
I'm really looking forward to seeing you (again).
4 ______

Ending your email
Hope to see you soon.
5 ______

Writing Time

6 Write an email inviting a friend to a celebration. In your email, you should:

- ask your friend how they are.
- offer an invitation.
- give details of where and when the celebration is taking place.
- add some details to the invitation which will help persuade your friend.

TIPS

In an informal email, your language can be quite chatty. For example, it's natural to ask questions. You can use exclamation marks too, but be careful: don't use too many.

WORDLIST Celebrations | Phrases for special occasions | National celebrations | Sounds

anniversary /ˌænəˈvɜːsəri/
bang /bæŋ/
buzz /bʌz/
celebrate /ˈseləbreɪt/
celebration /ˌseləˈbreɪʃən/
champagne /ʃæmˈpeɪn/
cheer /tʃɪə/
Cheers! /tʃɪəz/
clap /klæp/
Congratulations! /kənˌgrætʃʊˈleɪʃnz/
crackle /ˈkrækəl/
cultural festival /ˈkʌltʃərəl ˈfestəvəl/
custom /ˈkʌstəm/
decorations /ˌdekəˈreɪʃnz/
die for /daɪ fə/
dinner party /ˈdɪnə ˈpɑːti/
display /dɪˈspleɪ/
especially /ɪˈspeʃəli/
experiment kit /ɪkˈsperəmənt kɪt/
family get-together /ˈfæməli ˈget tə ˌgeð ə/
fancy /ˈfænsi/
fireworks /ˈfaɪəˌwɜːks/
fizz (n./v.) /fɪz/
flag /flæg/
free of charge /friː əv tʃɑːdʒ/
futuristic /ˌfjuːtʃəˈrɪstɪk/
Have fun! /hæv fʌn/
hold (an event) /həuld ən ɪˈvent/
house-warming party /haʊs ˈwɔːmɪŋ ˈpɑːti/
Independence Day /ˌɪndəˈpendəns deɪ/
keen on /kiːn ɒn/
leaving party /ˈliːv ɪŋ ˈpɑːti/
limo /ˈlɪməʊ/
Mother's Day /ˈmʌðəs deɪ/
name day /neɪm deɪ/
national symbol /ˈnæʃənəl ˈsɪmbəl/
no worries /nəʊ ˈwʌriəs/
parade /pəˈreɪd/
public holiday /ˈpʌblɪk ˈhɒlədi/
religious ceremony /rɪˈlɪdʒəs ˈserəməni/
rickshaw /ˈrɪkʃɔː/
school prom /skuːl prɒm/
shamrock /ˈʃæmˌrɒk/
skateboard /ˈskeɪtˌbɔː(r)d/
soya bean /ˈsɔɪəbiːn/
space hopper /speɪs ˈhɒpə/
spectators /spekˈteɪtəs/
stroke /strəʊk/
tea ceremony /tiː ˈserəməni/
Thanksgiving Day /θæŋksˈgɪvɪŋ deɪ/
tradition /trəˈdɪʃən/
traditional costume /trəˈdɪʃənəl ˈkɒstjʊm/
tuxedo /tʌkˈsiːdəʊ/
unforgettable /ˌʌnfəˈgetəbəl/
wedding reception /ˈwedɪŋ rɪˈsepʃən/

WORD FRIENDS

blow out candles
bring good/bad luck
celebrate a birthday
follow the tradition of
hire a limo
let off fireworks
make a toast
put up decorations
throw a (street) party
turn eighteen/a year older
(un)wrap presents

VOCABULARY IN ACTION

1 Use the wordlist to find:

1 five sounds *bang, ...*
2 four ways of travelling *limo, ...*
3 three things you might do during a birthday party *blow out candles, ...*
4 two national celebrations *Independence Day, ...*
5 one word we say when someone has had a baby/ got engaged/etc.

2 Choose the correct option.

1 In your country, what things are supposed to (*bring*)/ *make* good and bad luck?
2 At what times of the year do you usually *put up* / *wrap* decorations in your house?
3 When did you last *throw* / *make* a party?
4 Do you usually make a wish when you *let off* / *blow out* the candles on your birthday cake?
5 Have you ever *hired* / *celebrated* a limo?

3 In pairs, ask and answer the questions in Exercise 2.

In my country, people say horseshoes bring good luck.

4 4.18 **PRONUNCIATION** Listen. For each phrase, draw a line between the words that link together.

1 let off fireworks
2 put up decorations
3 blow out candles
4 make a toast
5 throw a street party

5 Match the words in Exercise 4 that link together with their pronunciation.

a /θrəʊwə/ ______
b /setɒf/ ______
c /pʊtəp/ ______
d /meɪkə/ ______
e /bləʊwaʊt/ ______

Revision

VOCABULARY

1 Complete the words in the sentences.

1 My parents love cooking and they often invite friends over for a d*inner* p*arty*.
2 We've just moved into a new house and we're having a h____-w_______ p____.
3 She got a new job, so we threw her a l______ p____ on her last day.
4 Every M_____'_ D__ we give our mum breakfast in bed!
5 My n___ d__ is 25 November. Everyone called Katerina celebrates on this day.
6 When my cousin got married, they had their w______ r________ in a big hotel.

2 Complete the text with the words below.

costumes custom ~~festival~~ follow parade get-together good luck New Year's Eve

I love Chinese New Year! The Chinese New Year [1]*festival* lasts for fifteen days. On [2]________, we usually have a family [3]________ and have a large meal. At midnight, it's the [4]________ to open the doors and windows of your house to let the old year leave. On the last day of the festival, there is a [5]________. There are lots of brightly coloured animal [6]________. I like the lion dance, which is supposed to bring [7]________. Many people also [8]________ the tradition of giving children money in red envelopes!

GRAMMAR

3 Join the sentences using relative pronouns. Add commas where necessary.

1 This is the Rex Hotel. We had our prom here.
This is the Rex Hotel, where we had our prom.
2 I like these shoes. My mum bought them for me.
____
3 Mia is a friend. I met her at a New Year's Eve party.
____
4 We met Dina. Her albums have sold millions of copies.
____
5 We're going to stay on the island. My parents got married there.
____

4 Circle the correct option.

1 Can you tell me what time *the lesson starts* / *does the lesson start*?
2 Do you have any idea where *is Anna* / *Anna is*?
3 I was wondering who *you saw* / *did you see* after the cinema.
4 Could you tell me why *are you* / *you are* late?
5 Do you know if *they live* / *do they live* here?
6 I was wondering where *did you buy* / *you bought* that shirt – I'd love one the same!

SPEAKING

5 4.19 Complete the dialogues with the correct form of the verbs in brackets. Listen and check.

A: What are your plans for the weekend?
B: I'm planning [1]*to visit* (visit) my cousin in London. I can't wait [2]________ (see) him. What about you?
A: I need [3]________ (finish) my French essay.
C: What have you got planned for the holidays?
D: Nothing much. I could do with [4]________ (have) some rest after the exams. I just need [5]________ (relax). What about you?
C: I'm planning [6]________ (go) surfing in Greece. I dream of [7]________ (try out) my new surfboard.

6 In pairs, practise the dialogues in Exercise 5. Add your own new ideas for plans.

DICTATION

7 4.20 Listen. Then listen again and write down what you hear.

SELF-ASSESSMENT Think about this unit. What did you learn? What do you need help with? **WORKBOOK p. 110**

BBC CULTURE

What is a virtual festival?

Video gaming festivals: staying in to have fun

When you think of festivals, do you think street parades, traditional events and colourful costumes? Well, think again! Nowadays, it's fashionable to stay indoors with your screens! Why? It's to celebrate video-gaming, which is one of the most popular hobbies around. There are lots of big gaming festivals in the world and the UK is one of the main centres because most gamers communicate in English.

Insomnia, which is the biggest festival in the UK, is held every year near Birmingham and attracts thousands of young people. It's an amazing get-together where you can meet the world's most renowned players. Some of these celebrities are only eleven or twelve years old! There are tournaments of popular games like Mortal Kombat. Minecraft is also everywhere, which shows that it is a real cultural phenomenon.

Although the festival happens inside and everyone is glued to screens, these events have a lot in common with traditional festivals. There are many fans who form long queues to watch celebrity gamers on big stages. There are incredible light displays and giant screens everywhere. At first sight, it looks more like a rock concert!

We interviewed a teenager at the Insomnia festival in Coventry to see what she thought:

Marcela: 'This is the best party I've ever been to! I've travelled across the world to be here. There's a real sense of community. I've met a lot of people who I only knew from the internet. We share our love for video games and discuss how best to play them. It's great for my English because that's what everyone speaks online and here too!'

GLOSSARY
fashionable (adj) popular at a particular time
renowned (adj) famous
phenomenon (n) sth that happens or exists in society, culture, nature, etc.
be glued to (phr) give sth your full attention
isolated (adj) without much contact with other people

EXPLORE

1 Look at the photo. In pairs, discuss the questions.

1 Where do you think the people are?
2 What are they doing?
3 What kind of festivals for young people do you know? Would you like to go to any of them? Why / Why not?

2 Read the text and choose the correct option.

1 The article says that staying in is now *more* / *less* trendy than going out.
2 Gaming events are popular in the UK because *of the great facilities* / *English is the common language*.
3 Some of the most famous players are *pre-teens* / *young adults*.
4 Video game events are more *similar to* / *different from* traditional events than you think.
5 The celebrity video gamers are *in the audience* / *on stage like superstars*.

3 Choose the correct summary for Marcela.

a I can share my experience with people about playing video games.
b I have met a lot of people with similar interests who I never knew existed.

4 In pairs, discuss the questions.

1 Do you agree with Marcela? Why? / Why not?
2 Are similar events popular where you live?

EXPLORE MORE

5 9.5 Watch Part 1 of the video and complete the sentences with the words below. There are three extra words.

changing employees followers inspiring legend legitimate skills surprising

1 If you know the game, you can appreciate another player's ________ and technical ability.
2 One teen thinks that gaming is a(n) ________ sport.
3 Some gamers have a lot of fans and ________.
4 Siv has two ________.
5 The reporter concludes that gaming is ________ all the time.

6 9.5 Watch the video again. Choose the correct option.

1 Some of the gamers play with *headphones* / *microphones* only.
2 *One commentator* / *Two commentators* appear on a giant screen to comment on the gamers' play.
3 Josh and his mum play *drums* / *guitars* with their video game.
4 The gamer Siv has *blonde* / *dark* hair.
5 *One or two* / *A lot of* people fall asleep at the event!

7 9.6 Watch Part 2 of the video. Mark the sentences T (true) or F (false). Correct the false sentences.

1 ☐ BMX and parkour are not part of the Festival of Neighbourhood.
2 ☐ Stick says that graffiti dates back to very ancient times.
3 ☐ We see the dance troop, Zoo Nation, performing in an open space.
4 ☐ The festival celebrates both art and sport.
5 ☐ The Southbank has always been a favourite place for urban artists.

8 What's your opinion of the two events? Which of these events would you like to go to? Why? Which of them would be more popular where you live? Why? Discuss in pairs.

YOU EXPLORE

9 CULTURE PROJECT In groups, plan your own urban event or festival.

1 Choose the main focus of the event (e.g. sport, street art/graffiti, dance, music concerts).
2 Write a short script to describe your event or festival.
3 Present your event to the class.

1.2 Present Simple, Present Continuous and state verbs

Present Simple and Present Continuous

She often takes the bus to school. (routine)
He lives in Madrid. (permanent situation)
He's talking to his friends now. (present action)
She's from Brazil, but she's studying in the UK. (temporary situation)

State verbs

Some verbs don't normally have a continuous form: *like, love, prefer, wish, hate, want, need, believe, know, remember, understand, be, cost, belong, mean, seem.*
Some verbs can be state or dynamic, depending on the meaning.
I think he's right. (opinion)
What is he thinking about? (mental process)
I see her – she's round the corner. (see with eyes)
I'm seeing Peter a lot these days. (meet up with)
I have a dog. (possession)
I'm having lunch. (action)
The soup tastes/smells lovely. (quality)
I'm tasting/smelling the soup. (action)

Some verbs work both in the simple and continuous forms, but with no change in meaning.
I feel tired./I'm feeling tired.

1 Choose the correct option. Which verb can be used in the Present Simple or Present Continuous?

Hi Sara,

How are you? I [1]*'m enjoying / enjoy* my new school. There are lots of after-school clubs and I [2]*belong / 'm belonging* to the Drama Club now. We [3]*'re meeting up / meet up* every Friday. At the moment the club [4]*prepares / is preparing* for a show and they [5]*'re wanting / want* me to be in it. I [6]*think / 'm thinking* about it and I [7]*like / am liking* the idea, but I [8]*feel / 'm feeling* anxious about it. What [9]*do you think / are you thinking* I should do?

Sam

2 Do you belong to a club or have a hobby? Write a few sentences using the Present Simple and Present Continuous and the phrases below.

- I belong to …
- My hobby is …
- I usually/often/always …
- At the moment I/we …

1.4 Past Simple, Past Continuous and Present Perfect

Past Simple

She arrived yesterday. (finished action)
They studied every day. (repeated action)
Watch out for spelling changes in regular verbs:
study – studied drop – dropped

Past Continuous

Last night/At six o'clock she was talking to her friend. (action in progress)

Past Simple and Past Continuous

I was climbing the mountain when I fell.
While I was sleeping, the phone rang.
(background action interrupted by another action)

Present Perfect

She's just left the party. (result in the present)
They've never been to India. (experience)
Adverbs such as never, ever, just, yet, recently and already are often used with the Present Perfect.

Present Perfect and Past Simple

I've been to this theatre before. I came here with my parents last year. (experience/recent event and a completed action in the past)

1 Choose the correct option.

1 It *was raining / rained* when I *woke up / was waking up.*
2 While I *had / was having* my breakfast, my friend *sent / was sending* me a text.
3 I *was jogging / jogged* in the park when I *met / was meeting* my friend.
4 He *was breaking / broke* his leg when he *learned / was learning* to ski.

2 Complete the questions with the correct form of the verbs in brackets.

1 *Have* you ever *won* (win) a competition?
2 What ______ you ______ (do) at 8 a.m. this morning?
3 What ______ you ______ (have) for dinner yesterday?
4 ______ the sun ______ (shine) when you ______ (get up) this morning?

3 In pairs, ask and answer the questions in Exercise 2. Tell the class about your partner.

4 Write an email to a friend you haven't seen for a month. Tell him/her any interesting things that have happened since you last met.

2.2 Past Perfect

We use the Past Perfect to talk about an action that happened before a particular time in the past. For this reason, we often use it with the Past Simple.
We had done our homework.
They hadn't seen our house.
Had he bought the present?
Yes, he had./No, he hadn't.

8 p.m.	9 p.m.	9.30 p.m.	10 p.m.
	Maria left.	I arrived.	

Maria had left the party when I arrived.

Time expressions
after, already, before, by the time, just, never, until

We had finished our lunch by the time our other friends arrived.
Before she watched the documentary, Sally hadn't thought much about pollution.
I hadn't heard about Luke's news until Kelly told me.
He started recycling more after he had learned where his rubbish went.
They had never been to the café before.

1 **Complete the text with the Past Perfect or Past Simple form of the verbs in brackets.**

Until last year, I [1]*had read* (read) about solar energy only in my school books and I [2]________ (never/see) a solar panel. Then last year my uncle [3]________ (fill) one of the fields on his farm with solar panels. Before that, he [4]________ (grow) potatoes in the field. My uncle [5]________ (not think) of doing it before, but another local farmer gave him the idea. [6]________ I ever ________ (imagine) that one of my uncle's fields [7]________ (can) produce renewable energy? No, never!

2 **Write a few sentences about things you had and hadn't done by the time you were five. Use the Past Perfect and the Past Simple, and a suitable time expression.**

By the time I was five, I had learned to walk and talk. I hadn't learned to ride a bike – I learned that when I was about seven. I had never …

3 **Write six true sentences about yourself. Use the Past Perfect and the Past Simple with six different time expressions.**

2.4 *used to*

We use *used to* to talk about actions that happened regularly in the past, but that don't happen anymore or about things that were true in the past, but aren't true now.

We used to stay with my gran every summer holiday.
She used to have long hair.

In the negative and question form, we drop the *-d*:
I didn't use to play basketball when I was younger.
Did he use to have a dog? Yes, he did./No, he didn't.

We can't use *used to* to talk about things that happened once. We use the Past Simple.
~~We used to go on holiday to Brazil last year.~~
We went on holiday to Brazil last year.

We can use both the Past Simple and *used to* to describe regular actions in the past.
We used to go/went on holiday to Brazil every year.

1 **Complete the dialogue with *used to* and the correct form of the verbs in brackets.**

Teacher: Did you know that I [1]*used to go* (go) to this school?
Student: No, really? What [2]________ it ________ (be) like?
Teacher: It [3]________ (be) much smaller. Not so many people [4]________ (live) in the town. We all [5]________ (walk) to school every day. Families [6]________ (not have) cars, so there was less traffic and less pollution!

2 **Make questions with *used to* from the prompts.**

My country twenty years ago

1. many people / recycle / plastic and paper?
2. the countryside / in your country / be / more or less polluted?
3. people / waste / less energy?
4. people / throw away / more or less rubbish?

3 **In pairs, ask and answer the questions in Exercise 2. Tell another pair about your answers.**

A: Did many people use to recycle all their plastic and paper?
B: No, I don't think many people used to recycle twenty years ago.

4 **Choose one of the questions from Exercise 2 and write a few sentences about your town.**

3.2 Present Perfect Continuous

We use the Present Perfect Continuous for:

- actions that started in the past and continue in the present.
  I've been waiting for two hours. (I'm still waiting.)
- actions that started in the past and have results in the present.
  She's been playing basketball all morning. (She's feeling tired now.)
  Have they been watching the fashion show?
  Yes, they have./No, they haven't.

Time expressions

all day/night, recently, How long ...?
since last Friday/October/Saturday/I woke up
for two hours/three years/a long time/ages

1 **Complete the sentences with the Present Perfect Continuous form of the verbs below.**

collect practise save wait ~~write~~

1 Anna *has been writing* her own fashion blog since January.
2 We ______ for Jack for half an hour – and he's still not ready!
3 My brother ______ baseball caps since he was little. He's got over fifty!
4 They ______ their dance for the show all morning.
5 I ______ my money to buy a jacket.

2 **Complete the questions with the Present Perfect Continuous form of the verbs in brackets.**

1 There's chocolate all round your mouth! *Have* you *been eating* (eat) chocolate cake?
2 You've got lots of nice clothes. ______ you ______ (shop) recently?
3 Your jacket's really wet! ______ it ______ (rain)?
4 Your jeans are really dirty. ______ you ______ (play) outside?

3 **Write three sentences about yourself. Use the Present Perfect Continuous and the verbs below.**

collect learn practise read save

I've been reading a really good book about the fashion business.

3.4 Present Perfect Simple and Continuous

Present Perfect Simple
They've sold a lot of jewellery. (focus on the result)
She hasn't finished her homework. (focus on the result)

Present Perfect Continuous
She's been making her own jewellery for ages. (focus on the duration of the activity)
We've been trying on lots of clothes today. (focus on the fact that the activity is unfinished)

We can use *since* and *for* with both tenses.
Don't forget that with state verbs (*have*, *know*, *be*, etc.) you can only use the Present Perfect Simple.
How long has Mark known Tom?
They've been friends for a long time.

1 **Complete the sentences with the Present Perfect Simple or Continuous form of the verbs in brackets.**

1 I *haven't had* (not have) anything to eat since breakfast.
2 I ______ (learn) English since I was six.
3 I ______ (never/like) going to the hairdresser's.
4 I ______ (sit) in the classroom for half an hour.
5 I ______ (know) my best friend for five years.

2 **In pairs, say if the sentences in Exercise 1 are true for you.**

3 **Complete the text with the words below.**

been ~~bought~~ continued for have making since wearing

Have you [1]*bought* any jeans recently? Did you know that jeans are one of the most popular items of clothing? People have been [2]______ them [3]______ more than 140 years. Over the years, jeans have [4]______ both work clothes and fashion clothing. Their style has changed many times [5]______ the start of their history. Young people [6]______ been setting new fashion trends for decades, whether it's baggy jeans or skinny jeans. Surprisingly, the original indigo blue colour has [7]______ to be a favourite over the many years companies have been [8]______ jeans.

4 **Write a few sentences about your style. What clothes have you been wearing recently? What's your favourite item of clothing and how long have you had it?**

I've been wearing skinny jeans and large T-shirts a lot recently. My favourite item of clothing is ...

4.2 Talking about the future

We use *will* for:

- decisions made at the moment of speaking.
  I won't have any dessert, thanks.
- predictions, what we think will be true in the future.
  I think people will work less in the future.

We use *be going to* for:

- plans.
  Rachel's going to work in the café.
- predictions based on what we know now.
  I'm not going to have time to go out with my friends.

We use the Present Continuous for arrangements, often with *this evening, next week, in the summer, at the weekend, on Wednesday*, etc.
Joe isn't helping at the shop this weekend.

We use the Present Simple for timetables, often with times or dates.
The bus arrives at half past two.

1 Make questions from the prompts. Use the future form in brackets.

1 what time / this lesson / finish? (Present Simple)
What time does this lesson finish?
2 what / you / do / this weekend? (Present Continuous)
3 you / buy / anything this weekend? (be going to)
4 what / the weather / be / like / tomorrow? (will)

2 In pairs, ask and answer the questions in Exercise 1.

3 Choose the correct option.

A: Hi, Adam. What [1]*are you doing* / *will you do* after school?
B: I [2]*'m helping* / *help* my uncle. He owns a tennis club and I serve drinks in the café there. Maybe you can meet me afterwards.
A: Sounds good! I [3]*won't do* / *'m not doing* anything after school. I [4]*'ll meet* / *'m going to meet* you there. What time [5]*will you be* / *are you being* free?
B: My shift in the café [6]*is finishing* / *finishes* at six o'clock.

4 You plan to watch a film at the cinema tonight and want to invite your friend. Write a short email to your friend saying what you are going to see, what time the film starts and why you think your friend will like it.

4.4 Future Continuous

We use the Future Continuous to talk about an action that will be in progress at a certain time in the future.
In the summer, Harry will be working on his grandfather's farm.
She won't be relaxing on a beach.
Will you be flying over the Atlantic this time tomorrow?
Yes, I will./No, I won't.
What will you be doing?

Time expressions

- *in ten minutes/a week/a month/a year/the future*
  In two years, I'll be finishing school.
- *at 6.45 this evening/midnight/10 a.m. tomorrow*
  At eleven o'clock tonight I'll be sleeping.
- *next spring/month/year*
  Next winter, I'll be teaching children how to ski.
- *soon*
  I'll be working on a new project soon!

1 Complete the dialogues with the Future Continuous form of the verbs in brackets.

1 A: *Will* you *be looking* (look) for a full-time job when you leave school?
B: No, I ______ (start) a beauty therapy course at college.
2 A: ______ you ______ (earn) any money this summer?
B: Yes, I will. I ______ (help) my uncle on his farm.
3 A: ______ you ______ (study) this afternoon?
B: No, I ______ (work) in my parents' shop.

2 Complete the email with the Future Continuous form of the verbs in brackets.

Hi Lily,
I got the summer job at the beach café! So we [1]*'ll be working* (work) together this summer.
I can't wait! I'm so pleased I [2]______ (not stay) at home all summer. I hope we [3]______ (do) the same hours. I [4]______ (start) on 28 July.
I [5]______ (just/clean) tables in the beginning.
I [6]______ (not take) orders for the first week.
Anyway, speak soon!
Katy

5.2 Zero, First and Second Conditionals

Zero Conditional
If you freeze water, it expands. (scientific fact)
Sarah starts to sneeze if she smells flowers. (always true)
First Conditional
We'll look at the NASA website later if we have time. (the result of another action)
Unless it's a clear night, we won't see many stars. (possibility in the future)
Second Conditional
If I was/were older, I'd train to be an astronaut. (unreal situation)
If my little sister offered to help me, I'd be amazed. (unlikely situation)
Be careful!
- When the *if* clause is at the beginning of the sentence, we put a comma (,) after it.
- *Unless* means 'if not'.
- You can use *was* or *were* with the first person of the Second Conditional, except for *If I were you.*

1 Make sentences from the prompts. Use the Zero or First Conditional.

1 water / freeze / if / you / cool / it to 0°C
Water freezes if you cool it to 0°C.
2 you / burn / if / you / stay / in the sun any longer
3 Emma / always / call / if / she / be going to / late
4 we / get / better pictures for our school project / if / we / use / a drone

2 Complete the questions with the Second Conditional form of the verbs in brackets.

1 What *would* you *do* (do) if you *won* (win) a competition to go into space?
2 If you ______ (discover) a new planet, what ______ you ______ (call) it?
3 If you ______ (can) travel anywhere, where ______ you ______ (go)?
4 ______ you ______ (do) a bungee jump if your best friend ______ (ask) you to?

3 In pairs, ask and answer the questions in Exercise 2.

4 Write a few sentences to answer each question. Use the Zero, First and Second Conditionals.

1 What do you usually do if you have free time?
2 What will you do this weekend if you and your friends are free?
3 What would you do if you won the lottery?

5.4 Third Conditional

We use the Third Conditional to talk about an action in the past that did *not* happen.
If I had known you were coming, I wouldn't have gone out. (I didn't know you were coming, so I went out.)
You wouldn't have broken the camera if you had been more careful. (You weren't careful, so you broke it.)
Would you have done the parachute jump if it had been less windy? (You didn't do the parachute jump because it was windy.)

1 Complete the sentences with the Third Conditional form of the verbs in brackets.

1 If she *hadn't studied* (not study) Science, she wouldn't have become an astronaut.
2 They ______ (not do) the mission if they had known about the dangers.
3 If they hadn't filmed the first landing on the moon, no one ______ (believe) it!
4 We ______ (miss) the comet if we had gone outside later.
5 If you ______ (see) the film *Gravity*, you would have really enjoyed it.
6 Peter would have won if he ______ (answer) all the questions correctly.

2 Make questions from the prompts. Use the Third Conditional.

1 what / you / do / today / if / you / not go / to school?
What would you have done today if you hadn't gone to school?
2 where / you / go / on your last holiday / if / you / win / the lottery?
3 if / you / arrive / late at school this morning / what / happen?
4 what / you / wear / today / if / the weather / be / different?

3 In pairs, ask and answer the questions in Exercise 2.

I would have slept for twelve hours!

4 Write a few sentences to answer the question below. Use the Third Conditional.

If you had been born 100 years ago, how would your life have been different?

6.2 Reported statements and questions

Statements

Reported speech tells us what someone said earlier. We usually use the verbs *said* (*to me*) or *told* (*her*).
The verb tenses change as follows:
'I feel sick.' → He told them (that) he felt sick.
'She's taking her medicine.' → They said (that) she was taking her medicine.
'Tim broke his arm.' → She said (that) Tim had broken his arm.
'They will be tired after school.' → We said (that) they would be tired after school.
'I can't get to sleep.' → She told him (that) she couldn't get to sleep.

Questions

When we report a *yes/no* question, we use *if*.
'Do you need to sit down?' → She asked me if I needed to sit down.
When we report a *Wh-* question, we use the question word. We do not use the auxiliary verb *do/does/did*.
'Where do you live?' → He asked where I lived.

Other changes

We often change pronouns, time and place expressions.
'Annabel is allergic to my cat.' → He told us that Annabel was allergic to his cat.
'I'll come back tomorrow.' → She said she would come back the next day.
'You can wait here.' → The nurse said that the girl could wait there.

1 **Rewrite the sentences and questions in reported speech.**

1 'You're allergic to cats.'
The doctor told me that *I was allergic to cats*.
2 'Where are you going?'
Jack asked me ______________ .
3 'I've lost my appetite.'
She told me that she ______________ .
4 'Are you feeling dizzy, Emily?'
Mum asked Emily ______________ .
5 'I'll get your prescription for you, Tom.'
She told Tom that she ______________ .

2 **In pairs, ask and answer the questions. Tell another pair about your partner.**

1 What do you usually take for a sore throat?
2 What can people do to sleep better at night?
3 Do you ever get travel sick?
4 Can you name five examples of healthy food?

6.4 Reported commands and requests

Requests

We usually use *ask* (*me/him*/etc.) to report requests (verb + person + *to*-infinitive).
'Can you read the information, please?'
She asked him to read the information.
In negative requests, we use *not* before the *to*-infinitive.
'Please don't forget your appointment.'
She asked us not to forget our appointment.

Commands

We usually use *tell* to report commands (verb + person + *to*-infinitive).
'Take the tablets with water.'
The doctor told her to take the tablets with water.
In negative commands, we use *not* before the *to*-infinitive:
'Don't worry.'
She told us not to worry.

1 **Rewrite the sentences in reported speech. Use the verbs in brackets.**

1 'Can you lend me your surfboard?' Adam said to Jenny. (ask)
Adam asked Jenny to lend him her surfboard.
2 'Don't use your mobile phone now!' the teacher said to the student. (tell)
3 'Please help me with the shopping,' the man said to his children. (ask)
4 'Stand up,' the teacher said to the pupils. (tell)
5 'Can you follow me?' the nurse said to the visitor. (ask)
6 'Take a deep breath, please,' the doctor said to his patient. (ask)

2 **Complete the reported commands and requests in the email. Use the Past Simple.**

Hi Theo,

Guess what I did with Matt last weekend? Bungee jumping! When Matt [1] *asked me to go* (ask/go) with him, I really wasn't sure. I was a bit nervous because I'd never done it before. Anyway, he [2] ______ (tell/not worry). He said I would love it! He was right – it was great fun. I [3] ______ (tell/call) me next time he was going. He [4] ______ (tell/bring) you too next time, and I said that would be great. So what do you think?

Sophie

7.2 The Passive: Present Simple, Past Simple, Present Perfect, *can* and *must*

We use the Passive when the person doing the action is not known, not important or obvious.

Present Simple and Past Simple
Facial expressions are used to show emotions.
They weren't told about the party.
Was the message sent?

Present Perfect
The problem hasn't been discussed yet.
Has the activity been explained to you?

can* and *must
Drinks cannot be taken into the theatre.
Tickets must be bought in advance.

If we want to say who did the action, we use *by* + the agent (the person or thing that does the action).
The speech was made by the head teacher.
She was contacted by an environmental organisation.

1 Make passive sentences from the prompts. Use the tense given in brackets and add *by* if necessary.

1 the letter / write / by you? (Past Simple)
Was the letter written by you?
2 we / not show / the film about communication (Present Perfect)
3 some hand gestures / consider / rude (can)
4 an email / send / after every meeting (Present Simple)
5 the school rules / follow / all students (must)

2 Complete the text with the words below.

annoyed are be been bought is ~~spent~~

Every year more than $500 billion is [1] *spent* on advertising worldwide. Television commercials [2] ________ still used by many companies, but the biggest growth has [3] ________ seen in online advertising. This is because an online advert can [4] ________ seen by a much larger number of people. Also, much less money [5] ________ spent on advertising a product online. You might be [6] ________ by pop-up adverts on websites, but the products they advertise are [7] ________ by many people anyway!

3 In pairs, ask and answer questions about the text. Use the Passive.

How much money is spent … ?

7.4 The Passive with *will*

We use *will* + *be* + past participle to talk about the future using the Passive.
The information will be repeated later.
You won't be given any homework today.
Will the show be advertised on TV?

Be careful!
Sometimes you can form two different passive sentences from one active sentence:

Active: They will teach French to students.
Passive: French will be taught to students.
Students will be taught French.

1 Rewrite the sentences in the Passive with *will*.

1 They won't understand his pronunciation.
His pronunciation *won't be understood*.
2 They will advertise their product.
Their new product ________.
3 We won't give out flyers this year.
Flyers ________.
4 We will discuss good posture in the next lesson.
Good posture ________.

2 Make questions from the prompts. Use the Passive with *will*.

1 when / the workshop / hold?
When will the workshop be held?
2 who / it / teach / by?
3 which / topics / cover?
4 what / each student / give?

3 Read the flyer. In pairs, ask and answer the questions in Exercise 2.

Free workshop:
Improve your body language!

Every Tuesday, from 4 to 5 p.m., in the sports hall, with Mr Baker

We will cover topics such as:

- making eye contact.
- improving posture.
- how to make the most of your voice.

We will give each student their own folder with information. A fun and useful workshop for all students!

8.2 Ability

Present
We can/can't draw.
Can he sing? Yes, he can./No, he can't.
He is able to/isn't able to read books in Russian.
Are they able to come? Yes, they are./No, they aren't.

Past
She could/couldn't hear the story.
Could she paint? Yes, she could./No, she couldn't.
They were/weren't able to finish the book.
Were they able to help? Yes, they were./
No, they weren't.

manage to
We use *manage to* when we're talking about specific achievements.
We managed to/didn't manage to go to the party.
Did Ann manage to complete her painting?
Yes, she did./No, she didn't.

Future
They'll be/won't be able to come to the meeting.
Will you be able to join us? Yes, I will./No, I won't.

1 Complete the sentences with the words below.

able could ~~couldn't~~ managed to will

1 I *couldn't* write my name until I started school.
2 After watching the play, the students were ________ to write about it.
3 Next year we'll be able ________ see the film version of this book.
4 We ________ to get the book we wanted from the library.
5 The teacher ________ be able to help you.
6 He ________ paint very well when he was just five years old.

2 In pairs, ask and answer the questions.

1 What couldn't you do last year that you can do now?
Last year I couldn't do handstands. Now I can do handstands and cartwheels.
2 Can you paint or draw?
3 Will you be able to meet up with your friends this weekend?
4 Did you manage to finish all your homework last night?

8.4 Obligation and prohibition

Obligation
We use *must* or *have to* to talk about present obligation, but we only use *have to* for past or future obligations.
She had to/will have to help him.
You must be home before 9. / You have to be home before 9.

Lack of obligation
We use *not have to* to show lack of obligation in the present, past and future.
We don't/didn't/won't have to read the book.

Prohibition
We use *must not* or (*not*) *allowed to* for something prohibited.
We mustn't/aren't allowed to touch the sculptures.
We can only use *be allowed to* for the past or future and to form questions.
I wasn't/won't be allowed to touch the sculptures.
Are they allowed to touch the sculptures?
Yes, they are./No, they aren't.

1 Choose the correct option.

1 You *don't have to* / *mustn't* be good at art to enjoy it.
2 We *don't have to* / *aren't allowed to* leave until we have finished.
3 You *don't have to* / *mustn't* be late for class.
4 It was raining, so we *must* / *had to* finish our paintings inside.

2 Read what Ben says. In pairs, ask and answer questions about him.

1 At school we mustn't use mobile phones.
2 At weekends I'm allowed to stay up late.
3 At home I don't have to wash the dishes.
4 When I was younger, I wasn't allowed to play computer games.
5 Next year I'll be able to learn another foreign language.

A: Is Ben allowed to use a mobile phone at school?
B: No, he isn't.

3 Write sentences like Ben's that are true for you.

At school we mustn't take food or drink into the classroom.

9.2 Defining and non-defining relative clauses

Defining relative clauses

We don't use commas in defining relative clauses.
That's the hotel where our prom will be held.
Tom's the boy whose birthday we're celebrating.

We can use *that* instead of *which* or *who*.
I'd like to find some shoes which/that go with this dress.
These are the boys who/that helped me.

When *that, which, who* or *where* is the object of a defining relative clause, you can leave it out.
I'm wearing the prom dress that I bought last month./
I'm wearing the prom dress I bought last month.

Non-defining relative clauses

We use commas in non-defining relative clauses.
Lee, *who* is my best friend, is a really good dancer.
Liam, *whose* sister is in my class, is a DJ.

We can't use *that* instead of *which* or *who*.
~~This jacket, that was a present from my mum, is my favourite.~~
This jacket, which was a present from my mum, is my favourite.

1 Complete the sentences with *who, which, whose* or *where*.

1 This is the house ***where*** we were living when I was ten.
2 Look at the ring ________ I got for my birthday.
3 My brother, ________ wedding was last Saturday, is now in Bali with his wife.
4 These are the earrings ________ I bought my mum for Mother's Day.
5 This is the field ________ they'll let off the fireworks after the show.
6 Amanda, ________ made my costume, is an Art teacher at the local college.

2 Look at the sentences in Exercise 1 again. Which relative clauses are defining and which are non-defining? In which sentences can you leave out the relative pronoun?

3 Write down the name of a person, the name of a place and a favourite possession which are special to you. In pairs, take it in turns to tell your partner why they are so important. Use relative clauses.

She/He is the person who …
This is the place where …
This is the watch/guitar that/which …

9.4 Direct and indirect questions

We often use indirect questions when we want to ask something more politely. The word order in indirect questions is the same as in statements and we don't use the auxiliary verbs *do, does* or *did*.
We use different expressions like: *could you tell me, I was wondering* and *do you know*.

***Wh-* questions**

Direct: When does the festival take place?
Indirect: Do you have any idea when the festival takes place?
Direct: Who did you take to the prom?
Indirect: I was wondering who you took to the prom.

***Yes/No* questions**

Direct: Does the fireworks display start at 9 p.m.?
Indirect: Do you know if the fireworks display starts at 9 p.m.?

1 Complete the indirect questions.

1 Where's Sam?
Do you have any idea ***where Sam is***?
2 Did you hear that bang?
I was wondering ________.
3 What is the national flag of your country?
Could you tell me ________?
4 What do I need to wear to the party?
Do you have any idea ________?
5 Do you believe that black cats bring bad luck?
I'd like to know ________.

2 In pairs, write one or two indirect questions for each situation.

1 I'm hungry – I hope dinner's soon!
I was wondering when dinner will be ready.
Could you tell me what time dinner will be ready, please?
2 I've no idea what this food is!
3 I hope the parade finishes soon – I'm tired!
4 Is it the custom to make a toast? I don't know!

1 4.21 **There are seven questions in this part. For each question, choose the correct answer, A, B or C.**

Tip: Choose the answers that you think are correct the first time you listen, then check your answers on the second listening.

Example: Which challenge does the girl want to do?

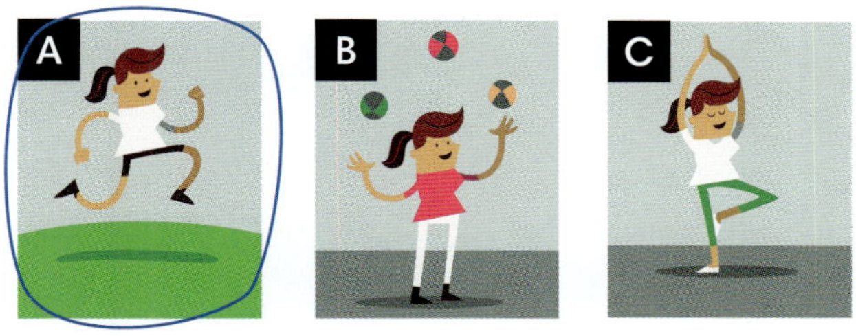

1 What did the boy enjoy on his first day at school?

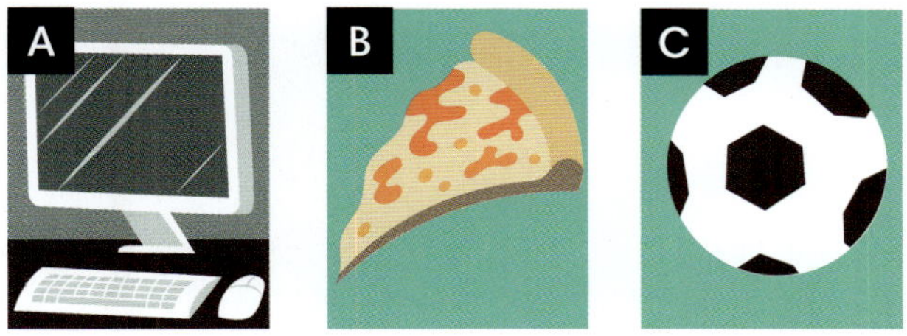

2 Which experience did the girl find most difficult?

3 What is the boy concerned about in his city?

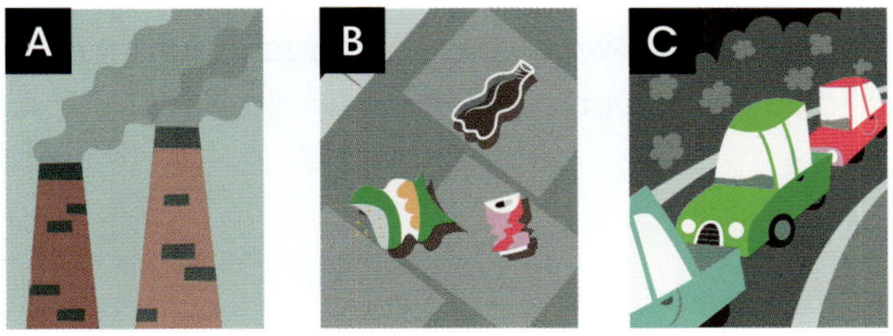

4 What can you recycle at school?

5 Which place are the people going to clean?

6 What has the boy just bought?

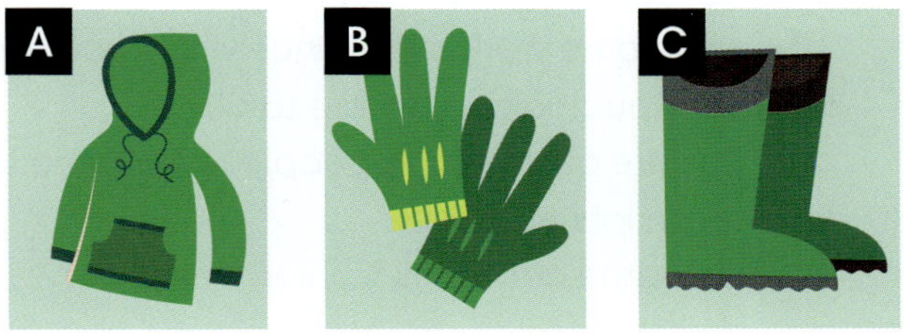

7 Which boots does the girl buy?

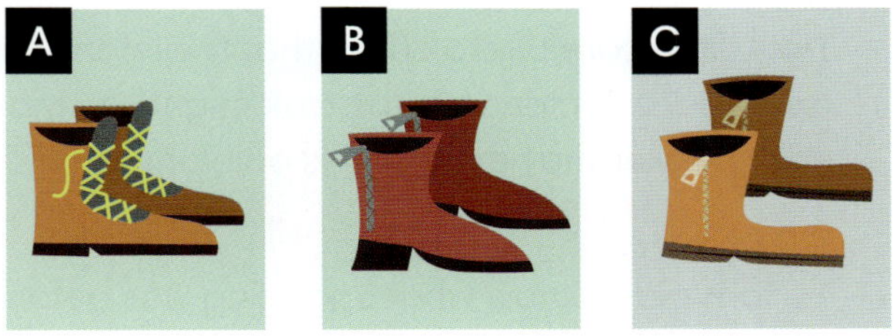

2 4.22 **You will hear part of an interview with a young fashion designer called Jake. For each question, choose the correct answer a, b or c.**

Tip: The questions come in the same order as the information in the recording. If you miss the answer to a question, leave it and move on to the next question, then try to answer it the second time you listen.

1 What is Jake planning to do in the summer holidays?
  a relax and have a rest
  b prepare for a fashion show
  c go on holiday with his parents
2 Who first suggested that he should design clothes?
  a his sister
  b his aunt
  c his parents
3 According to Jake, what quality do you need in order to be successful?
  a You need to be very creative.
  b You must be organised and reliable.
  c You need to be determined.
4 What makes Jake's clothes so popular?
  a You make them yourself in the shop.
  b Customers can choose exactly what the clothes look like.
  c They are cheaper than clothes in High Street shops.
5 What does Jake intend to do when he leaves school?
  a work full-time on his own business
  b go to college to study fashion design
  c get some work experience with a fashion designer
6 What would Jake most like to do?
  a inspire other young people to become successful
  b earn lots of money
  c become a famous fashion designer

3 4.23 **You will hear a conversation between a boy, Tom, and a girl, Tara, about upcycling. Decide if each sentence is correct or incorrect. If it is correct, choose the letter A for YES. If it is not correct, choose the letter B for NO.**

Tip: Listen carefully to check that the information in the recording exactly matches each sentence. For example, a sentence in the task might say that the speakers agree on an idea, but in the recording only one speaker may express this opinion.

		YES	NO
1	Tom didn't know what upcycling was before this conversation.	A	B
2	Tom thinks it's easier to upcycle things than to buy new ones.	A	B
3	Tara believes that individuals should try to create less rubbish.	A	B
4	Tom and Tara agree that governments should do more for the environment.	A	B
5	Tara persuades Tom that he should buy upcycled clothes.	A	B
6	Tom suggests that Tara should start a campaign to teach people about upcycling.	A	B

Tip: Relax and try to sound confident as you answer the personal questions in Part 1.

1 **Students A and B, answer the questions below.**

1. What's your name?
2. What's your surname? How do you spell that?
3. Where do you come from?
4. Do you study English at school? Do you like it?

2 **Students A and B, choose TWO questions to ask your partner.**

1. Can you describe your personality?
2. What is the most challenging thing you have had to do recently? Why was it challenging?
3. What things do you do to help the environment?
4. What's your favourite piece of clothing? Why do you like it?

3 **Work in pairs. Look at the pictures and do the task together.**

Tip: Discuss all the pictures and give your opinion on each of them, then agree which is best.

Your school has decided it wants to do more to help the environment. Talk together about the things it could do and then decide which is best.

Here are some pictures to help you.

1 **4.24 There are seven questions in this part. For each question, choose the correct answer A, B or C.**

Tip: Look at the pictures and think about what words you might hear, but remember that some words are mentioned in the recording to distract you.

Example: Which job is the girl going to apply for?

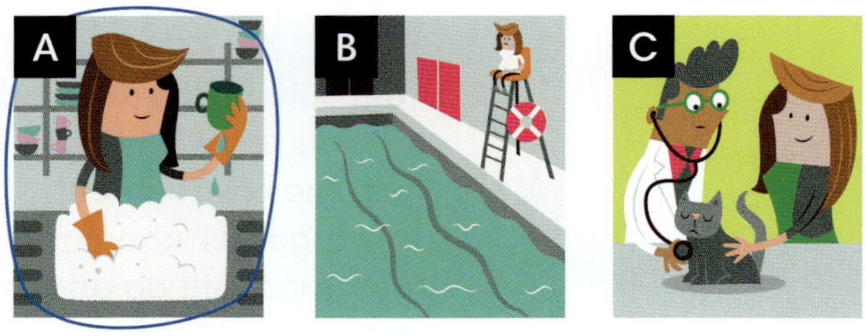

1 What time is the boy's interview?

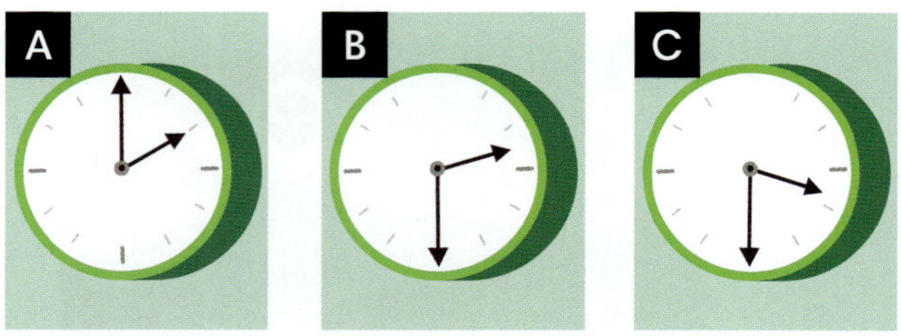

2 How much will the girl be earning this summer?

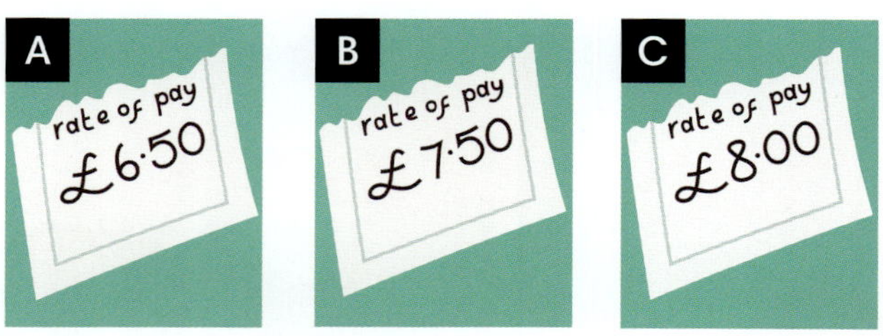

3 What is the boy hoping to see in the sky tonight?

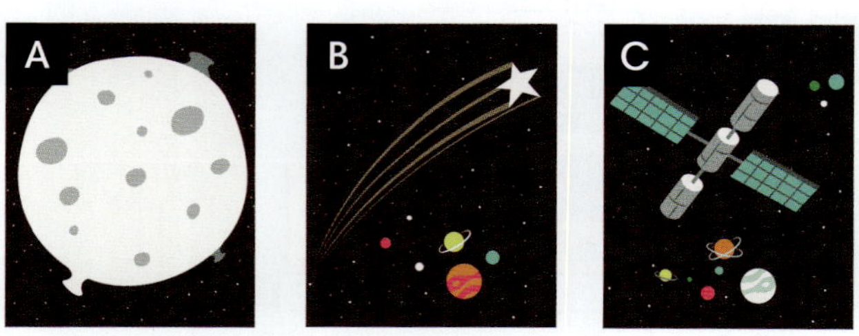

4 What would the girl like to do?

5 What is the girl suffering from now?

6 What should the boy do?

7 What extreme sport did the boy enjoy?

2 4.25 **You will hear part of an interview with a young woman called Kizzie who has just got onto an astronaut training programme. For each question, choose the correct answer a, b or c.**

Tip: Read each question carefully. All the answers might seem correct, but only one answer will match the recording exactly.

1 How is Kizzie feeling about starting her training?
   a impatient and ready to start
   b slightly nervous about everything she will have to learn
   c excited that she will soon meet the others on the training programme
2 Kizzie first became interested in space
   a at school.
   b through a friend at university.
   c after watching a TV programme.
3 The training to become an astronaut
   a involves only practice and not theory.
   b lasts for over two years.
   c involves a short trip to the International Space Station.
4 When do most astronauts have health problems?
   a during take-off and landing
   b after about three months in space
   c when they return home after their trip
5 What is Kizzie not looking forward to about going to the space station?
   a eating horrible food
   b missing members of her family
   c working very hard on experiments
6 What would Kizzie like to do one day?
   a travel to Mars
   b encourage other young people to become interested in space
   c make discoveries that could help people

3 4.26 **You will hear some information about a new museum. Complete the gaps with the missing information.**

Tip: Some of the gaps may be numbers. You can write these as words or as figures.

Museum of Space

- **Date of opening:** [1] ________
- **Number of exhibition rooms:** [2] ________
- **Ticket price for under-sixteens:** [3] ________
- **Price includes entry to the** [4] ________
- **Life-size model of part of the** [5] ________
- **Visit website at** [6] ________

Tip: Answer the questions clearly, then try to add more information (e.g. some extra details or your opinion).

1 Students A and B, answer the questions below.

1 What's your name?
2 What's your surname? How do you spell that?
3 Where do you come from?
4 Do you study English at school? Do you like it?

2 Students A and B, choose TWO questions to ask your partner.

1 What job would you like to do in the summer holidays? Why?
2 What would be your ideal job in the future? Why?
3 When was the last time you were ill? What was the problem?
4 Would you like to try any extreme sports? Why? / Why not?

3 Work in pairs. Look at the pictures and do the task together.

Tip: Remember that this is a discussion, so ask your partner what he/she thinks about each idea as well as expressing your own opinion.

A friend wants to get a job in the summer holidays to earn some money. Talk together about the types of job your friend could do and then decide which is best.

Here are some pictures to help you.

4 **Work in pairs. Take turns to tell your partner about a photograph. Your photographs will be of people having health checks.**

Tip: It's important to talk about who you think the people in the photographs are, what they are doing and how they might be feeling. You can make guesses if you are not sure.

Student A

It's your turn first. Look at the photograph and tell Student B what you can see in it.

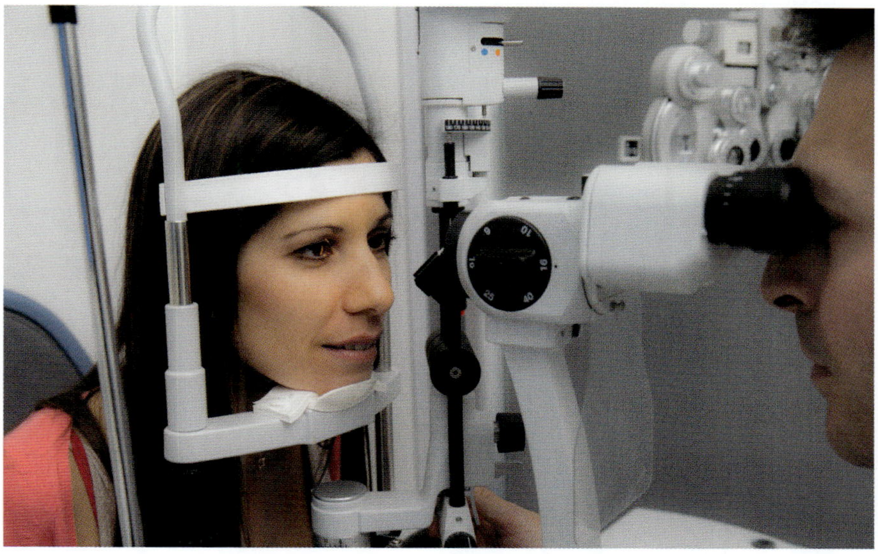

Student B

Tell Student A what you can see in the photograph.

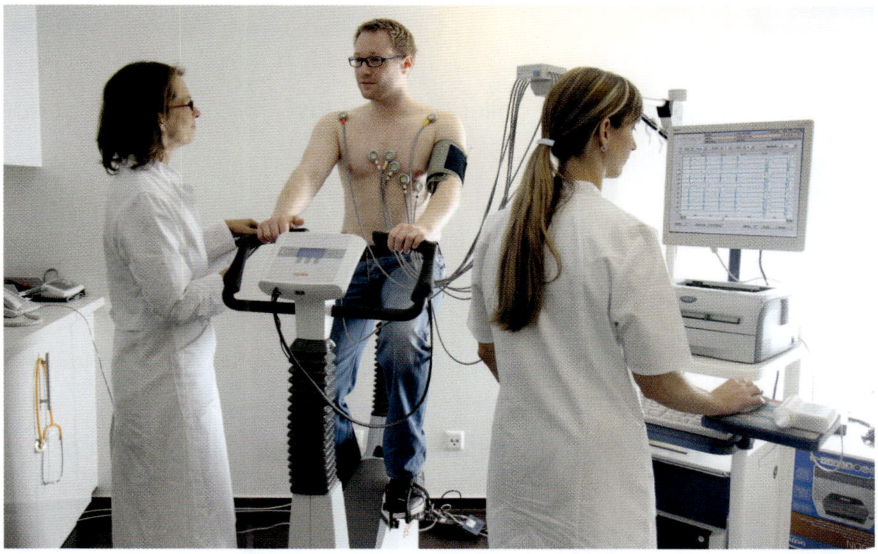

5 **Work in pairs. Talk to each other about what you do now to keep healthy and what other activities you could do.**

Tip: Remember that this is a conversation, so you should show that you are interested in what your partner is saying. You can use phrases like: *Really? That's interesting. I see.*

1 4.27 **There are seven questions in this part. For each question, choose the correct answer A, B or C.**

Tip: Look at the three pictures for each question and think about the differences between them. This will help you to focus on the right information when you listen.

Example: How did the girl learn about the new perfume?

1 What did the boy enjoy most at the exhibition?

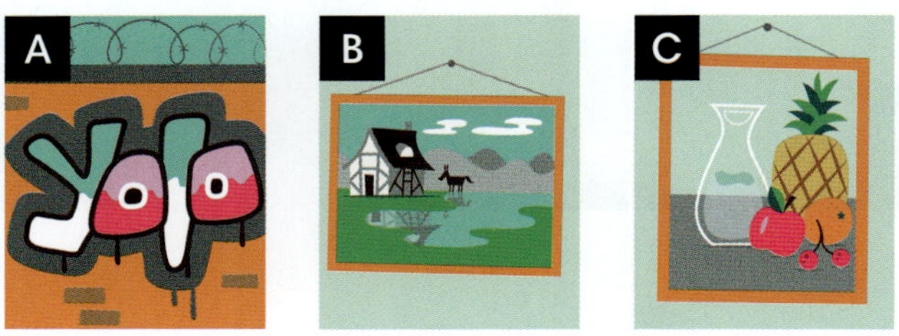

2 What time will the art gallery close today?

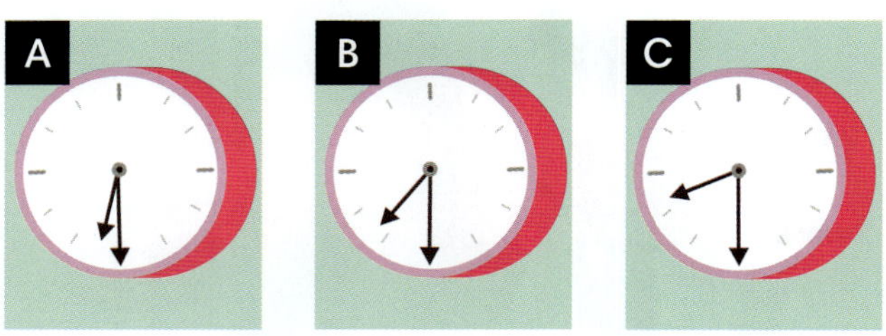

3 What could the girl do before she started school?

4 What does the boy always look at first on the news website?

5 What is the date of the school prom?

6 What does the boy want at his birthday party?

7 What event is the girl looking forward to?

2 4.28 **You will hear some information about a parade. Complete the gaps with the missing information.**

Tip: You should write between one and three words in each gap.

SUMMER PARADE

- **Place to meet:** 1 ________
- **Time parade starts:** 2 ________
- **Remember to bring** 3 ________
- **Mr Kean will bring** 4 ________
- **Mrs Denton will help with** 5 ________
- **Day ends with a** 6 ________

3 4.29 **You will hear a conversation between a boy, Jack, and a girl, Tess, about animal communication. Decide if each sentence is correct or incorrect. If it is correct, choose the letter A for YES. If it is not correct, choose the letter B for NO.**

Tip: Some questions ask about the opinions of the speakers, so listen carefully for expressions they use to respond or give their opinions.

		YES	NO
1	Tess agrees with Jack that birds don't really have a language.	A	B
2	Jack is surprised when Tess tells him how far whale sounds can travel.	A	B
3	Jack knows from personal experience that dogs can communicate with humans.	A	B
4	Other animals don't understand the body language of dogs.	A	B
5	Tess and Jack are both very interested in how chimpanzees communicate.	A	B
6	Jack isn't interested in reading Tess's book on animal communication.	A	B

Tip: Remember to add reasons and examples to support your answer and try to use a wide range of vocabulary.

1 Students A and B, answer the questions below.

1. What's your name?
2. What's your surname? How do you spell that?
3. Where do you come from?
4. Do you study English at school? Do you like it?

2 Students A and B, choose TWO questions to ask your partner.

1. How do you usually communicate with your friends?
2. Do you enjoy watching adverts on TV? Why? / Why not?
3. What kinds of art do you like looking at? Why?
4. Do you prefer books or films? Why?

3 Work in pairs. Look at the pictures and do the task together.

Tip: Use a range of expressions for agreeing and disagreeing with your partner about the different ideas, and remember you must reach agreement about which one is best.

You and some friends are organising a summer music festival at your school. Talk together about the different ways you could advertise the event and then decide which is best.

Here are some pictures to help you.

4 **Work in pairs. Take turns to tell your partner about a photograph. Your photographs will be of celebrations.**

Tip: Try to describe the whole scene in the photograph, and also some of the details. Remember to talk about how you think the people are feeling and why.

Student A

It's your turn first. Look at the photograph and tell Student B what you can see in it.

Student B

Tell Student A what you can see in the photograph.

5 **Work in pairs. Talk to each other about what kinds of special occasions you and your family celebrate together.**

Tip: Try to make sure that you and your partner both get a chance to speak. Remember to agree and disagree with your partner, and ask them for their opinion.

Fracking

The world needs energy to survive. We have relied on fossil fuels for a long time, but traditional fossil fuels like coal and oil are getting more difficult and expensive to access. A possible alternative is the process called 'fracking'. Although the technique is not new – it has been used for sixty-five years – companies have recently been using it a lot more in countries like the USA and Canada. New technology has made the process much easier. Now they want to use it in the UK, but many people are against the idea.

What is fracking?

Fracking is another name for 'hydraulic fracturing'. This is the method used to extract shale gas from rock deep below the surface of the earth. Shale gas is a natural gas which is trapped inside the rock and the only way to release it is by cracking the rock. With hydraulic fracturing, big machines drill a well down through the water table into the rocks – sometimes more than a kilometre down. Then the drilling turns horizontally and continues for thousands of metres. Water, sand and chemicals are forced into the rock at very high pressure. This fractures the rock, making lots of small fissures, and the natural shale gas comes out.

Why is fracking a good thing?

The supporters of fracking believe that it is a safe and cheap way of getting essential energy. There are huge amounts of shale gas on our planet and using fracking to access it will give people a cheap and reliable source of energy for a long time. In fact, many say that it is the only realistic source of energy for the future. People also believe that replacing coal with more natural gas is better for the environment, air quality and people's health.

Why is fracking a bad thing?

Many people are against fracking because they believe it is dangerous. One concern is that during the process, toxic chemicals and gases may leak into the water system. Another fear is that the drilling and fracturing may lead to small earthquakes. To reach the shale gas there need to be many, many wells in one area. This, combined with the constant transport of water needed for the process, will make enormous areas industrialised, noisy and busy. There are also worries about the vast amounts of water needed for fracking.

1 Look at the picture. In pairs, discuss what you think is happening and why.

2 The process in the picture is called fracking. Choose the correct answer. Then read the article quickly and check your answer to Exercise 1.

Fracking is related to

a recycling waste water.
b extracting fossil fuels.
c renewable energy.

3 Read the text again. Answer the questions.

1 How long has fracking been used?
2 Which countries use fracking a lot?
3 What is the word *fracking* short for?
4 Why is it difficult to extract shale gas?
5 What are the advantages of fracking?
6 How might fracking affect the environment?

4 Read the second paragraph again and look at the diagram. Work in pairs. Student A, close your book and describe the process of fracking to your partner. Student B, check your partner's description. Help and correct him/her where necessary.

5 In pairs, discuss the advantages and disadvantages of fracking. One of you should argue in favour and the other against.

6 PROJECT Use the internet to find out more about fracking in your own or a neighbouring country. Make notes about:

- where it has happened or where it is planned.
- what the consequences for the environment might be.
- what local people's reactions are.

7 PROJECT Create a short presentation. Write a paragraph about fracking in your own or a neighbouring country and add pictures, statistics and comments. Share your presentation with the class.

ART AND DESIGN

Fashion

CLIL 2

FASHION

In historical terms, the idea of fashion design is quite new. Charles Worth, who was from England, is thought to have been the first fashion designer. He set up his fashion house in Paris in 1858. Before Worth, people usually asked dressmakers to create what they, the client, wanted. Charles Worth did the opposite – he told his customers what to wear! He set trends and established the job of a fashion designer. Design houses like his started to employ artists to sketch pictures of clothes to show their clients, instead of making complete garments.The clients made choices and orders from the drawings. The fashion houses started to earn a lot of money. Today fashion houses and top designers control what we all wear, from hats to shoes and everything in between. There are three types of clothes that designers and manufacturers produce today.

Haute couture

This is the most expensive and exclusive clothing to buy. A garment is made specifically to fit one person only. The fabric that is used is very good quality and the garment is almost completely created and sewn by hand. Because of the cost of creating the clothes, haute couture doesn't make a big profit, but it is excellent for the reputation of the designer and fashion house.

Ready-to-wear

Ready-to-wear clothes are not as expensive as haute couture. They are produced using good quality fabrics and they are well-designed and made. However, these clothes are not created for individual people but for the general public. They are sold in standard sizes, in shops. Usually, there is only a limited number of clothes of the same design, so this means that not everyone is wearing the same dress or jacket. The designers' collections of ready-to-wear are shown during fashion weeks in cities around the world twice a year.

Mass market

Most people buy this type of clothing. After top fashion designers show their collections in fashion weeks, the high street clothing companies wait to see which trends, styles and colours become popular. Then they make their own versions using cheaper materials and methods of production. These clothes don't always last long and people throw them away regularly and replace them.

1 **Match the list of skills a fashion designer needs with the pictures. Then put the skills in the order you think they are required when designing and making clothes.**

- ☐ sewing
- ☐ cutting a pattern
- ☐ knowing about textiles
- ☐ sketching designs
- ☐ using a dummy
- ☐ understanding colour theory

A

B

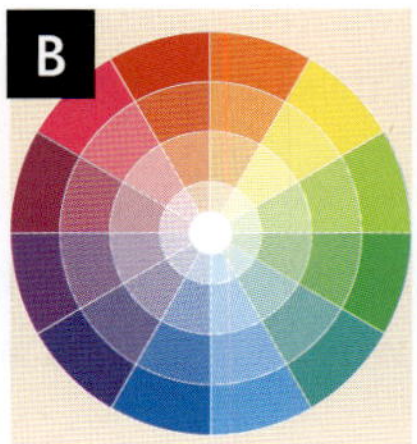

C

D

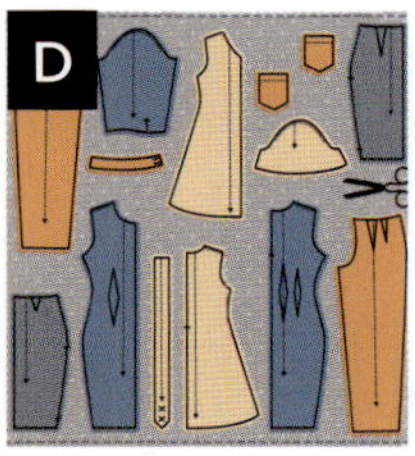

E

F

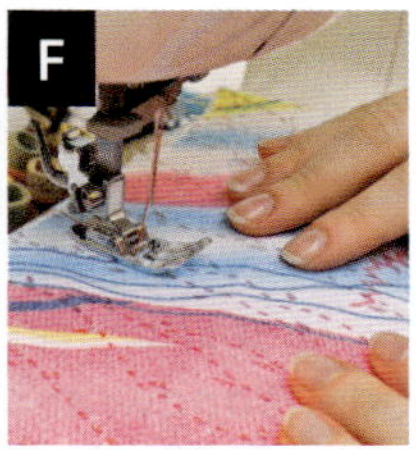

2 **Read the article quickly. What is it about?**

a the history of clothes and styles
b fashion design today
c the cost of buying clothes

3 **Read the article again and answer the questions.**

1 Why was Charles Worth important?
2 How did he change the way people ordered clothes?
3 Why is haute couture expensive?
4 Where can people see new ready-to-wear trends?
5 Why can't people buy cheap versions of catwalk fashion soon after the shows?

4 **PROJECT** **Use the internet to find out about a famous fashion house in your country. Make notes about its most famous designer(s), its history and its recent designs.**

5 **PROJECT** **Create a fact file about the fashion house. Add pictures. Share your fact file with the class.**

MUSIC David Bowie

David Bowie and space

1 David Bowie was one of England's greatest singers. He lived from 1947 to 2016 and for five decades his music touched people all over the world. He was not only a singer but also a songwriter and an actor, and he influenced many people who work in the music industry today. People will remember Bowie for his music, of course, but also for his imagination and the wonderful characters he created on stage, including the outrageous Ziggy Stardust. His continued success was because of his ability to reinvent himself as a musician again and again. He started singing pop songs, then rock, then glam rock and in the 2000s he even experimented with the styles of industrial and jungle.

2 One theme that Bowie used many times in his songs was space. From fantasies about going into space to aliens coming to visit us, his songs and albums show a deep interest in the subject. Perhaps his most famous song about space, which he first released as a single in 1969 and then re-released in 1975, is *Space Oddity*. It was released just before the USA launched Apollo 11, which landed on the moon on 20 July 1969. The lyrics of the song tell the story of a fictional astronaut, Major Tom, who is sent into space and goes on a space walk, but ground control loses contact with him.

3 *Space Oddity* became one of Bowie's signature songs. It also became famous again in 2013 for a very important reason. The Canadian astronaut Chris Hadfield, was on board the International Space Station and filmed himself singing *Space Oddity*. It was the first video ever shot in space. Bowie is remembered for *Space Oddity*, but he also wrote many other space-themed songs which also became popular. For example, his album called *The Rise and Fall of Ziggy Stardust and the Spiders from Mars*.

A

B

C
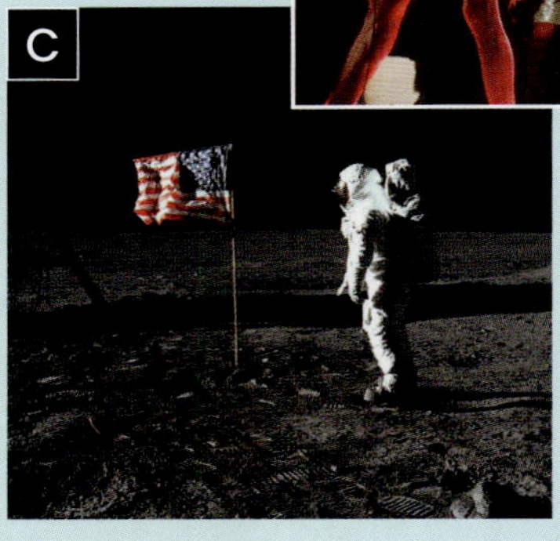

1 Have you heard of David Bowie? What do you know about him? Do you know any of his songs? Tell the class.

2 Read the article quickly and check your ideas from Exercise 1. In which paragraphs are photos A–C mentioned?

A ☐ B ☐ C ☐

3 Read the article again and complete the fact file.

David Bowie

Born: ……

Died: ……

Reason for success: ……

Types of music: ……

Famous single: ……

Released: ……

Re-released: ……

Location of unusual recording: ……

Date: ……

Famous album: ……

4 Work in pairs. Each of you should choose and read ONE of the short texts (A or B) below about songs which were played in space.

A *Across the Universe* by The Beatles
This was the first song that was beamed directly into space on 4 February 2008. It was sent from a seventy-metre dish at the Deep Space Network near Madrid. It celebrated the fortieth anniversary of the song, the forty-fifth anniversary of the DSN and the fiftieth anniversary of NASA.

B *Reach for the Stars* by will.i.am
This was transmitted from the planet Mars to Earth by NASA's Curiosity Rover, on 28 August 2012. NASA and will.i.am wanted to encourage young people to study Science. It travelled 300 million miles and was the first song ever broadcast from another planet.

5 Take turns to ask and answer about the information in your text. Ask questions with *what*, *who*, *when* and *why*.

6 PROJECT Use the internet to find out more about a famous singer/songwriter from your country. Make notes about:

- his/her career.
- why he/she became famous.
- any other interesting information.

7 PROJECT Create a short presentation. Write a paragraph about the singer/songwriter. If possible, use actual recordings to accompany your presentation. Share your presentation with the class.

SCIENCE The brain

Healthy brains

1 Our brains are very complicated organs. As they get older, the nerve cells (neurons) die, connections between nerve cells (synapses) are lost and the brain gets smaller and lighter. This affects all our brain functions – our memory, our thinking skills and our emotions. However, people's brains age at different speeds. Why is that? And can we protect the brain against ageing?

2 Scientists used to think that the speed of brain ageing was a result of genetics, that it ran in the family, but now they say only twenty-five percent of the differences are a result of genetics. Seventy-five percent are a result of our upbringing and lifestyle. So, it is possible for people to do things to keep their brains young.

3 Exercise plays an important role. Some exercise such as table tennis, which is fast and competitive, and where you have to think very quickly, can increase the size of the cortex. This improves the connections between nerve cells and affects our ability to solve problems. It can also make us happier and less depressed. Exercise like fast walking can increase the size of the hippocampus, which helps our memory. This might be because aerobic exercise can create new neurons.

4 Food, of course, is also important. Scientists believe that anthocyanin, a natural plant colouring, helps the brain stay young. It can be found in vegetables and fruit that are blue, purple and red, such as purple sweet potatoes, red cabbage, blackcurrants, blueberries and blackberries. It is also believed to help form new nerve connections.

5 Research has also shown that education plays a big part in protecting our brains as we get older. The more new things we learn when we're younger (and throughout our lives), the better for our brains. Some people believe that learning a second language is one of the best ways to keep our brains healthy.

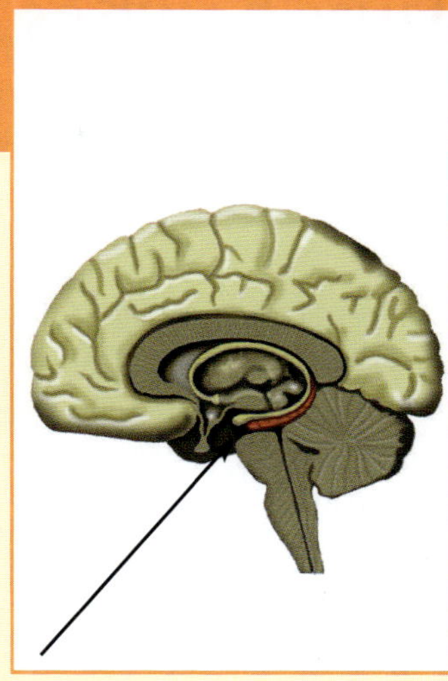

h______ c______

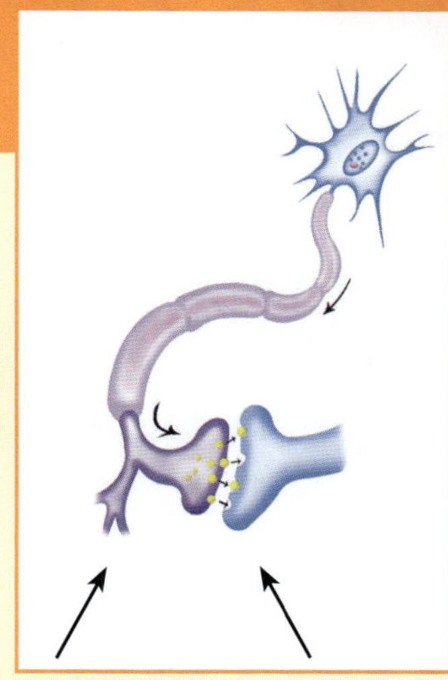

n______ s______
c______

a______

a______ e______

1 **In pairs, discuss the questions.**

1 How do you think our brains change as we get older?
2 What sort of things can people do to improve their memory as they get older?

2 **Read the article quickly and check your ideas from Exercise 1. Then label the pictures.**

3 **Read the article again and match paragraph headings a–e to paragraphs 1–5.**

a ☐ Colours are important
b ☐ In the family?
c ☐ Make it grow
d ☐ Natural changes
e ☐ Challenge is good

4 **Write one sentence to summarise each of the paragraphs.**

5 PROJECT **Use the internet to find out more about research into brain function. Make notes about:**

- what the research/experiment was.
- where it was carried out.
- what the results were.
- how it can help the brain.

6 PROJECT **Create a short presentation. Write a paragraph about the new research. Add some pictures. Share your presentation with the class.**

A

B

C

D

Guy Fawkes and the Gunpowder Plot

1 One of the most well-known national celebrations in the UK is 5 November, which is called Guy Fawkes Night, or Bonfire Night. It commemorates an event from 1605, but this was not an event that happened – it was an event that *didn't* happen! If the event had taken place, English history would have been very different.

2 It was all about religion. At that time in England the people were either Roman Catholic or Protestant (Church of England). Elizabeth I, who was a Protestant queen, persecuted the Catholics badly. When James I became king – although he was also a Protestant – Roman Catholics hoped he would be kinder to them. Unfortunately, this didn't happen and a group of Roman Catholic activists planned to blow up the Palace of Westminster when the King opened Parliament; this plan was called 'the Gunpowder Plot'. The leader of the group was Robert Catesby and he organised the smuggling of thirty-six barrels of gunpowder into the basement of the building. Guy Fawkes, who was the explosives expert, stayed to light the fuse. If all this gunpowder had exploded, it would have destroyed a huge area in the centre of London. Unfortunately for the plotters, Guy Fawkes and the gunpowder were discovered at the last minute and the plan failed. All the members of the gang were eventually found and executed.

3 After the plot, Parliament passed an act which made 5 November a national day of thanksgiving, and it has been celebrated ever since. On this day, people build bonfires and make a type of doll, called the 'guy' which is put on the top of the bonfire to burn. It is a festive evening with lots of fireworks and parades in many towns. The 'guy' represents Guy Fawkes and the fireworks represent the explosion that didn't happen. Traditionally, children used to make the 'guy' and take it round the streets asking people for 'a penny for the guy.' However, this custom has almost disappeared. The celebrations on 5 November take place all round the country. However, there is one place where they don't burn a 'guy'. This is St Peter's school in York – it is Guy Fawkes' old school. Another interesting traditional ceremony is every November, before the state opening of Parliament, the Yeomen of the Guard still search the Houses of Parliament.

1 **Do you know anything about a national celebration in another country where people celebrate the life of an important person from the past?**

2 **Read the article quickly. In which paragraphs are photos A–D mentioned?**

A ☐ B ☐ C ☐ D ☐

3 **Read the article again and say why these names and numbers are important.**

1 1605
2 Elizabeth I
3 James I
4 Palace of Westminster
5 Robert Catesby
6 36
7 St Peter's School
8 Yeomen of the Guard

4 **Work in pairs. What new information did you learn from the text? What was the most interesting part? Why?**

5 **Work in pairs. Read two people's comments about Guy Fawkes Night. Who do you agree with? Why?**

A It's important to commemorate things like this. It's fun to put a guy on the bonfire and watch him burn. In some places they burn a guy that looks like a politician! Great fun!

B In my opinion, it's a horrible tradition! Burning something that represents a person – that's just old-fashioned and scary. Maybe we should just light a bonfire.

6 PROJECT **Use the internet to find out more about a national celebration in your country. Make notes about:**

- when it takes place and what happens.
- the history behind the event.
- how the celebration varies in different parts of the country.
- any other interesting information.

7 PROJECT **Create a short presentation. Write a paragraph and add some pictures. Share your presentation with the class.**

CULTURE 1 Explore Canada

1 **Read about Canada. What is the most important language in each region?**

1 Ontario
2 Quebec
3 Nunavut

2 **Read about Canada again. Complete the sentences with place names.**

1 The capital city of Canada is ________ .
2 The Niagara Falls is a popular place for visitors in the ________ region.
3 A lot of maple syrup comes from ________ .
4 People in the town of ________ don't see the sun for four months in winter.

3 **In pairs, answer the questions.**

And YOU

1 What are the most popular places in your country for visitors from other countries?
2 Are there regions in your country where the country's official language isn't the main language? Do people in these regions want to be independent? Give examples.
3 What food is your country or region famous for?
4 Are there any regions where not many people live? Why don't more people live there?

4 **Write a short paragraph about different regions in your country. Use your answers to Exercise 3 and the Canada examples to help you.**

CANADA

Continent	North America
Population	35 million
Offcial languages	English, French
Currency	Canadian dollar
Favourite sport	Ice hockey

Canada is the world's second largest country, but a lot of the land in the centre and north is empty. Canada is famous for its cold winters and beautiful mountains.

Ontario

Canada's biggest city, Toronto, and its capital, Ottawa, are in this region. Here, as in most of Canada, English is the most important language. A lot of people come here to visit the Niagara Falls and the Great Lakes.

Quebec

Canada's second biggest city, Montreal, is here. Most people in Quebec speak French and about forty percent want Quebec to be an independent country. Most of Canada's famous maple syrup comes from this region. Canadians love eating it with pancakes and even have the leaf of the maple tree on their flag.

Nunavut

Nunavut is the biggest region in Canada, but only 33,000 people live there. There are no trees and the land and sea are frozen for most of the year. It is easier to travel by snowmobile than by car. At Grise Fiord, the furthest north of Nunavut's towns, there are four months without daylight in winter and four months without night in summer. Most people in Nunavut are Inuit. They speak the Inuit language, but they don't live in igloos. They have houses with TVs and the internet.

CULTURE 2 Explore the Republic of Ireland

1 Read about the Republic of Ireland. Which of the things below are mentioned?

business dancing mountains religion technology tradition TV

2 Read about the Republic of Ireland again. Choose the correct option.

1 *All* / *Some* of Ireland is in the United Kingdom.
2 Irish is the main language in *some* / *all* schools in Ireland.
3 In Irish dancing, you have to move your *feet* / *arms* very fast.
4 Some people say that *not many* / *many* Irish people talk a lot.

3 In pairs, answer the questions. And YOU

1 Was your country ever ruled by another country? Which one? Did this change your language or other parts of your culture?
2 What type of dancing is your country famous for? Have you ever tried it?
3 Is there anywhere in your country that has a strange tradition? What is it?

4 Write a short paragraph about your country. Use your answers to Exercise 3 and the Republic of Ireland examples to help you.

The Republic of Ireland

Continent	Europe
Population	4.8 million
Offcial languages	English, Irish
Currency	euro
Capital city	Dublin

Culture

Ireland has had a strong cultural influence on the English-speaking world. It has produced many great writers, including Oscar Wilde and George Bernard Shaw; actors, including Pierce Brosnan and Colin Farrell; and musicians, including U2. Irish step dancing – fast foot movements while the body and arms don't move – has also become popular around the world.

Language

About thirty-eight percent of the population speak Irish as a first or second language. Most people speak English. However, more and more children are going to Irish-speaking schools and there are several Irish TV channels, radio stations and newspapers.

North and South

For many centuries Ireland was ruled by the English, but in the early twentieth century most of the island became an independent country, the Republic of Ireland. Northern Ireland, however, continued to be part of the United Kingdom. The two parts of Ireland have a shared culture, but there are some religious differences. In the north, most people are Protestants; in the south, most people are Catholics.

The Gift of the Gab

At Blarney Castle in the south of Ireland, you can find the Blarney Stone. According to tradition, if you kiss this special stone, you will have the 'gift of the gab' – the ability to talk well and persuade people easily. Some people think that the Irish are the most talkative people in the world. Have they all kissed the Blarney Stone?